THE
BOOK OF FESTIVALS

by

DOROTHY GLADYS SPICER

Author of *Folk Festivals and the Foreign Community*

WITH A FOREWORD

by

JOHN H. FINLEY

DETROIT

Gale Research Company   Book Tower

1969

This is an unaltered reprint of
the 1937 edition published in New
York by The Womans Press

Library of Congress Catalog Card Number 75-92667

ISBN 0-8103-3143-8

If a man be Gracious and Courteous to Strangers, it shewes he is a Citizen of the Worlde; and that his Hearte is no Island, cut off from other Lands, but is a Continent that joynes them.

Francis Bacon, *Of Goodness and the Goodness of Nature*

TO THE MANY GRACIOUS AND COURTEOUS

"CITIZENS OF THE WORLDE"

WHO HAVE CONTRIBUTED TO THIS BOOK

CONTENTS

The Book of Festivals

PREFACE

FESTIVALS, like Yggdrasil, the ancient tree of the universe, spread their branches over the entire world. A well of wisdom lay at Yggdrasil's roots, and from its waters the giant Mimir refreshed himself each day. Infinite folk wisdom lies at the foundation of the beautiful old festivals of Oriental and Slav, Latin and Teuton. If we would know these festivals and, through them, the races which have cherished their growth, then we, like Mimir, must drink often and long at the source of wisdom.

The BOOK OF FESTIVALS has been written in an effort to show that festivals are but one of many common forces that unite nations and give continuity to cultural thought. The same festival runs through the folk life of different peoples, regardless of racial origin, geographical location or religious belief. The human emotion that prompts the festival is precisely the same whether the celebration occurs in India, America, Finland or Greece. Although festivals may vary from country to country in name and manner of observance, in spirit they remain always the same. Festivals are the outward expression of man's common heritage of fear and thanksgiving, joy and devotion. Thanksgiving for harvests and increase of flocks, fear of hostile natural forces, joy in sunshine, rain and renewal of life, gratitude to the unseen gods—these are the emotions from which festivals spring.

The BOOK OF FESTIVALS is intended as a handbook for libra-

vii

rians, teachers, students, social workers, festival and pageant directors, travelers, writers and others who may wish, for either practical or æsthetic reasons, to delve more deeply into the festal heritage of different peoples.

The festivals described have been selected on the basis of nationality—with the two exceptions of the Hindus and the Mohammedans. As explained in the text, it would be impossible to make any accurate list of Indian holidays as such, because of the many different religious groups represented in India. Since Mohammedan holidays are observed widely in Albania, Arabia, Bosnia, China, Egypt, India, Mesopotamia, Persia, Syria and other countries, and to some extent in Turkey, a special section is devoted to this religious group. In general, the holidays of a country's predominant religion have been selected as typical of the country.

Since it was impossible to include the festivals of all nationalities in the compass of a single volume, the basis of selection has been made to correspond, in the main, to the European and Oriental nationality groups most widely represented in the United States.

The principal religious, national and local holidays of different races have been described, although less emphasis has been placed on political anniversaries than on days associated with old folk practices and beliefs.

The "Story of the Calendar" in Part II, the "Glossary of Familiar Religious and Festival Terms" in the Appendix, and the tables of Easter dates on pages 357–358, 370–371, furnish sufficient data to enable the reader, given the Easter date, to compute the principal movable feasts of any year or nationality. The "Selected Bibliography on Festivals" provides the student with additional data on the holiday celebrations of different lands.

The festivals and customs that the author has not witnessed herself have been described from oral accounts, supplemented by

viii

Preface

authoritative written sources. Although all data have been checked and rechecked from many different sources, a degree of error is inevitable because calendar systems differ in different parts of the world, memories of childhood customs sometimes dim with time, and folk practices vary, not only from country to country but even from village to village in the same country.

Although the author has indicated, whenever possible, specific localities where given customs occur, her informants sometimes have been unable to supply these data. At times festival rites have been variously interpreted because they represent a curious blending of pagan and Christian survivals. In many countries only the custom remains, its original significance long since having been forgotten.

The author acknowledges her indebtedness to the sources given in the Bibliography. Although it is impossible to list the names of all who have contributed to the book, the author wishes to thank the following individuals and organizations for their generous help in aiding her research on festival observances:

The librarians of the New York Public Library, who have edited the festival sections mentioned after their names: Dr. Joshua Block, chief of the Jewish Division, Jewish; Dr. Victor Nicholov Sharenkov, Bulgarian; the late Mr. Moses Ferid Germerd, Mohammedan; Mrs. Claire Huchet Bishop, French; Miss Marie Cimino, Italian. Acknowledgment also is made to Mrs. Anna Heifetz for her translations from the Russian; to Mr. Charles F. McCombs, superintendent of the Main Reading Room, for the research privileges so kindly extended during the preparation of the book; and to the many other staff members who have rendered courteous assistance. Mrs. Jan Matulka of the Webster Branch Library has contributed valuable information on the Czechoslovakian section.

The many foreign consulates in New York City which have edited the festival sections of their respective countries. Special appreciation is expressed to: Mr. Charles Hallaert, consul of

The Book of Festivals

Belgium; Mr. Josef Hanč, consul of Czechoslovakia; Don Guido Colonna di Paliano of the Italian consulate; Mrs. Dorothy Mezs of the Latvian consulate; Dr. A. Furneé, vice-consul of the Netherlands; Dr. Irena Piotrowska, director of the Polish Art Service and Miss Mayra Werten of the International School of Art, both of the Polish consulate; Mr. J. Saavedra de Figueiredo, vice-consul of Portugal; Mr. Luis Careagra, acting consul general of Spain.

Foreign organizations and travel and information bureaus that have supplied valuable information and editorial assistance. Acknowledgment is made to Mr. S. A. Mokarzel, editor of *Al-Hada;* Miss Hanna Astrup Larsen, editor of the *American-Scandinavian Review,* editor of Norwegian and Danish sections; Mr. Holger Lundbergh, of the American Swedish News Exchange, Inc., editor of the Swedish section; the American Russian Institute; Mr. Habib I. Katibah, Arab National League, editor of the Syrian section; Mr. James Karabatos, editor of *Atlantis,* Inc.; Mrs. Virginia Creed Mettesich, publicity manager of the Austrian State Tourist Department; China Institute of America; Miss Selma Leeman, Finnish Book Concern, and Miss Nina Strandberg of the Finnish Travel Bureau, editors of the Finnish section; Mr. Hans Portack, manager, German Railroads Information Office, editor of the German section; Mr. Nalin S. Sen, resident manager of the India State Railways; the International Institutes of the Young Women's Christian Associations. Special acknowledgment is made to Miss Lola de Grille and Miss Kyra Malkowsky of the New York International Institute for editing the Hungarian and Russian sections; to Miss Rose Chew of the San Francisco International Institute for editing the Chinese section; to Miss Lucille O. Azevedo of the New Bedford International Institute and Miss Emily Silva of the Providence International Institute for data on the Portuguese; Mr. Stephen Goerl, manager of the Hungarian Official Travel Information Bureau; Mr. Angel Rosas of the Mexican

Preface

Tourist Information Bureau; Mr. Knut Olesen, manager, Norwegian Travel Information Office; Mr. Peter P. Yolles, managing editor of *Nowy Swiat;* Mr. Frederick Dossenbach, director of the Swiss Federal Railways, editor of the Swiss section; Mrs. Concha Romero James, director of Division on International Cooperation, Pan American Union, Washington, D.C., editor of the Mexican section.

The following individuals whose knowledge and experience have contributed to the book: Miss Inez Cavert; "Dagmar"; Dr. Taraknath Das, formerly of the Department of Politics, Catholic University of America, and lecturer in the Department of History, College of the City of New York, who has edited the Hindu section and made many helpful suggestions; Mr. George Demetriades, secretary of the Greek Cathedral of the Holy Trinity Church, editor of the Greek section; Miss Mabel Ellis; Dr. Leon Feraru, professor of Romance Languages and chairman, Modern Languages and Literature, Long Island University, editor of the Rumanian section; Mrs. Elpinike A. Frasher, editor of the Albanian section; Miss Katina Katsaras, who has assisted in preparing the manuscript and in editing the Greek section; Mrs. Olle Kukepuu, of the Estonian Educational Society, editor of the Estonian section; Mr. Vladimir M. Lugonja; Swami Nikhilananda, who has selected much of the material on Hindu festivals; Miss Virginia Olcott; Mr. and Mrs. Olaf Olesen; Reverend Cyril C. Roosens, pastor of St. Albert's Church, who has assisted with the Belgian section; Dr. Elisha H. Simonian, pastor of the Holy Cross Armenian Apostolic Church, editor of the Armenian section.

DOROTHY GLADYS SPICER

White Plains, New York
March 1937

xi

FOREWORD

THIS admirable work which has gathered into its pages so much of the joy of festival days of many peoples needs no preface except the prayer that Pippa, the mill girl in Browning's "Pippa Passes," makes in the morning of her one holiday in all the year:

Oh, Day, if I squander one wavelet of thee,
A mite of my twelve hours' treasure
The least of thy gazes or glances,
(Be they grants thou art bound to, or gifts above measure)
One of thy choices or one of thy chances,
(Be they tasks God imposed thee or freaks at thy pleasure)
My Day, if I squander such labor or leisure,
Then shame fall on Asolo, mischief on me!

And if anything is to be added, there is nothing better than the poetic catalogue of Europe's folk contributions to America—including the "handsels," the "first gifts"—written in prose by that great and beloved citizen, Franklin K. Lane, for "America's Making"—

America is a land of but one people, gathered from many countries. Some came for love of money and some for love of freedom. Whatever the lure that brought us, each has his gift. Irish lad and Scot, Englishman and Dutch, Italian, Greek and French, Spaniard, Slav, Teuton, Norse, Negro—all have come with their gifts and have laid them on the Altar of America.

xiii

All brought their music—dirge and dance and wassail song, proud march and religious chant. All brought music and their instruments for the making of music, those many children of the harp and lute.

All brought their poetry, winged tales of man's many passions, folk songs and psalm, ballads of heroes and tunes of the sea, lilting scraps caught from sky and field, or mighty dramas that tell of primal struggles of the profoundest meaning. All brought poetry.

All brought art, fancies of the mind, woven in wood or wool, silk, stone or metal—rugs and baskets, gates of fine design and modeled gardens, houses and walls, pillars, roofs, windows, statues and painting—all brought their art and hand craft.

Then, too, each brought some homely thing, some touch of the familiar home field or forest, kitchen or dress—a favorite tree or fruit, an accustomed flower, a style in cookery or in costume—each brought some homelike, familiar thing.

So did Franklin Lane describe in this swift enumeration the folk gifts of legend and "old and antique song" to America. This BOOK OF FESTIVALS preserves in full detail authentic memories of what America should not be permitted to forget of beauty and joy.

PART I

THE FESTIVALS OF DIFFERENT PEOPLES

FESTIVALS OF THE ALBANIANS

Shën Vasili, Saint Basil; Mot'i Ri, New Year's Day.

January 1

This day is observed by both Mohammedan and Christian Albanians as the beginning of the New Year. The first person who steps over the threshold must bring a log for the fire. As he is thought to bear good or bad luck for the coming year, he is treated with great respect. Sweets are served bountifully, to insure a year filled with sweetness. Every household prepares a New Year's cake in which a coin—often an antique gold piece—is hidden. The mother cuts the cake into as many portions as there are members in the family, as well as a piece for the ikon, one for the house and one for the business. The first piece of cake goes to the head of the house. The person receiving the coin is thought to prosper in his undertakings throughout the year Presents, especially handkerchiefs, are exchanged on this day.

Ujët e Bekuar, Epiphany.

January 6

In native villages the morning church service is followed by Blessing the Waters. The priest lowers the cross into the icy-cold water of a river or lake. Bystanders dive in after the sacred object. The one who recovers the cross collects coins from the villagers. In some parts of the country jars of water are brought to be blessed at the village fountain. Long straws

3

are placed in the mouth of each jar. Later one of these straws is tied to each of the fruit trees, with a wish for fertility. In some communities the church ikons are "sold for the day," in order to raise money for the church. The Dove ikon, being of special significance because of its symbolic connection with Christ's baptism, brings the highest price. It is taken to the home of the "purchaser," upon whom special blessing is thought to rest. Friends visit his house during the day, and at night the priest carries the ikon back to the church.

SHËN JANI, Saint John the Baptist.   *January 7*

This great church holiday is observed by religious services. Since *Jani* is a popular name in Albania, friends and relatives visit all the Johns of the neighborhood and offer their congratulations.

*JAV'E BARDHË, The White Week.[1] *The week, beginning with Monday, that immediately precedes the Great Lent*

During this period, butter, cheese, milk and all kinds of sweets, but no meat, are eaten.

*TË LIDHURAT, Carnival Sunday.
                            The last day of the White Week

At the Sunday service preceding Lent each person asks forgiveness for sins he may have committed against friends or relatives during the past year. Young people kiss the hands of their elders and men kiss one another in the performance of this

---

[1] Stars indicate movable feasts that depend on Easter. A table of the Eastern Orthodox Easter dates and movable feasts is given on pages 370–371. Mohammedans, of whom there are many in Albania, observe the Mohammedan festivals described on pages 236–239. See also Mohammedan calendar, pages 372–374.

4

sacred rite. No one thinks of taking communion during Lent without first performing this act of reconciliation. In the evening people dress in all kinds of gay masquerade costumes and visit from house to house. Everywhere they are welcomed with sweets and merrymaking, since Carnival Sunday is the last day of gaiety before the Great Lent begins.

*KRESHM'E MADHE, The Great Lent. *The period of fasting between Carnival Sunday and Easter*

Gypsies go from door to door, asking for the sweets left over from the preceding night. Many Christians fast completely during the first three days of Lent. The Church warns against rigorous fasting, except when people are strong enough to bear it, since death following fasting is looked upon as suicide.

Të Dyzet Dëshmimtarët, Forty Saints' Day.
March 9 O.S. (March 22 N.S.)

This church holiday honors the Forty Saints who were drowned for their faith and, while dying, miraculously received crowns of glory. Any saint who has been given no special day is remembered on this date.

Dit'e Verës, Spring Day.　*March 9 O.S. (March 22 N.S.)*

On the Eve of this day children go to fields and mountains in search of fragrant sprays to decorate the doorways. The boys and girls sing special songs to the newly awakened spring. Mothers twist together red and white threads, which they tie around the children's throats and wrists, so their sons and daughters may keep strong and healthy throughout the coming year. Red and white, to the Albanian, symbolize a clear skin, and therefore perfect health.

The Book of Festivals

VANGJELIZMOJ, Annunciation.   *March* 25

This church festival celebrates the Angel Gabriel's announcement to the Virgin Mary of Christ's coming birth.

*DIT'E DAFINËS, Palm Sunday. *The Sunday preceding Easter*

Church services are held in memory of Christ's triumphal entry into Jerusalem. Branches of laurel are blessed in the sanctuaries and taken home by the worshipers. The blessed laurel is placed near the ikons, where it remains indefinitely.

*E PRËMTE E ZEZË, Black Friday.

The Friday preceding Easter

In the churches an almost life-sized picture of Christ is elevated above a table, which is covered with costly material embroidered with the story of Christ's death and burial. Each family brings flowers to decorate this "tomb," which is watched over throughout the day. Shortly after midnight the priest performs the burial service. He remembers in prayer the deceased members of each family.

*PASHKËT, Easter.

Easter, the great holiday of the Albanian calendar, continues for three days. Everyone dons new clothes and attends the traditional church service. Each worshiper breaks a colored egg with his neighbor. "Christ is risen," says the first man. "He is risen indeed," is his neighbor's response. Until the Day of Ascension, friends greet one another in this way whenever they meet. The customary Easter dinner includes roast lamb and unleavened bread. Easter is a great day for visiting. Each guest is presented with two colored eggs.

6

SHËN GJERGJI, Saint George. *April* 23

On this day it is customary to picnic near the springs. Tradition decrees that everyone shall weigh himself while holding a stone and a sweet-smelling twig. Saint George's Day is significant not only as a religious festival but also as the name-day of George Castriota (Scanderbeg), Albania's national hero.

*NALTËSIMI, Ascension. *The fortieth day after Easter*

This church festival is observed forty days after Easter, in commemoration of Christ's ascension to heaven after his resurrection.

*PESËDHETORI, Pentecost. *The fiftieth day after Easter*

Celebrated seven weeks after Easter, this church festival commemorates the descent of the Holy Ghost upon the disciples.

*SHËN TRINIA, Trinity. *The fifty-seventh day after Easter*

Picnics in the open are a feature of this day, which is celebrated in the churches as a feast to honor the Holy Ghost.

SHËN NAUMI, Saint Naum.
June 20 (*also observed on December* 23)

This holiday is observed in honor of Saint Naum, the patron of the mentally defective.

SHËN PETRUA DHE SHËN PAVLI, Saint Peter and Saint Paul.
June 29

A church holiday commemorates the martyrdom of the two great Christian evangelists.

7

NALTËSIMI I VIRGJERESHËS, Assumption of the Virgin Mary.
August 15

This is a church holiday to commemorate the Virgin's bodily taking-up into heaven.

TË VIELAT, Gathering of the Fruits.   *Sometime in September*

Friends and neighbors and hired workers help in gathering the grape and fruit harvests. All are given a share of grapes, figs and other fruits. The new wine is made at this season, as well as preserves, such as quince, fig and grape. A great dinner and general rejoicing mark the end of the harvest.

SHËN MITRI, DHIMITRI, Saint Demeter.   *October* 26

On this day the houses are prepared for winter. Warm sheepskins, woven rugs and blankets are all brought out, and the rooms are made snug and comfortable in anticipation of the cold winter.

SHËN MIHAILI, SHËR MILLI, Saint Michael.   *November* 8

This day is observed in honor of Saint Michael, the saint who brings men's souls to heaven. Legend states that Saint Michael is deaf to the prayers of the relatives of the dying because once the saint was so moved by pity for a dying man's family that he returned to God without his soul. God, in his displeasure, sent the angel to the bottom of the sea for a stone which, when opened, was found to contain a worm and a fresh leaf. "If I care for even a worm," said God, "how much better shall I provide for my children on earth!" Whereupon, the Lord sent a thunderbolt which deafened Saint Michael forever.

Festivals of the Albanians

DIT'E FLAMURIT, Flag Day, Independence Day.   *November* 28

This is the anniversary of the country's independence, in 1912, and likewise of the raising of the Albanian flag, in 1443, by George Castriota (Scanderbeg). Albanians in the United States observe the day with historical plays, lectures, balls and other educational and social events.

SHËN KOLLI, Saint Nicholas.   *December* 6

This special church holiday honors the fourth century Bishop of Myra, who protects sailors and is patron of school boys.

DUKE GDHIRË KRISHTLINDJET, Christmas Eve.   *December* 24

Village lads rise at three or four o'clock in the morning of December 24 and go to the surrounding mountains, where they light huge bonfires. Later in the day, children armed with gaily decorated sticks called *rabushes,* go from house to house singing of the birth of Christ. In return, the singers are given coins and *kollendra*—round bread with a hole in the center— which they carry away on strings suspended between their *rabushes.* The Christmas Eve meal includes pancakes, made without butter or oil, and special holiday sweets. Before leaving the table each person fills his spoon or fork and leaves it on his plate with a wish for abundance throughout the coming year. Then all members of the family seize the table and move it up and down, chanting, "May there be plenty in this house, may the time for a wedding be near." The remainder of the evening is spent in roasting chestnuts, eating figs and sitting around the fire, which burns with a branch of freshly cut cedar.

KRISHTLINDJET, Christmas.   *December* 25

After early morning Mass the day is spent in feasting and visiting. The holiday meal consists of a meat or chicken broth, into which lemon juice and egg have been whipped, and of tripe, chicken or lamb, and unleavened bread. *Byrek,* a pie made with milk, eggs, cheese, butter and vegetables, or *mesnik,* a kind of meat pie, often are features of the meal.

SHËN STEFANI, Saint Stephen.   *December* 26

This day is spent in a continuation of the Christmas festivities.

FESTIVALS OF THE AMERICANS

POSSIBLY few peoples can boast a richer festal heritage than the Americans. The early colonists brought with them from England, Holland, France, Germany and many other countries the holiday customs of the homelands. These old-world traditions, transplanted to new-world soil, gradually assumed a character more or less unique to the various colonies.

The first Christmas Day in New England must have been a dreary affair, especially to the womenfolk, who possibly made secret comparisons with other and happier Christmases spent among relatives and friends in far-away England. For the men of the Pilgrim band that first Christmas was a busy one, spent in cutting timber and toiling to make community shelters.

"Munday, the 25th day," writes Mourt, "we went on shore, some to fell tymber, some to saw, some to rive, and some to carry; so no man rested all that day. . . . Munday the 25th being Christmas day, we began to drinke water aboord, but at night the master caused us to have some Beere." In this way the first Christmas came and went, with nothing but the cheering mugs of beer to remind our Puritan ancestors of the "wanton Bacchanallian Christmasses" spent in England in ". . . revelling, dicing, carding, masking, mumming," and other excesses scorned by all good seventeenth century churchmen.

As time went on, the Puritans looked upon the "wicked Papistrie" of Christmas with more and more intense hatred. There was a period when colonists who observed the day with feasting and merrymaking, or even with the cessation of toil, were forced to pay a five shilling fine. It was not until the end of the nineteenth century, indeed, that Christmas was celebrated in New England as today—with merrymaking, the exchange of gifts and the eating of festive foods.

Christmas in Virginia always was a gracious season, even in the days of Captain John Smith. An early account of one of the Captain's expeditions describes a cheerful holiday spent in the wilds, where, despite inclement weather, the little party managed to "make merry" according to the best British traditions. In the words of a contemporary account:

"The extreme winde, rayne, frost and snow caused us to keepe Christmas among the salvages, where we were never more merry, nor fed on more plenty of good Oysters, Fish, Flesh, Wild fowl and good bread, nor never had better fires in England."

Christmas in New York must have been a jolly affair, for our Dutch ancestors, true to their hearty heritage of abounding good cheer, were wont annually to observe the "anniversary of Saint Nicholas, otherwise called Santa Claus." A record of 1773 states that ". . . a great number of the sons of that ancient saint celebrated the day with great joy and festivity."

Perhaps one of the most interesting accounts of Christmas in early America is preserved in a letter written December 26, 1795, by Theophilus Bradbury to his daughter, Mrs. Hooper. Mr. Bradbury ". . . had the honor" of dining with George and Martha Washington in company with other prominent men of his time. He describes the arrangement of the festal board, with its "elegant" centerpiece, decorated with ". . . a pedestal of plaster of Paris with images upon it." The dishes of food were placed all around this centerpiece. We almost can hear Mr. Bradbury smack his lips as he adds, ". . . and there was an elegant variety of roast beef, veal, turkeys, ducks, fowls, hams, etc.; puddings, jellies, oranges, apples, nuts, almonds, figs, raisins, and a variety of wines and punches."

Thanksgiving was the Puritan's substitute for Christmas. If Christmas was under the ban as a reaction against the excesses with which the festival was observed in contemporary England, there were, at least, no inhibitions to mar the jollity of Saint Pumpkin's or Saint Pompion's Day, as churchmen derisively called Thanksgiving. That first great harvest festival was marked not only by feasting and fellowship with Indian guests. There were also shooting and target practice, not to mention "other recreations," regarding which we should give much to know.

"Our harvest being gotten in," wrote Edward Winslow on December 11, 1621, to an English friend, "our governor sent foure men on fowling, so that we might after a more speciall manner rejoyce together, after we had gathered the fruit of our labors; they foure in one day killed as much fowle as with a little helpe beside, served the company almost a weeke, at which time amongst other recreations, we exercised our Armes, many of the Indians coming amongst us, and amongst the rest their greatest King Massasoyt, with some ninetie men, whom for three days we entertained and feasted, and they went out and killed five deere, which they brought to the Plantation and bestowed on our Governor, and upon the Captain [Standish] and others."

As time went on, the Thanksgiving festival assumed greater importance as a social factor in New England life. After the Revolutionary War, fireside games were permitted in the homes as features of the great day. Pumpkin pie was one of the most important foods added to the wild turkey, venison, fruits and vegetables of the Puritans' first harvest feast. In 1705 Thanksgiving was put off from the first to the second Thursday in November, because Colchester, Connecticut, had not received its supply of molasses in time to make the Thanksgiving pumpkin pies!

Thanksgiving and Christmas were by no means the only festivals which the colonists enjoyed. A writer of 1699 said of the New Englanders that "Election, Commencement and Training Days are their only Holy days." Election Day, with its famous " 'lection cake" and " 'lection beer," the school commencements, with their impressive exercises, farewell dinners and famous "Commencement Cake"; the annual parade of Artillery Day— all were notable events in the calendar of early New England.

Another holiday of special note was Pope's Day, better known, perhaps, as Guy Fawkes Day, which boys still observe in some parts of New England and New York by lighting bonfires on November fifth. In the old days the festival was celebrated heartily with bonfires and parades of masqueraders, who carried aloft "popes" or "guys" of straw, for, according to old almanacs,

"Gun powder plot
we ha'n't forgot."

The playing of "idle tricks because 'twas the first of April," hanging doorknobs with baskets of flowers on May Day Eve, and seeking one's Valentine on February 14, all are part and parcel of America's festal heritage which has descended to modern times from the brave old days of yore.

NEW YEAR'S DAY. *January* 1

On New Year's Eve watch-night services are held in churches and brilliant parties featured in hotels and restaurants, "to watch the Old Year out and the New Year in." The day is spent in merrymaking and rejoicing. One of the gracious customs of older times was for men to call on their women friends on January first. Women called upon one another on January second. The usual refreshments were choice wines and sliced pound, fruit, gold and silver cake.

Festivals of the Americans

LINCOLN'S BIRTHDAY. *February* 12

On this day Americans pay tribute to the memory of their great national hero, Abraham Lincoln. The United States Congress reads from the works of Lincoln and listens to an address in his honor. Lincoln's birthday was observed publicly for the first time in 1887.

SAINT VALENTINE'S DAY. *February* 14

This day is widely celebrated among persons of all ages by the exchange of missives or gifts called "valentines." Although of uncertain origin, the festival has been observed in much the same manner ever since the fourteenth century, or possibly earlier. It is a favorite day for parties, especially among young people. Gay favors and decorations of red paper hearts and chubby cupids, fortune-telling games, and appropriate refreshments of frosted heart cakes and crimson candies, all pay fitting honor to the memory of good Saint Valentine, patron of sweethearts and lovers.

WASHINGTON'S BIRTHDAY. *February* 22

Congress observes the birthday of George Washington, first president of the United States, with speeches and readings from his works. Schools are closed on this day, which is observed with patriotic addresses, parties, masquerade balls, historical plays and entertainments.

SAINT PATRICK'S DAY. *March* 17

The anniversary of Ireland's patron saint is celebrated by Irish and Irish-Americans. The traditional "wearing of the green," patriotic meetings, huge parades, musical and social events make this day a gala event to all sons of the Emerald Isle.

*PALM SUNDAY.[1]   *The Sunday preceding Easter*

This church holiday is observed with special sacred music and the distribution of palms, in memory of Christ's triumphal entrance into Jerusalem.

*GOOD FRIDAY.   *The Friday preceding Easter*

Throughout the country Good Friday is observed with special music and church services.

*EASTER SUNDAY.

Churches are decorated with Easter lilies and other spring flowers. In many sections of the country, as on Mount Rubidoux, California, impressive open-air sunrise services are held on Easter morning. Magnificent musical programs are featured in the churches. On this day the traditional new spring clothes are donned. In New York City the annual "Easter parade" on Fifth Avenue is an event of special interest to all fashion devotees. To American children Easter is a gala event, since colored eggs, brought by the Easter bunny, are sought in many mysterious corners! In addition to dyed eggs there are baskets of colored candy and chocolate eggs, chocolate chicks, bunnies, and all kinds of stuffed plush rabbits, ducks and other toys.

*EASTER MONDAY.   *The Monday after Easter*

In England and other countries where egg rolling is a feature of the Easter festivities, the custom probably originally symbolized rolling away the stone from the mouth of Christ's sepulchre. The tradition of egg rolling has been retained in

[1] Stars indicate movable feasts that depend on Easter. See table of Easter dates and movable feasts on pages 357–358.

American life, although its symbolism has long since vanished. Every Easter Monday hundreds of children are invited to an egg-rolling party on the sloping White House lawns. Egg games and contests are participated in by the young visitors, who are guests of the First Lady of the Land.

APRIL FOOLS' OR ALL FOOLS' DAY.   *April* 1

Since early times the first of April has been associated in the United States, as in many other countries, with playing harmless pranks on friends and neighbors. The origin of the custom is uncertain. Many agree, however, that probably it dates back to France and the adoption of the reformed calendar in 1564, when the beginning of the New Year was put back from March 25 to January first. Mock gifts were sent on April first (the day which originally culminated the New Year feast), in the hope of discomfiting folk who had forgotten the change in dates.

MAY DAY.   *May* 1

The first of May is one of the oldest and best loved festivals that have been transplanted to the United States from British soil. At Ma-re Mount, in 1628, the Puritans celebrated May Day, the old pagan festival of Flora, before the very eyes of the scandalized Governor Bradford. Not only did the young people insist upon setting up "an idoll May Polle," as the Governor calls the Maypole, described by Thomas Morton as ". . . a goodly pine of 80. foote long," but according to the latter authority they even "brewed a barrell of excellent beare," and provided ". . . good May songs, dancing hand in hand around the Maypole and performing exercises . . . in a solemn manner, with Revels and merriment after the old English custome." Although May Day celebrations were looked upon with keen disfavor by the Puritan Fathers, the custom of observing the day with merrymaking and gladness has persisted through the years. In some places May baskets still are hung on doorknobs, while May queens, Maypole dances and May songs are all important features of the festivities, which are observed in the parks and playgrounds of almost every metropolitan center.

MEMORIAL DAY.   *May* 30

Originally this day was called Decoration Day, as the anniversary was dedicated, in 1868, to decorating the graves of Civil War soldiers. Since then it has become customary to look after the graves of all soldiers, as well as of relatives and friends.

FOURTH OF JULY, INDEPENDENCE DAY.   *July* 4

July 4 is the anniversary of the adoption of the Declaration of Independence in 1776, by the Continental Congress. This great secular holiday of the United States is celebrated with patriotic speeches, red, white and blue decorations, parades and exhibitions of fireworks.

LABOR DAY.   *The first Monday in September*

This holiday, to honor laborer and worker, is the same occasion that is celebrated on May first in other countries. Labor Day is observed by meetings conducted by labor leaders, parades of labor organizations, picnics and outings.

COLUMBUS DAY, DISCOVERY DAY.   *October* 12

The anniversary of the discovery of America, in 1492, by Christopher Columbus is observed not only in the United States but also in Latin America and many cities of Italy and Spain.

Festivals of the Americans

Patriotic addresses, special church services and musical programs are among the chief features of the day's celebration.

HALLOWEEN, ALL HALLOWS' EVE.
October 31, *the evening preceding All Saints' Day*

Popular fancy has peopled this night, which originated in a curious mixture of Druid practice, classic mythology and Christian belief, with ghosts, witches, devils and spirits of the dead. Although All Hallows' Eve retains religious significance for many nationalities, to young people of the United States it is an occasion for traditional games, amusing ceremonies and love charms for foretelling the future. In many communities boys and girls, masked and dressed in grotesque costumes, go from house to house, ringing doorbells and wishing a "Happy Halloween." In return for their visits the children are treated with nuts, candy, apples and other goodies. In some places Halloween has degenerated into an occasion for boisterous pranks and wanton destruction of property.

ARMISTICE DAY.   *November* 11

Throughout the nation the ending of the World War in 1918 is observed with a three-minute pause at eleven o'clock in the morning. The grave of the Unknown Soldier in Washington is decorated with a wreath, and impressive services are held in honor of the men who gave their lives in the performance of patriotic duty.

THANKSGIVING DAY. *The last Thursday in November, by proclamation of the President of the United States*

The origin of this most truly American of all festivals dates back to Governor Bradford and the Pilgrims' Thanksgiving for their harvests in 1621. The typical American Thanksgiving dinner usually includes roast turkey and cranberry sauce, vegetables of every sort, apples, mince and pumpkin pies, raisins, nuts and sweet cider. Thanksgiving services are held in the churches.

CHRISTMAS. *December* 25

This is the greatest children's festival of the year. Boys and girls hang their stockings before the fireplace on Christmas Eve in anticipation of Santa Claus, who comes down the chimney with his pack of gifts. Fragrant fir trees, trimmed with colored lights, gay balls, tinsel, candies and little toys are set up in hundreds of homes. Gifts and cards are exchanged, Christmas trees are lighted in public parks, community centers and churches, while seasonal parties and entertainments are featured extensively. In many rural sections of the country and in sections of some cities, candles, placed in the windows, light the paths of singers who go from house to house singing the "glad tidings." The Christmas dinner, which is similar to the Thanksgiving feast, is traditionally distinguished by a rich plum-pudding dessert. Holly wreaths, mistletoe and festoons of green and red give a gala aspect to homes and public places. Christmas decorations often are kept up until Twelfth Night. Special services, featuring the Christmas story and Christmas music, are held in the churches.

FESTIVALS OF THE ARMENIANS

THE Church of Armenia claims ancient lineage. According to national tradition, Saint Thaddeus and Saint Bartholomew visited the Armenians early in the first century and introduced Christianity among the worshipers of Ahura Mazda, "maker of heaven and earth, the father of the gods."

The new faith spread rapidly throughout the land. Tradition states that, in about the year 302 A.D., Saint Gregory the Illuminator baptized Dertad the Great, King of Armenia, together with many of his followers. Since Dertad probably was the first ruler to embrace Christianity for his people, the Armenians proudly claim that theirs was the first Christian state.

Despite persecution and suffering, the invasions of other faiths and the scattering of the race, the Church of Armenia has retained her national character throughout the centuries. From earliest times the Church has consciously kept alive, through her festivals and feast days, the main streams of national life. She has adopted from antiquity many of the most picturesque pagan ceremonials, invested them with new significance, and handed them down from generation to generation—proud reminders of the past. The festival of Christ's Presentation in the Temple, for example, retains many elements of the pagan spring festival in honor of Mihr, god of fire, on whose day it falls. The Transfiguration of Christ, called *Vartavar,* the "flaming of the rose," takes place at the same time as the ancient midsummer festival to Anahid, goddess of chastity. In olden days worshipers of-

21

fered a dove and a rose to the golden image of Anahid. Today some Armenian communities still free doves in honor of the transfigured Christ, and little children gather roses for his feast. By the same easy transition, the worship of Anahid was transferred to the veneration of the Virgin Mary, and the pagan cult of sacred tree and stone quite logically became the exaltation of the Holy Cross.

Not only through the adaptation of pagan tradition to Christian ritual did the Armenian Church identify herself with the national life of the people. By her government, democratic in character, she early became linked inseparably with the daily interests of the common people. All the officials of the Church are elected by the laity. The priest is the sole confessor of his flock. He fosters general participation in all church festivals and usually is present at all the family festivals which carry out the ancient traditions of the Armenian race.

GAGHANT, NOR DARY, New Year. *January* 1

This is a day of feasting and merrymaking. Boys go from house to house, singing New Year greetings and receiving gifts of nuts, sweets and coins. Each home prepares special New Year dishes, as well as many different kinds of dried and fresh fruits. At midnight the family meets around the table to receive blessings from the grandmother or the eldest member of the household. Good wishes are exchanged, presents opened, fruit, candies and nuts eaten. A lucky coin, baked in the New Year cake, foretells luck and riches to the one who receives it.

DZNOONT, Christmas; ASDVADZAHAÏDNOOTYOON, Epiphany.
January 6. Celebrated by Armenians in the United States on the Sunday following January 6 when this date comes on a week-day

The Christmas Eve supper consists of fried fish, lettuce

and boiled spinach. This last is said to have been eaten by the Virgin Mary on the Eve of Christ's birth. After Christmas morning services and a merry noonday meal, the men visit from home to home. The customary greetings are exchanged, "Christ is born and manifested today," and "Blessed is the manifestation of Christ." The call lasts for about a quarter of an hour, each guest being served with coffee and sweets. The holiday festivities continue for three days. On the third day the women make and receive calls.

VARTANANTZ YEV GHEVONTYANTZ, Saints Vartan's and Ghevont's Day.   *The Thursday preceding Lent*

This national holiday is in memory of Vartan, the Armenian national saint and patriot, and the 1,036 martyrs who fell, 451 A.D., in the religious war between Persia and Armenia. The Armenians lost the battle, but the King of Persia gave up his plan to have Armenia renounce Christianity and accept Zoroastrianism. The day is celebrated with patriotic speeches, lectures and music.

MIHR, Festival of Mihr; DYARNTARACH, Presentation of Christ in the Temple.   *Forty days after Christmas*

The pagan spring festival in honor of Mihr, god of fire, was adapted by the Church as the festival of Mary's sacrifice of two doves and the presentation of Jesus in the Temple. The original rite consisted of kindling fires in Mihr's honor in the open market-places, and of lighting a lantern which burned in the temple throughout the year. In the ancient Christian observance of the festival, fires were made in the church courtyards. The people danced about the flames, jumped over them, and carried home some of the sacred embers. Weather prophecies were made according to the direction in which smoke and

23

fire blew. The present month of February corresponds in name to the ancient Armenian month of *Mehakan* (Mihragan), translated freely as the Festival of Mihr.

*DZAGHGAZART, Palm Sunday.[1] *The Sunday preceding Easter*

In many Near Eastern Armenian communities where palms are difficult to obtain, olive branches, instead of palms, are distributed to worshipers at the church service.

*AVAK HINKSHAPTY, Maundy Thursday.
The Thursday preceding Easter

The priest enacts the symbolic "washing of feet," which Christ performed on his disciples. Twelve boys are chosen for the ceremony. After bathing their feet, the priest anoints them with oil. The story of Christ's betrayal is read and the choir chants hymns appropriate to the occasion. This service is observed in many Armenian parishes in the United States.

*DJERAKOLOYTZ, Day of Illumination; AVAK SHAPAT, Holy
Saturday.   *The Saturday preceding Easter*

The day before Easter is observed by special services in the churches.

*ZADIG, Easter.

At dawn of Easter Day people don their new clothes and attend early communion. The service ends at midday, when everyone partakes of the usual Easter feast of roast lamb, red-dyed eggs, and a bread made only at this season. Small boys

[1] See table of Easter dates on pages 357–358; and the Armenian calendar on pages 351–352.

play games with red eggs. Men visit from house to house in the afternoon and exchange the traditional greetings, "Christ is risen from the dead," and "Blessed is the resurrection of Christ." The guests are served with such dainties as coffee, sweets and bonbons.

*MERELOTZ, Festival of the Dead. *The day after Easter*

The day of memorial for the dead always is celebrated on Easter Monday. Picnic baskets loaded with food and drink are carried to the cemeteries, where priests offer prayers for the departed and mourners chant loud lamentations. This festival, on which food offerings to the dead often are given, may be regarded as a survival of pagan ancestor worship.

*HAMPARTZOOM, Ascension of Christ; VIJAG, Festival of Fortune. *The fortieth day after Easter*

This is one of the most romantic and picturesque of all Armenian holidays. It is customary for young girls to tell their fortunes from tokens thrown into a bowl of water drawn from seven springs. This is a joyous out-of-door occasion, celebrated with singing, dancing and playing games. Many charming superstitions exist in regard to Ascension Day. It is said that brooks and springs are filled with healing power at the hour of midnight. On Ascension Eve streams, stones, stars and other "soulless" objects are said to receive the gift of speech and to share one another's secrets.

*ETCHMIADZIN. *The second Sunday after Pentecost, or between May 24–June 27*

Etchmiadzin, the religious center of the Armenians, means "Descent of the Only Begotten." For many years this city was

25

the scene of pilgrimage by the faithful. The cathedral, where tradition says Christ appeared, contains many sacred relics, including the reputed hand of Saint Gregory. *Etchmiadzin* is a national holiday, celebrated by special church services.

SOORP RHIPSIME YEV SOORP GAIANE, Saints Rhipsime and
    Gaiane.   *June* 8

This festival honors Saint Rhipsime, who, accompanied by her nurse Saint Gaiane and thirty-eight virgins, fled from Rome to escape the carnal desires of the Emperor Diocletian. The maidens took refuge in Armenia, where they finally suffered death for their Christian faith. At Etchmiadzin, the religious center of Armenia, there are two churches in honor of these saints.

SOORP SAHAG YEV SOORP MESROB, Saints Sahag and Mesrob.
    The Thursday following June 15

The two fifth century Church Fathers who were leaders of Armenia's Golden Era are honored on this day. These saints completed the ancient alphabet, opened schools and translated the Bible into Armenian. In 1936, Armenians all over the world celebrated the 1500th anniversary of this translation of the Scriptures.

*VARTAVAR, Water Day; AYLAGERBOOTYOON, Festival of the
    Transfiguration of Christ.
    Ninety-eight days after Easter

In pagan times *Vartavar,* meaning "flaming of the rose," was celebrated at midsummer in honor of Anahid, goddess of chastity. On this day a rose and a dove were offered to the goddess. After Christianity was introduced into Armenia, the dove still remained as an important feature of the festival. In mountainous regions of the country, sheep, grain, flowers and doves were offered as sacrifices to the Christian God. The worshipers sprinkled water on one another, and the priest sprinkled the congregation, a ceremony suggestive of Christ's baptism in the Jordan. In some parts of the country the festival was the occasion of exhibits showing the community's progress in arts and handicrafts during the year. Races, games and competitions were held, and the victors were crowned with roses.

VERAPOGHOOM, Assumption of the Virgin Mary; HAGHOGHY ORTNOOTYOON, Blessing of the Grapes. *The Sunday nearest August 15, either before or after*

This is the festival of the Virgin Mary. Nobody is supposed to eat grapes until this day. A tray filled with grapes is blessed in church. After the ceremony, each member of the congregation is given a bunch of fruit as he leaves the sanctuary. Every woman named Mary entertains her friends on this day. Parties are held in homes and vineyards, where everyone eats grapes and rejoices in the harvest.

KUD KHACH, Holy Cross Day.
The Sunday nearest September 15

The day commemorates the discovery of the cross which, according to tradition, was buried on Calvary. Queen Helena, when she visited Jerusalem in 326, wished to find the cross on which Christ was crucified. Three crosses finally were excavated. The True Cross was identified through its power to resuscitate a dead body. At the annual church ceremony a cross is buried under sprays of the evergreen *rahan,* and each member of the congregation carries home a twig to insure a blessing.

The Book of Festivals

SOORP THADDEUS YEV SOORP PARTOGOMIOS, Saints Thaddeus and Bartholomew.   *The first Saturday in December*

These two disciples of Jesus preached Christianity in Armenia and finally were martyred for their faith.   These saints are known as the "First Illuminators" of the Armenian Church.

FESTIVALS OF THE AUSTRIANS

NEUJAHRSTAG, New Year's Day. *January* 1

The day is spent in merrymaking and enjoying family and friends. Dinner always is eaten in the middle of the day. Everyone dresses in his best clothes and spends the afternoon and evening in visiting friends and exchanging the season's compliments. According to old peasant belief, the weather of the twelve months is predicted by that of the twelve days following Christmas. On New Year's Day (or at any time between Christmas and Epiphany) people often amuse themselves by cutting an onion in two, carefully peeling off twelve coats of skin and sprinkling each layer with a pinch of salt. By the following morning, moisture has gathered in each layer of skin. Since the twelve layers correspond to the twelve months, the amount of dampness in each is said to indicate the rainfall for a given month.

*FASCHING, Carnival.[1] *The week preceding Ash Wednesday*

The Austrian carnival, which begins the week before Lent and ends on Ash Wednesday, is a season of great gaiety. For centuries the traditional *Schemenlaufen,* or Dance of the Phantoms, has been an outstanding event in the Shrovetide festivities

---

[1] Stars indicate movable feasts that depend on Easter. See table of Easter dates and movable feasts on pages 357–358.

of Imst, which is situated on the southern slopes of the Lech-
taler Alps. Only men participate in this festival, which symbolizes the combat between winter and spring. After a bitter
struggle, the evil winter spirits finally are routed and the spirits
of spring enter Imst with blessings for animals and crops. In
ancient times people of this community thought they could
frighten away destroying demons with grotesque wooden masks
which were painted realistically to represent various forces of
evil. Many of the masks worn by the modern performers have
been handed down from father to son for generations. The
dancers make a terrific din as they jangle bells, sing, shout and
surge through the squares of Imst—for evil spirits always must
flee before noise! The spirits of fertility and awakened life
finally conquer the demons of discord and darkness. About
three hundred performers take part in the famous procession-
dance.

*Karfreitag, Good Friday.   *The Friday preceding Easter*

In many sections of the country, church clocks are not allowed to strike on Good Friday. In some parts of Vienna, boys
indicate the time of day by going through the streets at regular
intervals with large round rattles, which are decorated with
flowers and bright ribbons. The rattles, when swung, make a
curious grating noise.

*Ostern, Easter.

Young and old, rich and poor, give and receive colored
eggs at this season. Sometimes the eggs are dyed in solid
colors, sometimes they are decorated with comic faces or beautiful flower designs. At Easter, eggs are served for breakfast,
dinner, supper, and for *Jause,* or afternoon tea. In addition to

the usual dyed eggs, children receive presents of chocolate, marzipan and candy-filled composition eggs, as well as little candy bunnies which delight the eye and satisfy the palate. Adults exchange presents of papier-mâché eggs containing such trifles as handkerchiefs, perfume and neckties. Eggs always are hidden, whether they are intended for children or adults. On this day wives usually receive gifts of flowers from their husbands. Women wear new gowns and fresh flowers when they attend the Easter morning church services.

STAATSFEIERTAG, Constitution Day.   *May* 1

This is a national anniversary in commemoration of the new constitution of 1934. The day is observed with political speeches, public demonstrations and musical programs.

*FRONLEICHNAM, Corpus Christi.
The Thursday following Trinity Sunday*

One of the most unique and beautiful of Austrian Corpus Christi festivals is celebrated each year in Hallstatt, on Hallstattersee. At an early hour peasants dressed in their richest costumes and costliest headdresses surge into the town square and gather about the temptingly arranged market booths. The band plays, people buy sweets, exchange gossip and drink to one another's health. After morning Mass, celebrated in the mystic dimness of the old Gothic church, a colorful procession slowly makes its way to the lake. There the priest, his altar boys and attendants enter a brilliantly canopied barge and slowly glide across the mountain-bound lake. The worshipers follow in other boats, until a long procession of craft is reflected in the clear waters. Flowers, fluttering church banners which are richly encrusted with gold and silver embroidery, lighted tapers and old

31

church chants add solemnity and beauty to the water procession in honor of the Eucharist. Similar ceremonies are held at Traunkirchen, where people go out in boats on the Traunsee, and at other lake towns in different parts of the country.

JOHANNESFEIER, Saint John's Eve.   *June* 23

Young people build bonfires on the hillsides or in the fields. In some parts of the country people say the hemp will grow as high as they jump over the Saint John's fires. In other sections, peasants leap over the fires three times, believing that by so doing they will become immune from fever. Boys dance about the fires with lighted torches which first have been dipped in pitch. In Lower Austria, peasants often build the fires before a village cross. The people toss flowers into the flames, meanwhile dancing about and singing old folk melodies. Before a bunch of flowers is tossed into the fire, the dancers pause and a set speech is made. Then the dancers again move into rhythmic action. They catch up the last words of the speech and sing it in chorus.

PASSIONSSPIELE THIERSEE, Passion Play at Thiersee.
July–September

Each year thousands of peasants and visitors from abroad witness the Sunday performances of *Christus,* the medieval passion play that is enacted by villagers of Thiersee, near Kufstein, in the heart of the Austrian Tyrol. The players, under the devout training of priest and choirmaster, enact the gospel story with simplicity and dramatic power, following closely the great Biblical narrative. The earnestness and devotion of both performers and spectators carry out the religious tradition that has been handed down for centuries among Tyrolean peasants.

Festivals of the Austrians

LEOPOLDSTAG, Saint Leopold's Day. *November* 15

Austria celebrates its annual harvest home festival on the birthday of Saint Leopold, the country's patron saint. This anniversary, also known as *Gaense Tag,* or Goose Day, because of the traditional evening dinner of roast goose, marks the official opening of the *Heurigen,* or "new wine" season. According to ancient custom, hundreds of pilgrims annually visit the saint's shrine at Klosterneuburg, Austria's twelfth century abbey. There they perform the ceremony of *Fasselrutschen,* "the slide of the Great Cask," in the abbey's famous wine cellar. Laughing boys and girls, heavy *Hausfrauen,* ruddy-faced men, fashionably dressed Viennese, rich and poor, all await their turn to perform the time-honored rite. Often the line of people extends from the dimly lighted cellar to a place far down the hillside. One by one the people mount the narrow staircase that goes to the rafters and the top of the cask. Each person seats himself on the smooth surface and then lets go. With breath-taking speed he shoots down the side of the cask and lands on the padded platform at its base. According to old tradition, the more violently he slides the better his luck in the coming year. The great cask, magnificently sculptured by a famous Viennese carver, holds 12,000 gallons of wine. It was completed in 1704 by an abbot who decided a fitting receptacle was needed for the famous Leopoldsberg wine which, even in early days, annually attracted hundreds of pilgrims to the abbey. After properly attending to the *Fasselrutschen* ceremony, everybody goes farther up the mountainside to visit Stiftskeller Hall and its lovely gardens. There the pilgrims feast and sing and drink new Heurigen wine. All over Austria wine-drinking picnics and parties are held on this day. Grinzing, with its pleasant gardens, is noted for its democratic gatherings of folk from every station in life. People bring huge basket luncheons which include "yards" of good Austrian sausage, and many other hearty

33

and delicious foods.   The picnickers gossip, eat and drink new wine, until count and butcher are brothers and class distinctions are forgotten.

Nikolaustag, Saint Nicholas' Day.   *December* 6

Saint Nicholas, the gift-giver of Austrian children, makes his rounds in person as a splendidly arrayed bishop, with long white beard, glittering robes and pastoral staff.   The saint's benign appearance is offset by his *Knecht Ruprecht,* an awe-inspiring black-faced servant who stands close by with a stout switch. Saint Nicholas rewards with gifts of sweets and nuts children who are obedient, study their lessons and know their catechisms. Naughty youngsters have reason to tremble, however, as Knecht Ruprecht·spanks them soundly and threatens further punishment unless they mend their ways.   Saint Nicholas' servant varies in character according to locality.   In some parts of Austria he is *Klaubauf,* a horrible horned monster.   In Styria he is known as *Bartel;* in Lower Austria he is called *Krampus* or *Gampus.*   Wherever and however he appears, children dread Saint Nicholas' attendant, who knows too much about their shortcomings and frightens them with threatening mien.   The Christmas markets open immediately after Saint Nicholas' Day. These markets are brilliant, glittering affairs where ingenious toys, fancy gingerbreads, nuts, sweets and all kinds of holiday foodstuffs are exhibited in tempting array.   Beginning with Saint Nicholas' Day, school children are taught to make Christmas-tree decorations.   They fashion fancy-colored papers into long chains, paint nuts silver or gold, and make baskets, paper stars and many other charming trifles.   When Christmas finally arrives it is a day of special delight to the children, who have labored long and diligently to prepare for the event.

Festivals of the Austrians

HEILIGER ABEND, Christmas Eve.   *December 24*

Shops, concert halls and theatres are closed on Christmas Eve, as Christmas is celebrated strictly within the family circle. Pious folk attend church early in the day and later go to Midnight Mass. The Christmas supper includes roast goose or, in some places, a certain kind of fish. Other favorite dishès are *Mehlspeise,* a round, hot tart, and the famous *Linzertorte,* or light pastry dessert-tart, which is filled with raisins and nuts and flavored with almond and rose oil. After the Christmas dinner the father reads the story of *Kristkindl* to family, guests and servants. Later everyone joins in singing the old and well-loved carols. At last a big bell is rung, the doors are flung open and the lighted Christmas tree exhibited in a blaze of glory. In homes of the wealthy each member of the household is assigned to a small table which holds wrapped gifts and plates filled with apples, nuts and every imaginable kind of sweet. In humble circles everyone sits at the same table and receives goodies, and the unwrapped gifts are placed beneath the Christmas tree. In peasant families the presents always consist of stout shoes, woolen socks, warm mittens or other practical articles.

CHRISTFEST, Christmas.   *December 25*

The day is spent quietly in the homes. Attending religious services, eating and visiting are the chief occupations of the holiday.

STEFANSTAG, Saint Stephen's Day.   *December 26*

In some Carinthian villages which are noted for their fine horses, youths follow the old custom of mounting unsaddled horses and racing them several times about the parish church.

The priest, meanwhile, blesses the animals and sprinkles them with holy water.

SYLVESTERABEND, Saint Sylvester's Eve.   *December* 31

Among peasants of Upper and Lower Austria, Saint Sylvester's Eve, like the Eves of Saint Thomas, Christmas and Epiphany, is regarded as a *Rauchnacht,* or "smoke-night," when rooms and outhouses must be purified with incense and holy water. The peasant is accompanied by his children and his wife, who carries a censer and basin of holy water. Together they visit every corner of the household. The sacred smoke and blessed water must touch rooms and stalls, cows, horses, pigs and chickens. Even the storerooms, with their stocks of grain, cheese and smoked meats, must be purified. This old household rite, which is practiced in many towns and cities as well as in rural communities, is said to drive out the evils of the old year and usher in the new with prosperity and luck. In Vienna the pig, the animal which follows man's footsteps wherever he goes, is the popular good luck symbol. Smart Viennese sometimes lead young pigs by pink satin leashes along the magnificent *Ringstrasse.* In many of the fashionable restaurants and cafés squealing pigs are set loose at midnight and everyone tries to touch them "for luck." In private homes a marzipan pig often is suspended by a ribbon from ceiling or chandelier. Just at midnight, when bells are ringing and whistles blowing, the guests rush forward and touch the pig. A gold piece, placed in the animal's mouth, symbolizes a wish for wealth throughout the coming year.

FESTIVALS OF THE BELGIANS

NIEUWJAARSDAG, New Year's Day.   *January* 1

Adults celebrate the first day of the New Year with conventional calls and the exchange of greetings and congratulations. For weeks before the holiday, children save their pennies to buy elaborately decorated papers on which to inscribe New Year's wishes to parents and god-parents. Often these papers are ornamented with roses, ribbons, golden cherubs and angels. The children practice composing and writing their letters in school until they make final copies without error or erasure. Then the messages carefully are hidden away from the parents. On the morning of the first, each boy or girl reads aloud his or her composition before the assembled family. Not only are wishes for a Happy New Year expressed, but promises are made to improve in behavior during the next twelve months. In Liége poor children visit from house to house and stop passers-by to wish them a Happy New Year and offer *nul,* or wafers stamped with pictures of the crucifix. The children receive small coins in return for the wafers, which people keep as charms during the coming year.

DRIEKONINGENDAG, Day of the Kings, Epiphany.   *January* 6

In many homes *Driekoningendag* is a great festival for the children, who celebrate it with a *gâteau des rois,* cake of the kings. Somewhere in the cake a bean is hidden. The child finding the bean in his or her portion is proclaimed king or queen of the feast. The ruler then chooses a royal consort. Crowned with paper crowns and attired in mock splendor, the monarchs reign over the merry party. Whatever they do the other boys and girls comment upon and imitate with great hilarity. In many places bands of children go from door to door singing about the kings and receiving gifts of pennies. One favorite ditty says:

> *"Three Kings, three Kings,*
> *Give me a new hat.*
> *My old one is worn out,*
> *My mother shouldn't know about it,*
> *My father has counted the money on the grille!"*[1]

SINT GUDULE, Saint Gudule.   *January* 8

The anniversary of Saint Gudule, patroness of Brussels, is observed with special solemnity in the great cathedral which bears her name. According to old legend, the seventh century saint, who was noted for her piety, was once on her way to early Mass when the Evil One extinguished her lantern. As Saint Gudule knelt down and prayed for help, an angel rekindled her lantern. In art Saint Gudule always is represented in company with the angel who is lighting her lantern.

CARNAVAL, Carnival.[2] The Sunday, Monday and Tuesday preceding Ash Wednesday

Carnival, which falls on the Sunday, Monday and Tuesday

---

[1] Since old Belgian charcoal stoves are decorated with open *grilles* on top, the verses mean that the money the father counted out fell through the *grille* and so was lost.

[2] Stars indicate movable feasts that depend on Easter. See table of Easter dates and movable feasts on pages 357–358.

Festivals of the Belgians

before Ash Wednesday, is celebrated throughout Belgium with varying degrees of gaiety. Among the most picturesque festivities are those of Binche, which dramatize Mary of Hungary's reception to the son of Charles V. The famous *gilles,* dressed in costly lace-trimmed and embroidered silk costumes and wearing brilliantly dyed ostrich-feather headdresses, dance through the streets to the accompaniment of music and throw oranges to the crowd. The *gilles* number about seven hundred. Before the war, carnival processions were held in the streets of almost every town. Nowadays there are fewer public demonstrations, although merrymaking, drinking, dancing and gaiety characterize this season everywhere. *Duivelsweek,* Devil's Week, is the name humorously given to the seven days preceding the Lenten fast.

*Vastenavond, Mardi Gras, Shrove Tuesday.
The Tuesday preceding Ash Wednesday

The last day before Lent culminates a long series of joyous carnival events which vary in character from city to city. *Koekebakken,* or pancakes, and *wafelen,* waffles, are *Mardi gras* delicacies in many households. In the environs of Liége a superstition exists that cabbage eaten on this day will prevent flies and caterpillars from destroying the cabbages growing in gardens. In some sections of the country boys and girls sing little ditties from door to door. In return they receive gifts of such gala foods as apples, nuts and strips of bacon. The children broil their bacon on long willow spits and hold high holiday before beginning the Lenten fast.

*Eerste Zondag van den Vasten, Sunday of the Great Fires.
First Sunday in Lent

In some parts of the Ardennes the first Sunday in Lent is called the "Sunday of the Great Fires," because bonfires are

built on the heights. For days preceding the festival children
of Grand Halleux go from house to house begging wood for the
fires. If people refuse to give fuel, the children chase them next
day and smudge their faces with ashes. In certain parts of the
country, young folk dance and sing about the fires. They jump
over the embers with a wish for good crops, good luck in marriage and freedom from colic. Seven Lenten fires seen on this
night are said to be a protection against witches. Sometimes
grown folk tell the children they will get as many Easter eggs
as they can count fires. According to old peasant belief, neglect
to kindle "the great fire" means that God will kindle it Himself
—that is, He will set fire to the house.

SINT GREGORY, Saint Gregory.   *March* 12

Saint Gregory, patron of school boys and scholars, is invoked on this day when lads and university students lock up
their masters and ask for a holiday. Sometimes the students
demand other favors as well, and often the harried professor is
forced to yield to their wishes.

*HALF-VASTEN, Mid-Lent.   *The fourth Sunday in Lent*

The Lenten fast is broken by a day of gaiety and fun, when
De Graaf van Half-Vasten, the Count of Mid-Lent, makes his
appearance and rewards good boys and girls with gifts.

*PALMZONDAG, Palm Sunday.   *The Sunday preceding Easter*

Small branches of boxwood are blessed in the churches and
later put in the cornfields to insure plentiful harvest. Sometimes, also, these branches are placed on the tombs of the dead,
with prayers for the souls of the departed.

Festivals of the Belgians

*WITTE DONDERDAG, Holy Thursday.
The Thursday preceding Easter

On this day the chimes cease ringing in the church towers and people say, "The bells have flown to Rome." The Ceremony of Foot Washing still takes place in cathedral churches and some old parishes which rich families have endowed for the purpose. Twelve old men from "God's House," as the almshouse is called, are selected on account of their character and piety to enact the rôle of the Twelve Apostles. The clergy bathe the feet of the men and give them bread and alms.

*GOEDE VRYDAG, Good Friday. *The Friday preceding Easter*

All the churches are draped in black in memory of Christ's Passion, and a general air of sadness prevails throughout the streets of cities and towns. In villages peasant women often wear mourning on this day. In the afternoon everybody attends the three-hour Passion service.

*ZATERDAG VOOR PASCHEN, Saturday before Easter.
The Saturday preceding Easter

The chimes that "flew to Rome" on Holy Thursday return at the Saturday Glory Service and ring joyously throughout the land. Children are told that the bells sow colored Easter eggs in the gardens. In some parts of the country, boys and girls rise early on Easter morning to find the eggs; in other districts egg hunts take place on Saturday. The eggs either are dyed in bright solid colors or else are decorated with bird and flower designs. Every garden overflows with eggs; they are in the crotches of trees, behind shrubs, in the grass, behind piles of stones. The children fill little baskets with their treasures. After having exhausted the resources of their own gardens, the

41

youngsters visit grandparents, uncles and aunts. Everywhere they go there are more eggs to hunt, for Belgian chimes are no less generous with Easter eggs than with their joyous Easter music!

*PASCHEN, Easter.

Easter is a religious holiday, characterized by impressive services in churches and magnificent recitals of organ and carillon music. Children are given presents of all kinds of eggs— hens' eggs dyed, chocolate cream-filled eggs and beautiful sugar eggs containing chocolate or almond paste.

PROCESSIE VAN HET HEILIG BLOED, Procession of the Holy Blood.   *The first Monday after May 2*

The city of Bruges annually holds an imposing procession in honor of the Sacred Blood. The ceremony was instituted in the year 1147, when the Earl Thierry of Alsace was said to have brought to Bruges from the Holy Land a drop of Christ's blood. The sacred relic, which is preserved in a marvelously wrought shrine, is carried in procession from the Chapel of the Holy Blood to the cathedral. There it is placed upon the altar and Mass is celebrated. The procession is composed of different groups which represent various episodes of historic and scriptural interest.

SINT DYMPHNA, Saint Dymphna.   *May* 15

According to tradition, Dymphna, daughter of a seventh century Irish king, fled to Gheel to escape her father's insane demand for an incestuous marriage. The king pursued his daughter to Gheel where he finally killed her. People gradually

42

came to regard Dymphna as the special patroness of the insane. Even in early times mental patients were brought to her tomb for a novena of prayer. A small infirmary finally was built next the church dedicated to Saint Dymphna. The fame of the community grew through the centuries until by 1852 Gheel was placed under state medical supervision. Today Colony Gheel is noted throughout the world for its "boarding out system" whereby mental patients are cared for as "paying guests" in homes of different villagers. On the day dedicated to the canonization of Saint Dymphna special church services are held and a religious procession goes through the streets with a stone from Dymphna's tomb. In olden times this relic was applied to patients as part of their treatment.

*KRUISDAGEN, Cross Days, Rogation Days.
                    The three days preceding Ascension Thursday

The priest, carrying the cross, leads the peasants to the fields, where he blesses crops and prays for rain and abundant harvests. The Litany of All Saints is chanted as the procession goes forth across the meadows and through upturned furrows.

*PINKSTEREN, Pentecost, Whitsunday.
                    The seventh Sunday after Easter

On this church holiday, which commemorates the descent of the Holy Ghost on the disciples, everyone who can goes on an excursion to the country. Parties of merrymakers visit places of historic or scenic interest—in the Ardennes, along the banks of the Meuse, to the famous *grottos* or ancient castle towns.

SINT MEDARDUS, Saint Medardus.   *June 8*

The anniversary of Saint Medardus, Belgium's rain saint,

43

is important in weather lore. According to an old folk rhyme, rain on Saint Medardus' Day means forty days of wet weather:

> *"S'il pleut le jour de Sint Medardus*
> *Il pleut quarante jours plus tard."*

CORPUS CHRISTI.   The Thursday following Trinity Sunday

Stately religious processions, led by the clergy, carry the Sacrament through the streets of the towns and villages. The procession stops at the various *repositoires,* or altars, erected before the houses of certain wealthy parish benefactors. There special services are held in honor of the Eucharist.

SINT JANS VOORAVOND, Saint John's Eve.   *June 23*

In some parts of rural Belgium bonfires are lighted on Saint John's Eve. Children go about from farm to farm, begging for wood in the following words:

> *"Wood, wood, lumber wood,*
> *We come to get Saint John's wood,*
> *Give us a little and keep a little,*
> *Until the Eve of Saint Peter's Day."*

According to old folk superstition, embers from the Saint John's fires protect houses and barns from fire, while jumping over the lighted fires is an antidote against diseases of the stomach.

SINT PIETER, Saint Peter.   *June 29*

In some country places Saint Peter's martyrdom still is observed by building bonfires in the saint's honor. The custom is rapidly dying out, but a few years ago children trundled wheelbarrows from farm to farm and begged fuel for Saint Peter's fires. Old and young made the bonfires, in commemoration of the fire before which Saint Peter warmed himself when he denied Christ. As the flames leaped high, children danced in a ring and sang:

> *"Saint Peter come and join us*
> *In our circle of pleasure."*

In some sections of the country people light candles on this night and say the rosary in memory of Saint Peter.

ZEGENING VAN DE ZEE, Blessing of the Sea.

Sometime during July

Each July mariners of the seaport town of Ostend follow their priest to the sea, where he blesses the waters and invokes divine protection on the parish seamen. All fishermen, mariners and others who are exposed to dangers of the water are allowed to participate in the ceremonies. After Mass in the cathedral, a procession composed of clergy, dignitaries and mariners, carrying votive offerings and church banners, slowly makes its way to the strand. Clergy and seamen enter boats and go out to bless the waves.

DAG DER NATIONALE ONAFHANKELYHEID, National Independence Day. *July 21*

This anniversary marks the beginning of Belgian independence and the accession to the throne of Leopold I. The nine Belgian Provinces, which for fifteen years had belonged to the Kingdom of the Netherlands, set up their own sovereign state in 1830. Prince Leopold of Saxe-Coburg ascended the throne on July 21, 1831, and was proclaimed first King of the Belgians. The day is celebrated annually with military reviews, patriotic speeches and *Te Deums* in the churches.

45

MARIA-HEMELVAART DAT, Assumption of the Virgin Mary.

August 15

After morning Mass in honor of the Virgin, the priest, holding aloft the Blessed Sacrament, leads a procession to the fields, to bless the fruits and grains. In Hasselt, capital of Limburg, the festival of *Virga Jesse* is annually celebrated on Assumption Day. Originally, the image of the Virgin, placed against a forest tree, presided over the crossroads near the present site of Hasselt. Travelers left offerings at the shrine and prayed for safe journeys. Gradually report of the miraculous power of the image spread, until by the fourteenth century, pilgrims from far and near came to worship at the shrine. Nowadays the ancient blackened image of the Virgin annually is crowned, clothed in a velvet mantle and carried through the town in triumphal procession. Arches, erected at different places, mark various dramatic episodes in Hasselt's history.

ALLER HEILIGEN DAG, All Saints' Day.   *November* 1

In the churches prayers are said to the memory of all the saints not mentioned on the calendar. Toward evening the All Souls' Eve services begin. People visit the cemeteries and decorate the graves with flowers and wreaths. Candles are lighted in memory of the deceased.

ALLER ZIELEN DAG, All Souls' Day.   *November* 2

Special "All Souls" cakes are made for this occasion. According to an old superstition, "the more cakes you eat on this night, the more souls you can save from Purgatory."

SINT HUBERTUS VAN LUIK, Saint Hubert of Liége.

November 3

Saint Hubert, the seventh century Bishop of Liége, is patron of dogs and the chase. According to legend, Hubert was a worldly young man who one day was following the chase when he had a vision of a stag with a shining cross between his antlers. Hubert was converted to Christianity and a chapel later was erected near the spot where the vision occurred. Saint Hubert's day marks the formal opening of the hunting season, when Saint Hubert's Mass is held in the churches. Each household prepares special loaves of bread which are blessed at the early morning service. The bread then is taken home, the sign of the cross made and everyone breaks fast by eating a piece of the blessed loaf. Dogs, horses and all other animals are fed the bread to protect them from rabies during the coming year. Sometimes people say an old folk rhyme as they carry home the loaves:

> *"I came all the way from Saint Hubert's grave,*
> *Without stick, without staff.*
> *Mad dogs, stand still!*
> *This is Saint Hubert's will."*

Every year hundreds of devout pilgrims visit the grave of Saint Hubert, who is buried in the city that bears his name.

SINT MAARTENS DAG, Saint Martin's Day.   *November* 11

This is a day greatly anticipated by Belgian boys and girls, who celebrate the festival with processions, bonfires and general merrymaking. In some parts of the country the saint calls in person on the Eve. If children have been good he bestows apples and goodies, but if they have been bad, he suggestively throws a whip on the floor. On Saint Martin's Day showers of apples and nuts sometimes are tossed into the room as boys and girls stand with their faces turned toward the wall. In Furnes, Bruges and some other places children carrying lighted paper lanterns march through the streets at night. They sing Saint Martin songs and ask for gifts of nuts and apples. *Gauffres,* special Saint Martin's Day cakes, are popular at this season.

47

SINT NIKOLAAS VOORAVOND, Saint Nicholas' Eve.   *December* 5

Children write annual letters to Saint Nicholas, the invisible gift giver, who slips down the chimney on this night and leaves toys in the empty shoes by the mantel.   Saint Nicholas rides a donkey and is attended by a black servant.   The saint sees everything.   He knows everything, but no child has ever seen or known him.   The father of the family always promises to post the children's letters because he alone knows how to reach the saint!   The children place carrots and pieces of bread in the chimney corner for Saint Nicholas' donkey, who doubtless is hungry from journeying over village housetops.   In the evening parents and children sit around the fire and tell stories about the life and works of Saint Nicholas.   The children sing charming little songs in his honor.   Suddenly a shower of sweets flies through the door.   Boys and girls scramble under tables and chairs and by the time the last candy is found, Saint Nicholas has vanished.

SINT NIKOLAAS, Saint Nicholas.   *December* 6

Boys and girls rise early and patter to the chimney to see what Saint Nicholas has left during the night.   Each child's shoes usually contain special treats such as an orange, a piece of marzipan, and *specalaus,* or a gingerbread figure of Saint Nicholas.   Often there are toys and useful gifts besides, such as sweaters, mittens, pretty woolen mufflers, dresses or suits.

KERSTAVOND, Christmas Eve.   *December* 24

Midnight services are held in many of the churches, where worshipers kneel before the lifelike representations of the Christ Child in the manger.   Many folk superstitions exist regarding this holy night, when, according to peasant belief, water turns to wine and people can look into the future.   In some parts of the country children go from door to door singing of Christ's birth and begging for gifts of nuts, fruit or other good things to eat.

KERSTDAG, Christmas.   *December* 25

Christmas is a religious holiday, observed by attending special services in the churches and wishing friends and neighbors a Merry Christmas. After church, in some parts of the country, the whole family gathers about the Yule log to celebrate *La Veillée*. Ghost stories and tales are told, old ballads sung and gin freely passed. Sometimes the gin is lighted as the log falls to ashes. Children await Christmas morning eagerly. If they are good and have said their prayers faithfully throughout the year, the Archangel Gabriel or, in some places, the Child Jesus, is thought to slip an *engelskoek,* an angel's cake (a kind of bun), under the pillows of sleeping boys and girls.

ALLERKINDERENDAG, LE JOUR DES INNOCENTS, Holy Innocents' Day.   *December* 28

On the day commemorating Herod's slaughter of Bethlehem's infants, Belgian children try to put their elders under lock and key and make them buy themselves out of bondage. Early in the morning boys and girls attempt to get possession of all the keys in the house. Whenever an unsuspecting adult enters a closet or room, he may unexpectedly find himself a prisoner. His freedom is not restored until he pays the forfeit the children demand—an orange, a toy, spending money, sweets —the ransom varying with his keeper's whim. The innocent person held for ransom is called "sugar uncle" or "sugar aunt."

SINT SYLVESTERS VOORAVOND, Saint Sylvester's Eve.
                                                           December 31

The boy or girl who rises last in the morning is nicknamed

a "Sylvester." As the "Sylvesters" have to pay forfeits to their brothers and sisters, each child tries to be the first one out of bed. According to an old saying, the young girl who does not finish her handwork by sunset on Saint Sylvester's Eve will remain a spinster for the next twelve months. In small towns and villages the last night of the year is spent in gay family parties. At midnight everybody kisses and exchanges wishes for a Happy New Year. In cities, restaurants and cafés are crowded with merrymakers, who drink and bid the old year a noisy farewell.

FESTIVALS OF THE BRITISH

NEW YEAR'S DAY.   *January* 1

The first of January is regarded as Scotland's great national holiday. Directly after midnight church services, people
often begin calling and wishing one another a Happy New Year.
According to old folk custom, the first person putting foot across
the doorsill on New Year's Day is called a "first-foot," and is
thought to bring good or bad luck for the coming year. To
make the luck good, the "first-foot" always brings a gift of
wine, ale or some holiday dainty. New Year's Day is spent in
visiting family and friends, exchanging greetings and good
wishes. In many villages groups of boys masquerade from
house to house, enacting a rude folk play of which Galashan is
hero. In return for their performance the lads receive small
money gifts.

TWELFTH DAY EVE, EPIPHANY EVE.   *January* 5

Wassailing the fruit trees is an ancient fertility rite which
still survives in Carhampton, near Minehead, and in other parts
of rural England. In olden times Devonshire farmers and their
helpers used to carry jugs of cider to the orchards. Surrounding one of the best-bearing apple trees, they would address it
with the following toast:

"Here's to thee, old apple-tree,
Whence thou mayst bud, whence thou mayst blow!
And whence thou mayst bear apples enow!
Hats full! Caps full!
Bushel-bushel-sacks full,
And my pockets full too! Huzza!"

According to old folk belief, the "Twelve Days" between Christmas and Epiphany are a mirror of the next twelve months. A mince pie or a plum pudding eaten on each of the fateful days is said to insure good fortune and prosperity for the coming year. The Twelfth Day cake, with a bean and a pea baked inside, is eaten at many parties. Whoever finds the bean in his share of the cake is proclaimed king of the revels, while the person getting the pea is queen. King and queen rule the feast, and the other guests imitate their actions with great hilarity.

SAINT AGNES.   *January* 21

The feast of the fourth century Roman virgin who suffered persecution under the Emperor Diocletian is regarded as a propitious time for spells and divination. By fasting all day and eating a salt-filled egg at night, a young girl will dream of her lover—who will appear and offer her water!

SAINT PAUL.   *January* 25

Country folk say the weather of the whole year depends upon this day. According to the *Shepherd's Almanack* for 1676, sun on Saint Paul's Day means a good year, rain or snow foretells indifferent weather, a mist means want, while thunder predicts twelve months of winds and death.

Festivals of the British

Saint Bridget, the sixth century Irish princess who was converted to Christianity and became the first Irish nun, is identified in pagan legend with Brighit, daughter of the sun. Brighit's ancient temple at Kildare was attended by royal vestal virgins who kept the goddess' fires eternally burning. Years later, when the pagan temple became the site of the Christian convent, Brighit, goddess of fire and guardian of dreams, was transformed into an Irish saint. Nowadays, children of some rural communities carry from house to house a doll called Saint Bridget's baby, and beg for money "to buy Saint Bridget's candles."

CANDLEMAS DAY.   *February* 2

Candlemas, the feast that commemorates the Purification of the Virgin Mary or the Presentation of Christ, derives its name from the custom of blessing candles in the churches. In Scotland, and in many other parts of Great Britain, candles are kindled on the altars in honor of this day. Tradition says it is bad luck to leave up the Yuletide greens after Candlemas Day. Herrick wrote the following lines about kindling a brand from the Yule log on Candlemas:

> *"Kindle the Christmas brand, and then*
> *Till sunne-set let it burne;*
> *Which quencht, then lay it up agen,*
> *Till Christmas next returne.*
>
> *"Part must be kept wherewith to tend*
> *The Christmas Log next yeare;*
> *And where'tis safely kept, the Fiend*
> *Can do no mischiefe there."*

SHROVE TUESDAY, PANCAKE DAY.[1]

The Tuesday preceding Ash Wednesday

Until the Reformation the tolling of the bell on Shrove Tuesday reminded village folk of confession and shriving by the parish priest. Later, however, the bell which once prompted people to attend church became a signal for making pancakes, and Shrove Tuesday popularly became known as Pancake Day. Pancake Day, with its pancake eating, singing for Shrovetide fare and customary sports of cock-fighting, football and "throwing the pancake," closely rivaled Christmas as a time of merrymaking and feasting. Poor Robin's *Almanack* for 1684 describes the ringing of the pancake bell, which was a summons for cooks to rush to the frying-pan, and for clerks and laborers to cease working and join in the day's festivities:

> *"But hark, I hear the pancake bell,*
> *And fritters make a gallant smell;*
> *The cooks are baking, frying, boyling,*
> *Stewing, mincing, cutting, broyling,*
> *Carving, gormandising, roasting,*
> *Carbonading, cracking, slashing, toasting."*

At Westminster School the traditional game of "Tossing the Pancake" is observed annually with its old-time enthusiasm. With great ceremony a pancake is tossed over the bar which separates the Upper and Lower Schools. The boys struggle to obtain the pancake and the one getting either the whole cake or the largest portion is rewarded with a money prize. In many parts of Great Britain, football games are another feature of the Shrove Tuesday sports. Shrove Tuesday is called by different names according to locality. In Northumberland and Scotland it is Fastern's E'en; in some other places it is Rope-pulling Day or Shuttlecock Day, after some of the holiday's favorite sports.

[1] Stars indicate movable feasts that depend on Easter. See table of Easter dates and movable feasts on pages 357–358.

SAINT DAVID. *March* 1

The anniversary of Saint David, fifth and sixth century patron of Wales, is celebrated annually with special services and processions of Welsh organizations and charitable societiés. The leek, Wales' national symbol, is worn on Saint David's Day to commemorate the legend that Saint David, when leading his people to victory against the Saxons, commanded them to wear leeks in their hats, to avoid confusion with the enemy.

*ASH WEDNESDAY. *The first day of Lent*

In Norfolk and Suffolk people say the direction of Ash Wednesday's wind foretells how it will blow throughout Lent. In olden times many special foods such as hasty puddings, peas, frumenty, fritters, fish and simnel cakes were eaten on Ash Wednesday.

SAINT PATRICK. *March* 17

The anniversary of Saint Patrick, Ireland's patron saint, is celebrated as the country's national holiday. Everybody "wears the green" to commemorate the legend of Saint Patrick and how he used the shamrock, with its three leaves growing from one stem, as symbolic of the Trinity doctrine. Parades, balls and special festivities honor the day of Ireland's saint, who freed the country from snakes and converted the heathen to Christianity.

*MOTHERING SUNDAY. *The fourth Sunday in Lent*

According to old custom, Mothering Sunday is the day when all children go home to visit their parents and take them gifts. The mother's traditional present is a simnel, a kind of

55

rich plum cake. In olden times parents and children usually attended morning church service and then ate a family dinner, which consisted of roast veal, rice pudding and other good things. The mother always was the center of the festivities, and nothing was omitted to add to her pleasure or enjoyment. Shrewsbury, Devizes, Bury and other towns still make the traditional simnels, which children present to mothers on this day.

*CARLING SUNDAY. *The fifth Sunday in Lent*

Since early times, the fifth Sunday in Lent has been called Carling Sunday, after the custom of eating carlings, or peas, which are soaked overnight, fried in butter, and seasoned with pepper and salt. In Lancashire, fig pies are another food typical of the day.

*MAUNDY THURSDAY. *The Thursday preceding Easter*

The name Maundy Thursday, generally thought to be from the Latin *mandatum,* a command or order, refers to Christ's words to his disciples, *Mandatum novum do vobis,* "A new commandment I give to you." From early times English laity and churchmen observed the ceremony of washing the feet of the poor and distributing alms, in commemoration of Christ's so doing. Although James II was the last English sovereign to perform the actual foot-washing ceremony, subsequent monarchs have continued the ancient practice of giving presents of money to the poor people selected for the ceremony.

*GOOD FRIDAY. *The Friday preceding Easter*

*"Good Friday comes this month, the old woman runs
With one or two a penny hot cross buns,*

56

Festivals of the British

Whose virtue is, if you believe what's said,
They'll not grow mouldy like the common bread,"

is written in Poor Robin's *Almanack* for 1733. Many folk-superstitions exist regarding the efficacy of Good Friday buns, which are thought to protect homes from fire and cure diseases of cattle and men. There are numerous local beliefs about work done on Good Friday. If you wash, the suds will turn to blood; if you hang out clothes, they will be spotted with blood; should you break a piece of crockery, however, you will have good luck, as the sharp points will penetrate Judas' body!

*EASTER.

The sun dances for joy on Easter morning, old folk say, in memory of Christ's resurrection. People used to rise at dawn and go forth to witness this miracle. In Sussex it was said that nobody ever really saw the occurrence because the devil always put something between the sun and the observer's eyes. To wear a new garment on Easter day is one way of getting good luck for the new year!

"At Easter let your clothes be new
Or else be sure you will it rue,"

says an old rhyme. Easter is considered important in weather lore. Rain on Easter Day means grass but little hay, while Easter sunshine predicts fair Whitsuntide weather. The Easter holidays—the Monday, Tuesday and Wednesday following the festival—always have been celebrated as a period for popular sports and recreation. Among the traditional amusements observed from ancient times are exchanging gifts of colored eggs, "playing at handball for a tansy cake," dancing on the village green, "heaving" or "lifting," "holly bussing" and other quaint customs. Many of them survive in certain localities. On Easter Monday and Tuesday, "lifting" still is observed in Cheshire. Possibly the custom originated in 1290, when Edward I gave sums of money to the members of his household who lifted or raised him from his bed, in commemoration of Christ's resurrection.   Today money presents continue to be given to those who "lift" members of their family at this season.

SAINT GEORGE.   *April* 23

The day of Saint George, patron saint of England, is celebrated with wearing the red rose and raising his flag (the banner of the Church of England), which is a red cross on a white background.   Saint George, who was made England's patron about 1344, later became the country's military protector.   On Saint George's Day the annual service of the Order of Saint Michael and Saint George is held in Saint Paul's Cathedral, London.

MAY DAY.   *May* 1

The English May Day rites, which originated in Roman times in honor of the goddess Flora, are continued with much of their old-time charm in many towns and villages.   In some localities Jack-i'-the-Green, the jolly leaf-covered mummer of olden days, still circles the Maypole with his chimney sweeps. In many places picturesque processions of white-clad May queens with garlanded attendants go through village streets and dance about the Maypole.   In English and Irish villages people put bells and flowers on their horses and drive them through the streets.   In Stratford-on-Avon the squire's horses are particularly gay, while merchants and livery men parade their animals with flower-decked harnesses and colored ribbon streamers.

FURRY FESTIVAL.   *May* 8

At Helsten, in Cornwall, Wales, the Furry Festival is celebrated each year on the day of the apparition of Saint Michael. According to legend, the town of Helsten is named from a great granite stone that once lay at the mouth of hell. One day the devil attempted to steal the stone. On his way through Cornwall, Saint Michael intercepted the devil, forced him to drop the granite block and flee. The Furry Festival celebrates this legend. The day begins with singing an ancient ballad, to the accompaniment of drums, kettles and other musical instruments. The singers then go to the schoolhouse and demand a holiday for the scholars. Later the merrymakers go to the woods in search of flowers and leaves, and return at nightfall in gay procession. To the accompaniment of the "Furry tune," played by the village fiddler, they dance in and out of the houses at will, ending their revels far in the night. The origin of the term "furry" as used in connection with the festival is obscure.

SAINT JOHN'S EVE.   *June 23*

Ireland, especially southern Ireland, still celebrates Saint John's Eve with bonfires, dancing, omens and prayers. Many authorities think the fires of Saint John originated in the bonfires the ancient Druids dedicated to Bel. Cattle driven between the fires were thought to become immune to disease during the coming year. Today people build countless bonfires on the hillsides. Young and old gather round and feed the flames with fragrant boughs. As the night spends itself and the flames grow low, old and young join hands and jump through the embers, wishing for abundance of grain and plentiful harvests. As the Druids tried to foretell the future by casting strange spells, so young Irish maids seek to learn their destinies by dropping melted lead into water and watching the shapes the metal assumes—a lover, a convent, a castle, a king. Many are the forms taken by the lead and many the "fates" girls read on the night of the blessed John.

SAINT SWITHIN. *July* 15

Saint Swithin, the ninth century Bishop of Winchester, is popularly regarded as responsible for the weather of the forty days following his anniversary. According to old folk rhyme:
> *"Saint Swithin's Day, if thou dost rain,*
> *For forty days it will remain:*
> *Saint Swithin's Day, if thou be fair,*
> *For forty days 'twill rain na mair."*

EISTEDDFOD. *First week in August*

The *Eisteddfod,* or annual national congress for the encouragement of Welsh music and literature, probably originated before the Christian era. The *Eisteddfod* as we know it dates back to the fourth century, when chieftains and rulers rewarded the meritorious performances of court musicians and bards. In the twelfth century the Prince of Wales showed special honor to Irish harpists and other musicians who had come to his court from foreign lands. In the latter part of the thirteenth century, when Wales was annexed to England, the King ordered the perpetuation of the *Eisteddfods.* Today the annual contests open with blowing trumpets "to the four corners of the world." This ceremony is followed by a speech of welcome and poetic addresses by the bards. Then there are all kinds of competitions—harp playing, solo and choral singing, dramatic presentations and poetic composition. The winners are honored with degrees and prizes.

ALLHALLOWS' EVE, NUTCRACK NIGHT. *October* 31

The last night of October, once observed as a solemn festival of the Church, gradually developed into a time of gaiety and fun, when girls and boys read fortunes from such simple

60

objects as apple parings, cabbages, seeds or nuts. Because nuts probably were the favorite means of fortune telling, Allhallows' Eve popularly became known as Nutcrack Night. Girls and boys placed nuts side by side on the glowing embers. If the nuts burned peacefully, it meant a happy married life, but if they flew apart, a stormy future was foretold. In Ireland girls named nuts after lovers, set them in a row on the grate, and watched results. If a nut jumped, an unfaithful lover was predicted, but if it blazed steadily, it proved a lad's affection.

ALL SOULS' EVE.   *November* 1

In Knutsford, Cheshire, and other old towns, girls still go "souling," or singing for cakes in remembrance of the dead. The young people travel about from house to house, chanting such ancient ballads as:

> *"Soul! Soul! for a soul-cake!*
> *I pray, good misses, a soul-cake!*
> *An apple or pear, a plum or a cherry,*
> *Any good thing to make us merry.*
> *One for Peter, two for Paul,*
> *Three for Him who made us all.*
> *Up with the kettle, and down with the pan,*
> *Give us good alms, and we'll be gone."*

In Cheshire the girls are rewarded with bunlike "soul-cakes," which, in olden times, doubtless were given for prayers for the dead, or as "a charity" for departed souls. Soul-cakes and souling customs vary from place to place, but "souling" practices always flourished best along the Welsh border.

GUY FAWKES' DAY.   *November* 5

The anniversary of the discovery of the plot to blow up the Houses of Parliament in 1605 is celebrated annually with bon-

61

fires and fireworks. In many places, especially in cathedral towns, effigies of Guy Fawkes, wearing his high hat and carrying a lantern, are taken about the streets by torchlight, and later are burned in blazing bonfires.

ANDRYS DAY, ANDERMESS, SAINT ANDREW'S DAY.

November 30

Patriotic Scotsmen, wherever they may be, annually observe the day of Saint Andrew, Scotland's patron saint. Banquets, parades and Saint Andrew's fairs are among the special festivities which mark the modern observance of the anniversary. In London it once was customary for Scotsmen to carry in procession a singed sheep's head, as a reminder of one of Scotland's favorite foods. In Eastling, Kent, England, squirrel hunting used to be the day's historic sport. In Scotland as elsewhere, Saint Andrew's Eve is a favorite occasion for love omens and charms.

CHRISTMAS. *December* 25

Christmas in the British Isles is a time of feasting and hearty good cheer. Yuletide is characterized by picturesque customs, old carols, blazing logs, holly and mistletoe. "He has more to do than the ovens in England at Christmas," says an Italian proverb, in describing the thoroughness with which British housewives prepare for the Yuletide feast. Every locality boasts its own traditional food. In Cornwall a saffron-colored currant cake is made for each member of the household. In the Highlands of Scotland new sowens, a kind of oatmeal husk porridge, once was popular as an early Christmas morning food. Shropshire has its wigs, or caraway buns, which people dip in ale on Christmas Eve and eat with a toast to the Christ Child.

Festivals of the British

At Queen's College, Oxford, the boar's head is carried in with the traditional carol:

> *"The boar's head in hand bear I,*
> *Bedeck'd with bays and rosemary*
> *And I pray you, my masters, be merry."*

In olden days the wassail bowl, or mixture of hot ale, spices and toasted apples, was prepared for friends and drunk with the greeting:

> *"Love and joy come to you,*
> *And to your wassail—too."*

Plum puddings always have been associated with British Yuletide feasts. One superstition declares that a pudding eaten before Christmas brings bad luck. After the holiday, however, it brings good luck. Twelve puddings (or mince pies, in some places) eaten between Christmas and Epiphany symbolize good fortune for the twelve months of the year.

CHILDERMAS DAY, FEAST OF THE HOLY INNOCENTS.

December 28

The Irish say that Childermas, the day that commemorates Herod's massacre of the Innocents, is "the cross day of the year." To begin work on this day was considered unlucky in Northamptonshire, while Cornwall housewives refused to scrub or clean on Childermas. It is recorded that Edward IV, whose coronation was set for Childermas, insisted upon postponing the ceremony, as he did not consider the day propitious for beginning his reign.

NEW YEAR'S EVE.

December 31

The festivities surrounding the closing of the old year and the beginning of the new are among the gayest of the Scotch calendar. Houses are scrubbed and put in order. Pies, cakes

63

and all kinds of choice holiday foods are prepared in anticipation of the family reunions in every home. On this night boys and girls go out in bands to seek their "Hogmany" or New Year gifts at the homes of well-to-do villagers. "Hogmany! Hogmany!" shout the children as they arrive. Then they sing traditional verses, which have been handed down for generations:

> *"Get up, goodwife, and shake your feathers,*
> *And dinna think that we are beggars;*
> *For we are bairns come out to play;*
> *Get up and gies our Hogmanay."*

The children receive rewards of apples, coins or New Year cakes in return for their songs. Older people "watch the old year out and the New Year in" at the midnight church services.

FESTIVALS OF THE BULGARIANS

Nova Godina, New Year's Day. *January* 1

For days before the New Year, housewives are busy baking *kolach,* toothsome little round cakes with holes in the center. On New Year's Eve, shortly after the village clock tolls the midnight hour, groups of boys shouldering red cornel switches, which are decorated with gaudy paper flowers, steal through the silent streets and rap smartly at the doors. As they knock, the boys sing the traditional greeting for good luck and a plentiful harvest:

> *"Happy, happy New Year,*
> *Till next year, till eternity,*
> *Corn on the cornstalk,*
> *Grapes in the vineyard,*
> *Yellow grain in the bin,*
> *Red apples in the garden,*
> *Silkworms in the house,*
> *Happiness and health*
> *Until next year."*

With a last tremendous rap the door flies open. The boys rush into the spicy kitchen, where their coming is awaited by the entire household. The lads gently switch good wishes into every member of the family, beginning with the aged grandmother and ending with the baby. In reward for their greetings the children receive money and dozens of the crisp little *kolach,*

65

which they slip over their rods. Then, with whoops of delight the boys are off to win more cookies before dawn touches the eastern hills.

YURDANOV DEN, Jordan's Day; BOGOYAVLENIYE, Epiphany.
January 6 O.S. (January 19 N.S.)

The ceremony of Blessing the Waters is performed annually in all Danube port towns. In Philippopolis, the most important town of southern Bulgaria, the priest throws the cross from the bridge into the swiftly flowing Maritza. The man who recovers the crucifix is allowed to carry it from house to house during the day and receive money gifts from the various families. At night he returns the cross to the priest, who bestows his blessing. In some parts of Bulgaria it is customary for housewives to rise early and carry to village fountains the family crucifix, the ikons and the ploughshare. The women wash these objects with salt and water, saying, "May the wheat be as white as the ploughshare, as wholesome as the salt." On Epiphany the clergy bless the parishioners' homes with holy water. According to folk superstition, if the water freezes on the priest's boxwood whisk, the year will be good and the crops fruitful.

BABIN DEN, Grandmother's Day.
January 7 O.S. (January 20 N.S.)

On this day it is customary for boys to duck the girls in the icy waters of rivers and lakes. This custom, of ancient origin, is to "make the girls healthy" throughout the coming year.

Festivals of the Bulgarians

ROZHDEN DEN NA TZAR BORIS III, Birthday of King Boris III.
January 30

The day is observed with special Masses, followed by military parades and public demonstrations.

DEN NA NEZAVISIMOST'TA, Independence Day.   *March* 3

This day celebrates the anniversary of the Treaty of San Stefano, in 1887, and Bulgaria's liberation from Turkish rule. It is observed with military parades, patriotic dramas, contests of the *yunaks,* or athletic societies, folk dancing, singing and picnics in the open.

*SIRNA SEDMITZA, Cheese Week.[1]
The week preceding Lent

During this week only such foods as cheese, milk, pure lard and fish are eaten. All quarrels are forgiven and everyone reconciles himself with his neighbor. In accordance with the strict rites prescribed by tradition, young people visit their elders, sons and daughters their fathers and mothers, godchildren their godparents. It is customary for the younger person to present a lemon to a man, an orange to a woman. Bowing three times, he kisses the older person's hand, begs forgiveness and says, "May your fast be light, may you enjoy a happy fast night." After supper the children indulge in all kinds of merry games. A favorite sport is to tie a piece of Turkish Delight to the end of a string suspended from the ceiling. As the string is set in motion, the child, holding his hands behind his back, tries to get a bite of the tempting morsel. Sometimes a hard-boiled egg or a piece of cheese is substituted for the

[1] Stars indicate movable feasts that depend on Easter. See table of Eastern Orthodox Easter dates and movable feasts on pages 370–371.

67

candy. In some parts of Bulgaria the evening is devoted to building bonfires, through which boys jump and about which girls dance—possibly a survival of an old charm to make crops fruitful.

*ZAGOVEZNI, Beginning of Lent.
The Monday following the last day of Cheese Week

Throughout Lent rigorous fasting is observed. According to an old Bulgarian proverb, the Four Evangelists love those who observe the four rules of abstinence. On the evening of the first Monday in Lent, the day of purification after Carnival, men foretell the weather by looking at the stars. If they are bright and the sky cloudless, a dry summer may be expected; if there is mist, cold days are coming; if it snows at night, the summer will be wet.

*SECOND MONDAY IN LENT.

The second Monday in Lent marks the beginning of spring housecleaning and the season's first planting.

*GLORIFICATION WEEK.   *The fifth week in Lent*

All church services of this week begin with hymns glorifying the Virgin Mary. It is customary for farmers to plant cabbages at this time and for lads to court their sweethearts and offer presents.

*LAZAROVDEN, Lazarus Saturday.
The Saturday preceding Willow Sunday

On this day willow branches are picked. Children go to the woods and gather the first spring flowers. Village boys and girls play a quaint game in memory of Lazarus, whom Christ

raised from the dead. The little lads pretend they are dead
Lazaruses. The little girls, on the contrary, are the Marys and
Marthas. They go from house to house in the community asking, "When is the Lord coming to raise our brother from the
dead?" The children receive pennies and little cakes at the
various homes.

*Vrŭbnitza, Willow Sunday; Tzvetnitza, Flower Sunday.
The Sunday preceding Easter

The willows are blessed in church. Later they are carried
home, placed near the ikon and used, when needed, as charms
against storm and hail.

*Strastna Nedelya, Passion Week.
The week preceding Easter

Throughout the week, fasting continues with renewed zest.
In general, people eat nothing but black bread, black olives,
stewed prunes or peas, and beans cooked in olive oil. Womenfolk busy themselves with preparations for the holidays. Easter
eggs, symbolic of the resurrection, are dyed and painted red,
the color of joy. The mistress of the house places the first
decorated egg beside the ikon, where it remains a symbol of luck
until the following year. Each family bakes many marvelous
almond-adorned Easter cakes, as it is customary to exchange
gifts of cakes and eggs on Passion Saturday.

*Strasten Chetvrŭtŭk, Passion Thursday.
The Thursday preceding Easter

The church bells toll for the last time before the midnight
Easter service. Everyone attends evening services, at which
priests three times chant the twelve Gospels.

69

*Raspeti Petŭk, Crucifixion Friday.

The Friday preceding Easter

In the morning people go to the public baths. Ashes from Good Friday fires are sprinkled in the hen-yards, with a wish for plenty of eggs in the coming year. The afternoon church service is symbolic of the mourning at Christ's sepulchre.

*Strastna Subota, Passion Saturday.

The Saturday preceding Easter

People take Easter eggs and cakes to church for blessing before placing them on the festive table. No work is done on this day.

*Velikden, The Great Day; Vuzkresenie, Resurrection Day.

An impressive midnight service is held in every church and cathedral in the land. In Sofia the ceremonies are particularly magnificent. Shortly before twelve o'clock, the traditional hour of Christ's resurrection, a procession composed of choir, laymen, and church dignitaries in gold and yellow vestments follows the archbishop from the cathedral to a temporary altar in the Alexander Nevsky Square. The square is filled with thousands of worshipers, each of them carrying an unlighted candle. At midnight the chimes peal forth, the archbishop blesses his people and then proclaims loudly, *"Hristos vosskresse"* (Christ is risen). Immediately the dark square is illuminated by thousands of twinkling candles. Each person greets his neighbor with the words, *"Hristos vosskresse"* (He is risen indeed). The Easter candles are reverently carried home and placed beside the ikons. Throughout the year they are used as protection against storm, disease or the evil eye. After the morning service the day is spent in feasting, merrymaking and visiting. The traditional dinner consists of roast lamb stuffed with rice and currants, cold ham, suckling pig, great piles of colored eggs, holiday cakes, and all kinds of fruits and sweets. Each guest who calls is given an Easter egg and some *kozunak,* or special holiday bread. In the afternoon young folk dance the *Horo,* or national dance, on the village green. Lads give their sweethearts eggs, wishing that the girls may be both white and rosy, like the eggs. The girls reply that they are not only white and rosy, but as sound, also, as the eggs the boys give!

*SVETLA NEDELYA, Week of Light.   *The week after Easter*

The week following Easter is called the Week of Light because peasants believe that in Jerusalem the sun did not set for eight days after Christ's resurrection.

GEORGIOVDEN, Saint George's Day.
April 23 O.S. (May 6 N.S.)

Peasants believe that to be born or christened on this day is to be blessed with wisdom and beauty. On Saint George's Day every household slaughters a lamb, smears the doorsills with its blood, and prays the home may be protected from witches, sickness and powers of darkness. Before killing the animal the head of the family bows three times before the holy ikon which hangs in a corner to the east. "Holy Saint George," he prays, "this year thou hast sent me this lamb; next year, I beseech thee, send me a larger one."

SVETI KIRIL I METODI, Saints Cyril and Methodius, Holy Day
        of Letters.   *May 11 O.S. (May 24 N.S.)*

This religious festival honors the two brothers, Cyril and Methodius, who in the year 855 invented the Bulgarian alphabet and translated the first church ritual into the native language. The two saints, who are patrons of Bulgarian education and culture, are honored throughout the country with special Masses, student parades and patriotic music. In Sofia an impressive High Mass, celebrated at the cathedral, is followed by all kinds of student demonstrations.

IMEN DEN NA TZAR BORIS III, Nameday of King Boris III.
May 15

The day is observed with special Masses, dinners and celebrations.

ILINDEN, Saint Elijah's Day. *July* 20 *O.S.* (*August* 2 *N.S.*)

According to peasant belief, Saint Elijah sends rain, hail and snow. When angry he rolls the wheels of his chariot across the stormy sky. To propitiate the saint, and prevent thunder and lightning from injuring cattle and people, every household observes the day with ceremonial rites.

BOGORODITZA, Assumption of the Virgin.
August 15 *O.S.* (*August* 28 *N.S.*)

On this day the grapes and vineyards receive the blessing of the clergy.

DEN NA BUDITELITE, Day of the Awakeners. *November* 1

This national fête is observed in honor of the great patriots, writers and revolutionaries, like Christo Boteff, the brothers Mladinoff, Sava Rakovsky and others, who helped to awaken the spirit of Bulgarian nationalism. These leaders, the patrons of Bulgaria's educational institutions, are nationally recognized

Festivals of the Bulgarians

with exercises in schools and universities and by patriotic societies. Thanksgiving services are held in the churches. Patriotic speeches, processions and folk music all are features of the celebration.

NIKULDEN, Saint Nicholas' Day.
December 6 O.S. (December 19 N.S.)

The saint who delivers from elemental perils is honored with a household festival. A traditional meal is prepared, which includes *sharan,* a special kind of fish, served with rice, and a ceremonial bread made for Saint Nicholas. When the feast is ready, the priest visits the houses and sanctifies the meal with prayers and blessings.

BUDNIVECHER, Christmas Eve.
December 24 O.S. (January 6 N.S.)

With the appearance of the first star the strict two weeks' fast which precedes Christmas is broken. The chief ceremonial food is *kravai,* a large round cake which the eldest daughter of the household decorates with the figures of a bird, a flower and a cross. The *kravai,* placed in the center of the table, is decorated with a lighted candle and surrounded by festive foods. After burning incense and offering prayers the father and mother of the family raise the loaf over their heads, saying, "May our wheat grow as high as this." Then husband and wife each break a piece from the loaf, for the saying goes that luck will follow the one getting the largest portion.

KOLEDA, ROZHDESTVO KHRISTOVO, Christmas.
December 25 O.S. (January 7 N.S.)

The day begins with a long church service. Children receive gifts from Grandpa *Koleda,* the ancient winter god. Before breakfast, wheat is put into a stocking. The head of the house sprinkles a little of the grain on the doorstep with the words, "Christ is born." The other members of the family reply, "He is born indeed." Then the wishing begins. Sparks are struck from the Christmas log, with a wish to each blow. Health to the farm and a plenteous crop are wished for; then the ashes are gathered, a coin hidden among them, and a wish made for an abundant harvest. The traditional Christmas dinner includes roast pig and *kravaitza,* or blood sausage.

NOVOGODISHNA VECHER, New Year's Eve.
December 31 *O.S.* (*January* 13 *N.S.*)

This is a great occasion for all kinds of fortune telling. A favorite method of looking into the future is to drop a leaf in water and let it remain overnight. If the leaf is fresh in the morning, sound health is predicted throughout the coming year.

FESTIVALS OF THE CHINESE

I

Days Observed in the Chinese Republic

The Chinese equivalent of the English name for many of the holidays cannot be given unless Chinese characters are used.

Yüan Tan, New Year's Day.   *January* 1

Dinners, parties, the exchange of presents, official gatherings and firework displays celebrate the beginning of the New Year.

This day is also the anniversary of the revolution of 1912, which resulted in the abdication of the infant Emperor and the founding of the Republic. Dr. Sun Yat-sen, China's first President, was inaugurated on this day.

Anniversary of the Death of Sun Yat-sen, 1925. *March* 12

Dr. Sun Yat-sen, China's best-known revolutionary leader and the first President of the Chinese Republic, organized the anti-Manchu forces, which finally caused the downfall of the Chinese Empire. The day is celebrated with memorial services throughout the Republic.

CANTON MARTYRS' DAY.   *March* 29

On this great Memorial Day tribute is paid to the seventy-two martyrs of the Yellow Flowers Hill in Canton, who died in 1911 in the cause of the Chinese Republic. The day is particularly celebrated in the Kwantung Province.

BIRTHDAY OF CONFUCIUS.
                        Twenty-seventh day of the Eighth Moon[1]

This anniversary commemorates the birth, in 551 B.C., of China's greatest philosopher and sage. Confucius died on the eleventh day of the Fourth Moon, in 479 B.C. He was buried outside the north gate of Ch'üfu, where his grave is the scene of annual visitation by thousands of devout pilgrims.

CHUNG-HUA-MING-KUO, Founding of the Republic. *October* 10

The Wuchang Revolution of 1911, which was led by Li Yang-hung and his troops, began the movement resulting in the overthrow of the Chinese Empire. This holiday, the most significant of modern China, is celebrated with the flying of flags, processions, public demonstrations, speeches and band music. In some localities, pictures of the revolutionary leaders and displays of revolutionary relics are exhibited.

BIRTHDAY OF SUN YAT-SEN.   *November* 12

The anniversary of the birth of the late President Sun Yat-sen is observed throughout China with special exercises and memorial services.

[1] This day, which is celebrated according to the lunar calendar, varies from year to year. See Chinese calendar, page 353.

Festivals of the Chinese

II

Days Traditionally Observed by the Older Chinese

Yüan Tan, First Day of the New Year. *First day of the First Moon—always between January 21–February 19*[2]

The first day of the year belongs to the family. A meatless dish is eaten in the homes, and the devout follower of old customs does not break his meat fast until the second day of the year. People don their best clothes. An offering is made to Heaven and Earth. Candles are lighted and incense burned before household gods and ancestral tablets. As nothing to cause bad luck must be done on the first few days of the year, business places are closed, and swearing and rough language are not tolerated.

Second Day of the New Year. *Second day of the First Moon*

As on the previous day, incense is offered to Heaven and Earth, to the household gods and to ancestral tablets. Calls are made upon relatives and friends. Congratulations and good wishes are exchanged. Guests are offered tea, sweets, melon seeds and mandarin oranges. Children give mandarin oranges to their elders "for luck."

Third and Fourth Days of the New Year. *Third and fourth days of the First Moon*

The festivities of the New Year are continued on these days. Among the older Chinese, red cards inscribed with good wishes and the giver's name are presented to relatives and friends. In China as in many other countries, red is the color of joy.

[2] Sometimes celebrated on the fifteenth day of the First Moon.

FIFTH DAY OF THE NEW YEAR.   *Fifth day of the First Moon*

Women sweep the houses on this day, for the first time in the New Year. In some parts of China they throw the sweepings into a stream, and in others on a dump heap, "to preserve the family luck."

BIRTHDAY OF MANKIND.   *Seventh day of the First Moon*

It is believed that bright clear weather on this day predicts numerous human births during the coming year. The first eight days of the New Year are looked upon as birthdays of fowls, animals, human beings and grains. Good weather on these days means that all creatures or grains born during the period will prosper. If skies are stormy, however, a gloomy fate is foretold.

TENG CHIEH, Feast of Lanterns.

Fifteenth day of the First Moon

This festival probably originated as a rite to welcome the lengthening of days and the return of spring after the dark winter months. In Northern China people hang lighted lanterns before their doors. In Southern China they celebrate the occasion by stringing gay lanterns from slender poles and forming processions of men and boys who carry all kinds of grotesque and beautiful lanterns. The great dragon lantern, which often measures between fifty and sixty feet in length and is manipulated by a dozen or more men, is a traditional feature of this picturesque procession.

CH'ING MING, Festival of Pure Brightness.
Beginning of the Second Moon (about March 21)[3]

This old festival of the dead used to be more widely ob-

[3] The date for the *Ch'ing Ming* is fixed for about one hundred and six days

served than it is in modern times. The graves of ancestors are swept with willows, put in order, and offerings of food and drink are made to spirits of the departed.

TUAN YANG CHIEH, Dragon Boat Festival.
Fifth day of the Fifth Moon

This great festival honors the patriotism of Ch'ü Yüan (328–298 B.C.), a statesman of the Chou Dynasty, who urged the Prince of Huai to accept certain reforms. The Prince repeatedly refused to listen to his minister's counsel, while the latter, in protest of his sovereign's indifference, drowned himself in the Tungting Lake. Since the festival originated by searching in boats for the body of Ch'ü Yüan, the modern celebration of the day consists largely in dragon-boat racing. Skilful crews of young men engage in swift contests on lakes and rivers. Prizes are awarded to the successful competitors. It is customary to decorate houses with artemesia and sweetflag, possibly to symbolize banishing the evil spirit of death. A special food consisting of banana leaves wrapped about rice and other ingredients and steamed is eaten on this day. Originally this food was intended as an offering to Ch'ü Yüan. The fifth day of the Fifth Moon marks one of China's three annual occasions for settling accounts.

CHI HSI, Festival of the Milky Way.
Seventh day of the Seventh Moon

This old folk festival honors the two stars Aquila, the Herd Boy, and Vega, the Weaving Maiden, which are situated on

after the winter solstice. Although *Ch'ing Ming* is supposed to fall on a certain day either in the Second or the Third Moon, the festival may be celebrated any time during the thirty-day period following this date. The lunar dates vary.

either side of the Heavenly River, as the Chinese call the Milky Way. According to ancient legend, the Weaving Maiden, daughter of the Sun God, was given in marriage to the Herd Boy. Instead of continuing to work with her former industry, the Weaving Maiden forgot everything except her own happiness. The Sun God, angry at his daughter's neglect of duty, commanded a flock of magpies to make a wingèd bridge across the Heavenly River, and banished the Herd Boy to the opposite shore. Husband and wife were forbidden to meet except once a year, on the seventh day of the Seventh Moon, when the magpies again form a bridge and the Maiden crosses to her husband's side. After a single day with the Herd Boy the Weaving Maiden sadly returns and resumes her duties. Should it rain on the night of the festival, the Maiden is doomed to remain on her side of the river until the following year. For this reason women and girls all over China offer incense and pray for fair skies on the seventh day of the Seventh Moon. They also pray for skill in handiwork, and offer the Weaving Maiden such gifts as small cakes, watermelons, vegetables and fruits.

CHUNG YÜAN, Festival of the Dead.
Fifteenth day of the Seventh Moon[4]

On this day people sacrifice to their ancestors and sweep the graves of the dead. At dusk boys carry lotus-leaf lanterns through the streets and sing quaint songs about how today the lanterns are lighted but tomorrow they will be cast aside. Offerings are made to the dead, especially to those "orphaned spirits" who have no living relatives to sacrifice for them. Gifts consisting of paper replicas of money, clothing and other worldly possessions are burned for the departed, in the belief that the souls in their spiritual existence receive the counterpart of these

---

[4] Celebrated on the fourteenth day of the Seventh Moon by many Chinese in the United States.

things. A special observance of the festival takes place at the monastery of Ch'ing Liang Shan, "Clear Cool Mountain," which is dedicated to Ti Tsang, ruler of Hades. Pilgrims go to the monastery to fulfil vows or to seek cures. During the tolling of the monastery bell, it is believed that the orphaned spirits are freed from suffering.

CHUNG-CH'IU, Mid-Autumn Festival, Harvest or Moon Festival.   *Fifteenth day of the Eighth Moon*

This festival, which marks the end of the harvest, is one of the most joyous events of the Chinese year. Most of the ceremonies center about the moon, which influences crops and harvests and is associated with the palaces of the immortals. Bakeries and candy shops feature large round moon cakes, made with flour and brown sugar, and ornamented with pictures of the moon and its palaces. Insofar as possible, all foods are prepared in round shapes, in honor of the moon. Tiny tile pagodas and amusing animals are prominent among the playthings offered to children. According to popular belief, beautiful flowers fall from the moon on this night. Women seeing the blossoms think they will be blessed with numerous offspring, and men with prosperity. Music, poetical writings, feasting and games are among the events that make this occasion memorable to young and old. Chinese folklore abounds in charming moon legends, many of which are celebrated in native song and poetry. This day is the third annual occasion for paying outstanding debts.

CH'UNG YANG, Festival of High Places.
                                    Ninth day of the Ninth Moon

According to legend, this festival is celebrated in memory of Fei Ch'ang-fang who, when warned in a dream of approaching calamity, fled to the hills and so escaped disaster. Today the anniversary is observed by picnics in the hills and the flying of countless kites, which are thought to carry aloft impending evils.

Tung Chih, Feast of the Winter Solstice.
Sometime during the Eleventh Moon[5]

On this long night all the members of the family unite, if possible, in worshiping the spirits of their ancestors. A feast is prepared for the departed, and prayers and incense are offered before the ancestral tablets. *Hun-t'un,* small bullet-shaped pork dumplings made from glutinous flour, are the popular food of this season. In Southern China the dumplings are meatless and often enclose small pieces of brown sugar.

Tsao Chün, Festival of the Kitchen God.
Twenty-third day of the Twelfth Moon[6]

On this night the entire family gathers in the kitchen to pay homage to the Kitchen God, whose gaudy picture is pasted against the chimney. A week before the old year ends, the god is thought to ascend to heaven, where he reports on the good or evil conduct of each member of the family. In some places people offer the god sweet foods, such as sugar cakes and confections, so he may speak none but sweet words. In other localities molasses is smeared over Tsao Chün's mouth, to make it so sticky he cannot open his lips! The Kitchen God's paper image is burned with great ceremony, for the household guardian rises to heaven in the flames.

[5] Always on the shortest day of the year.
[6] Celebrated in North China on this date; in the Kwantung Province on the twenty-fourth day of the Twelfth Moon.

Festivals of the Chinese

Cʜ'ᴜ Hsɪ, Night of the Thirtieth.

Twenty-ninth day of the Twelfth Moon

Amid the firing of crackers and general rejoicing, a new picture of the Kitchen God is pasted on the chimney. This ceremony symbolizes the return of the god to watch over the family's affairs. After debts have been paid and supplies for the New Year purchased, each family sits down to a special meal, "to round out the year."

FESTIVALS OF THE CZECHOSLOVAKS

Nový Rok, New Year. *January* 1

The night before the New Year, boys and girls drop bits of melted lead into cold water and try to read their fortunes in the various shapes it assumes. Another favorite method of fortune-telling is to place a lighted taper in a nutshell and set it on a tub of water. If the nutshell floats toward the center of the tub, its owner will go on a journey. If it stays near the edges, he or she will remain at home. If two nuts float toward each other, the boy and girl to whom they belong will wed within the year. Should the shells stay apart, however, another year of waiting is predicted. Sometimes this game is played on Christmas Eve. Housewives sprinkle their rooms with holy water and chalk crosses on the doors, to frighten away the witches and prevent them from entering the houses.

Den Svatých Tří Králů, Epiphany. *January* 6

In many parts of the country, boys dressed as the Three Kings go from door to door singing songs about the Magi and asking for alms. The boys mark the doors of the houses that receive them with three crosses and the initials K, M, B (Kaspar, Melchior, Balthasar).

Festivals of the Czechoslovaks

DEN KOMENSKÉHO, Komensky Day.   *March* 28

This anniversary marks the birthday of Jan Amos Komensky (Comenius), 1592–1670, noted educational reformer and theologian. Komensky recommended compulsory education, pointed out the obligation of the state to provide kindergarten training and schooling, and made the first successful attempt to use illustrated textbooks. The day is observed with appropriate lectures, music and educational exercises.

*VYNÁŠENÍ SMRTI Z VESNICE, Carrying Death Out of the Village.[1]   *Immediately preceding or during Lent*

This ceremony occurs at various times, according to locality. Shrove Tuesday, Ash Wednesday, the third or fifth Sunday in Lent—all are dates on which the festival may take place. In Bohemia children carry out of the village *Smrt,* the effigy of death. The straw image, which is decorated with colored rags and empty eggshells, is burned or thrown into the water. The children return to the village bringing flowers and garlands and singing of spring and the renewal of life. In some sections of Moravia boys carry a straw effigy through the fields. They dance about the straw man, chanting of the victory of spring. Then they parade through the village, demanding eggs because they have carried away death. Many variations of the custom occur in different parts of the country. On the fourth Sunday in Lent girls of the Libchovice district lead a flower-crowned queen through the village. The maidens announce the coming of spring and accept offerings of coins and goodies.

[1] Stars indicate movable feasts that depend on Easter. See table of Easter dates and movable feasts on pages 357–358.

*Květná Neděle, Palm Sunday.

> *The Sunday preceding Easter*

In some parts of the country pussywillows are blessed in church on Palm Sunday, in other sections on Easter. Later the willows are carried to the fields and waved over the grain, to insure it against rain and hail. The willows also are fastened to roofs, to protect houses from fire.

*Škaredá Středa, Ugly Wednesday.

> *The Wednesday preceding Easter*

Custom decrees that soot must be cleaned from the chimneys on this day.

*Zelený Čtvrtek, Green Thursday.

> *The Thursday preceding Easter*

According to a peasant superstition held in some places, the hawthorn weeps because it is the traditional tree from which the crown of thorns was fashioned. Epileptics pluck its branches, believing it will safeguard them from disease throughout the year. Parents waken children early and send them to bathe in the brooks, "so they may be cured of laziness." For breakfast children eat honey and "Judases"—rope-shaped cakes—in commemoration of Judas' fate. Honey is thought to protect people against serpent stings.

*Velký Pátek, Great Friday. *The Friday preceding Easter*

According to national legend, hidden treasures are revealed to those seeking them while the Passion Story is being read in church. The church bells are tied on Good Friday. As if to make up for their silence, however, the children make a terrific din by swinging rattles and loud clappers. After the evening service villagers run around the church to "drive out Judas." On this day the girls make the beautifully decorated eggs that are used in the Easter Monday sports.

*Bílá Sobota, White Saturday.

The Saturday preceding Easter

In the evening the last of the holy oil is burned before the church door. This ceremony is called the "burning of Judas." The peasant predicts that rain on White Saturday means a long season of wet weather. Keys rattled on this day are said to frighten away frogs, serpents and poisonous creatures.

*Velikonoce, Easter.

After the morning church service, at which the Easter food is blessed, every family enjoys its holiday dinner. The afternoon is spent in games, visiting among friends and in general rejoicing.

*Velikonoční Pondělí, Easter Monday.

The Monday after Easter

This is the greatest holiday of the year for the young people, who indulge in all the traditional Easter sports. The boys weave willow branches into *dynovacka,* or small whips, and decorate them with ribbons and flowers. They then carol for eggs and whip the girls "so they won't be lazy or have fleas." This custom, which probably dates back to purification by beating and is thought to bring good luck, still is observed in both city and rural communities. The girls reward their tormentors with flowers and elaborately decorated Easter eggs. Boys and girls sing and dance on the village green—the boys wearing brave new blouses, and the girls bright ribbons and freshly starched skirts.

DEN SVATÉHO JIŘÍ, Saint George's Day.   *April* 23

Young girls practice many different ways of fortune-telling on this day. Sometimes they weave garlands, which they either toss into trees or throw into the rivers. If a wreath catches on a branch and remains in the tree, it is prophesied that the girl will marry. If it falls to the ground, she will be an old maid. If the current carries away the wreath thrown into the river, the girl will leave the village. If it catches on a reed, however, its owner will remain at home. Many girls tuck the wreaths under their pillows at night, in the belief that they will dream of their future husbands.

PÁLENÍ ČARODĚJNIC, Burning of the Witches, May Day Eve.
                                                         April 30

According to an old folk superstition, witches once tried to enter people's homes on this night and do them harm. Sand or grass was sprinkled on the doorsteps, as it was thought that the witches had to count the grains or blades before entering the houses. Now the "Burning of the Witches" is celebrated in some parts of the country by building bonfires on the mountain tops. Brooms dipped in pitch are lighted and waved aloft.

PRVÉHO MÁJE, May Day.   *May* 1

On May Day Eve it is customary in many villages to raise a Maypole before the window of the most popular girl in the village. Boys also plant Maypoles at night before their sweethearts' windows, so the girls may see them the first thing on waking. The Maypole is said to represent the girl's life, and the longer it is, the more years she will live. Often the Maypole is a little tree, which is decorated with ribbons and colored egg-shells. The band plays in the village square and musicians go singing from house to house. Everyone sings, dances and re-joices in the beauty of spring.

*Svatodušní Svátky, Whitsuntide.

Beginning the fiftieth day after Easter

In some parts of Slovakia boys secretly carry decorated trees into the village at night and set them before the door or on the roof of the girl they love. The following day, the Whitsun king and queen march through the village, collecting gifts from house to house. In the village of Semic, the Whitsun king is beheaded. In other localities the Whitsuntide mummers some-times "bury the Carnival," represented by a lad dressed as a wild man.

Svatojánský Večer, Saint John's Eve.   *June 23*

Young folk, dressed in gay clothes, observe the pagan fire festival by building huge bonfires on the hilltops. A Maypole, decorated with wreaths and flowers, is a feature of the celebra-tion. Lads and maidens dance about the fires, singing love songs and tossing wreaths from one to another. The singed wreaths, thought to possess curative virtue, are preserved throughout the year. Certain herbs are gathered on this night, as they too are believed to have medicinal value.

Upálení Mistra Jana Husa, Martyrdom of Jan Hus.   *July 6*

Special commemorative exercises are held in honor of the

celebrated Bohemian religious reformer who was burned at the stake in 1415.

OBŽINKY, Sending Off Summer, Harvest Home.
End of August or middle of September

In many parts of the country, field workers celebrate the end of the harvest by fashioning a great wreath of corn and flowers. Ears of wheat, placed in the center, symbolize the sun. The woman who binds the last sheaf is known as the *Baba* in some localities. Sometimes, however, the *Baba* is a doll made from the grain, which is adorned with flowers and ribbons. In either case, the harvest wreath and the *Baba,* together with decorated rakes and scythes, are placed in a wagon and taken in triumphal procession to the owner of the farm. The scene is very gay, as ribbons are braided into the horses' manes and tails and the reapers wear their most colorful clothes. The farmer gives welcome to the laborers, who present him with the wreath and congratulate him on the good harvest. Then the farmer invites the reapers to a feast and everyone sings, dances and makes merry. In some parts of the country, people celebrate the last day of the harvest by dressing in gala attire and carrying decorated sheaves to the village square. Then the reapers sing, dance, eat and drink. Special cakes are made for this occasion. Sometimes they are large, sometimes small. They are always square, however, and filled with delicious plum jam, or a toothsome stuffing of sweetened cheese or poppy seed.

DEN SVATÉHO VÁCLAVA, Saint Vaclav (Wenceslas).
September 28

This is a national holiday in memory of the tenth century Christian duke who became Patron of Bohemia. Saint Vaclav was a friend of the poor and unfortunate. He founded the Prague Cathedral of Saint Vitus, where later his jealous brother, Boleslav, plotted his death. Tradition says that Saint Vaclav and his warriors sleep in Mount Blanik, whence they will issue at the time of Bohemia's greatest need.

OSLAVA STÁTNÍ SAMOSTATNOSTI, Independence Day.

October 28

This national holiday celebrates the founding, in 1918, of the Czechoslovak Republic. The day is observed with parades, speeches, athletic demonstrations and music.

VŠECH SVATÝCH, All Saints' Day. *November 1*

Each family remembers its dead. In some parts of Czechoslovakia, it is customary in the evening to eat special cakes and drink cold milk, to "cool souls that are roasting in Purgatory."

DUŠIČKY, All Souls' Day. *November 2*

People spend the day in the cemeteries, where they visit the graves of the dead and put them in order.

DEN SVATÉHO ONDŘEJE, Saint Andrew's Day. *November 30*

This is another great occasion for looking into the future. In some parts of the country a young girl who wishes to know how her husband will look, visits the woodpile at night. At random she pulls out a stick of wood. If she gets a crooked piece, he will be a hunchback, but if she draws out a straight, slender piece of wood, he will be slim and straight!

DEN SVATÉ BARBORY, Saint Barbara's Day.　　　*December* 4

On this day girls go out to the garden and pluck branches of cherry. These they put in water and tend carefully, to make them bloom by Christmas.

DEN SVATÉHO MIKULÁŠE, Saint Nicholas' Eve.　　*December* 5

The children believe that on this night the saint descends from heaven on a golden cord. On his back he carries a basket of apples, nuts and candies, with which he fills the children's plates and stockings. Gay masqueraders representing Saint Nicholas, an Angel and the Devil wander about as a trio on this night.

ŠTĚDRÝ VEČER, Christmas Eve.　　　　*December* 24

The day before Christmas is spent in fasting. With the appearance of the first star, however, the family solemnly partakes of the traditional supper consisting of roe soup, fish, *housky* (or *vánočky*), which is a braided bread, and a special cake rich with almonds and raisins. A child who does not touch food all day is promised he will see the Golden Pig, but somehow, no youngster has seen him yet! The Christmas tree is lighted, and beneath its branches is placed a "Bethlehem" or model of the manger scene. The evening is spent in merrymaking and telling fortunes with apples, nuts and candies. Whatever remains from the Christmas supper is taken out and fed to the farm animals, the bees and the trees, so that all living things may prosper and grow during the coming year. At midnight everyone attends the Midnight Mass, or the Angelic Mass as it is called in some parts of the country.

Festivals of the Czechoslovaks

VÁNOCE, Christmas.   *December 25*

The day generally is spent in the homes as a family holiday. In some places the village watchman goes about playing Christmas carols on a long musical horn. A few weeks before the holiday, the girls are likely to put branches of cherry into water, forcing them into bloom by Christmas Day. Then they tuck the sprays of blossoming cherry into their bodices and wear them to church. The boys try to snatch away the cherry blossoms. If a girl permits a lad to do so, it is a sign that she approves his courtship.

DEN SVATÉHO ŠTĚPÁNA, Saint Stephen's Day.   *December 26*

In certain sections of the country children masquerading as the Three Kings go from house to house on Christmas or the day following. They sing carols or *koledy*, and receive in return gifts of apples, nuts and cakes. Young Slovak shepherds often carry a Bethlehem, as they sing ancient carols about Christ's birth.

FESTIVALS OF THE DANES

NYTAARSDAG, New Year's Day.   *January* 1

The New Year marks the beginning of one of the most important social events in the calendar. Men and women don formal attire, attend church services and later call on relatives and friends to wish them a Happy New Year. The conventional call lasts for about a half-hour and the customary refreshments consist of wine and little cookies. The exchange of visits continues for about a fortnight.

HELLIGTREKONGERSDAG, HELLIG-TRE-KONGERS-DAG, Day of the
Three Holy Kings, Epiphany.   *January* 6

On this night, which closes the Yule season, young girls play all kinds of fortune-telling games. A time-honored way for a maiden to decide her fate is to walk backward, throw a shoe over her left shoulder and pray the Holy Kings to reveal the future. The man who subsequently appears in her dreams is thought to be the future husband.

FEBRUARY 14

On this day Danish young people exchange friendship tokens, which consist of pressed snowdrops accompanied by original verses. The sender signs her *Gaekkebrev,* or joking

94

letter as the message is called, with a series of dots, one dot standing for each letter in the name. If the person who receives the *Gaekkebrev* guesses the sender's name correctly, the sender is expected to reward her friend at Easter with a sugar or chocolate egg. If, on the contrary, the one getting a message fails to decipher the name, she is expected to pay the forfeit.

*Fastelavn, Fastelaven, Shrovetide.[1]

The Monday preceding Ash Wednesday

This is a holiday in the schools and one of the gayest events for boys and girls. Early in the morning, children armed with "Lenten birches," or switches decorated with gaily colored paper flowers, enter the rooms of parents and grandparents and beat their elders soundly. "Give buns, give buns, give buns," cry the children as they inflict resounding smacks with their switches. From the mysterious depths of the bedclothes are produced the traditional *Fastelavnsboller,* or Shrovetide buns, with which the tormentors always are rewarded. Probably this custom is a survival of the "Easter smacks" which in many lands were inflicted as a sort of purification rite. Many parties are held at this time of the year. An old Danish game, played extensively even in modern times, is called *Slaa Katten af Tönden,* or "beating the cat out of the barrel." An artificial cat (originally, a live animal) is enclosed in a wooden barrel decorated with paper flowers. Each player, armed with a wooden mallet, strikes at the barrel. The one who succeeds in smashing it is made king of the *Fastelavn* party. Various amusing games are played with the buns. Sometimes a bun is suspended from the chandelier by a string and the person who succeeds in snatching a bite of the tempting morsel receives the bun. In many Danish seaport towns the *Fastelavn* boat is a

[1] Stars indicate movable feasts that depend on Easter. See table of Easter dates and movable feasts on pages 357–358.

feature of the season's festivities. A great boat manned by twelve seamen is placed on a truck which is drawn by several horses. At the driver's side sit horn-players. The truck, followed by members of the Seamen's Guild, progresses slowly through the streets. The boat's approach is announced by a seaman bearing the national flag. The unique procession halts frequently during its progress through the town. "The ship is coming!" shout the townsfolk. The musicians play and the men perform dances, after which contributions are received for sick and needy seamen.

*SKAERTORSDAG, Holy Thursday.
The Thursday preceding Easter

Observed by special services in the churches.

*LANGFREDAG, Good Friday.   *The Friday preceding Easter*

Observed by special services in the churches. Hot cross buns are eaten on this day.

*PAASKEAFTEN, Holy Saturday.
The Saturday preceding Easter

This day is also observed by special services in the churches.

*PAASKE, Easter.

After the Easter morning services the day is spent quietly in the homes. Colored Easter eggs are a feature of the day.

*ANDEN PAASKEDAG, Second Easter Day. *The day after Easter*

This is a great holiday. The stores are closed and all

places of amusement, such as theatres, concert halls, clubs and restaurants, are crowded to capacity.

*STORE BEDEDAG, Great Day of Prayer.

The fourth Friday after Easter

This day of prayer dates back to the time of Christian VII, when Struensee, his Prime Minister, decided upon one great day of prayer instead of the many different penitential days then observed. On the Eve of *Store Bededag* the bells in every church announce the occasion. People attired in new spring garments stroll along the famous *Langelinie* or boulevard which faces Copenhagen's water front. *Hvedebröd,* a kind of square bread, is eaten on this night. The day following, stores and places of business are closed and special church services held.

MAIDAG, May Day (in the environs of Copenhagen). *May 1*

At Amager the old Danish May Day dances and ceremonies have been revived and are attended annually by hundreds of visitors from home and abroad. Lovers weave for one another *Skvovmaerker,* or wreaths made from a fragrant dried plant. These little wreaths are hung up in the homes.

*PINTSE, Pentecost, Whitsunday.

The fiftieth day after Easter

This is the greatest spring holiday. For weeks beforehand housewives are busy scrubbing and scouring and putting their homes in order. Since this is the season when the beeches begin to bud, Copenhagen people go on bicycles to parks and forests where they gather armfuls of young beech branches. With these they decorate their houses—a gesture of welcome to the spring. According to old folk belief the sun "dances" on *Pintse*

97

morn. Residents of Copenhagen still rise at dawn and go up to Frederiksberg hill to watch the sun rise and "see it dance." New summer clothes are worn on this day.

*ANDEN PINTSEDAG, Whit-Monday.

The fifty-first day after Easter

This day is celebrated with picnics, excursions and all kinds of out-of-door gatherings.

GRUNDLOVSDAG, Constitution Day. *June 5*

This is the anniversary of Denmark's Free Constitution, which was adopted in 1847, under Frederick VII. The day is observed with political speeches and demonstrations by various party groups.

SANKTHANSAFTEN, Saint John's Eve. *June 23*

Midsummer Eve—the longest night in the year—is celebrated with merrymaking and rejoicing and building bonfires in every town and village. In coast hamlets fires are made along the shore, people going out in boats to view the bonfires and sing in honor of the beautiful summer night.

JULEAFTEN, Christmas Eve. *December 24*

Christmas Eve is the greatest day of the Yuletide festival, which begins on Little Christmas Eve (the night of December 23) and continues well into the New Year. After a short church service held on the evening of December 24, people go home to feast and make merry within the family group. The traditional Christmas Eve dinner consists of roast goose stuffed with prunes and apples, red cabbage, doughnuts, cookies and rice pudding, or *gröd,* which is thickly strewn with quantities of sugar and cinnamon and has a huge butter "eye" in the middle. An almond, slipped within the pudding, causes much merriment and excitement, as the person finding it is rewarded with a gift. On Christmas Eve no living creature is forgotten. A sheaf of rye is placed outside for the birds' supper. Horses and cattle are given extra food and care, for, according to old folk belief, the manger animals stand at midnight in honor of the Christ Child's birth. Even the *Julenisse* is remembered. He is the wee gnome, thought to dwell in attic or barn, who looks after the household's welfare and brings gifts to the children. The *Julenisse* always is given a generous portion of the rice pudding, to which an extra lump of butter has been added. The Christmas tree is lighted as the climax of the evening's festivities. Presents are distributed and both children and parents sing and dance around the tree.

JULEDAG, Christmas.   *December* 25

After morning church services, visits are exchanged among friends and neighbors. Throughout the holiday season hospitality is offered—and accepted—in every household. According to old superstition, whoever enters a house at Christmas without partaking of the family's cheer will "bear away their Yule."

NYTAARSAFTEN, New Year's Eve.   *December* 31

Instead of "blowing in the New Year," as was customary in olden days, the Danes now "smash it in." For months ahead, boys save up worthless crockery. On New Year's Eve they break it against the doors of friends and neighbors. The most popular man in the town or village is he who has the greatest number of old pots and bowls smashed against his front door.

According to traditional etiquette, the master of the house rushes out and tries to catch his noisy guests, who run away after the bombardment. They do not run too quickly, however, because those who are caught are treated with cakes, cookies or hot doughnuts. Just at midnight the bells peal out the passing of the year. Bands of gay masqueraders swarm through the streets. Banquets, dances, dinners and gala parties are features of the evening's entertainment.

FESTIVALS OF THE ESTONIANS

Uus Aasta, New Year's Day.   *January* 1

Religious folk begin the new year at church, with prayer and communion. Cards and congratulations are exchanged and calls made on friends and relatives. Homemade beer and *sült*, a delicious jelly made from pigs' feet, are special delicacies of the day.

Kolme Kuninga Päev, Epiphany.   *January* 6

The Christmas holidays come to a close with Epiphany. Children return to school and servants to their places of employment.

Iseseisvuse Päev, Independence Day.   *February* 24

This day, which marks the anniversary of Estonia's freedom from Russian rule, in 1918, is celebrated with speeches, patriotic demonstrations and great concerts of national music. Someone has said that the "Estonian people sang themselves into freedom," because by their folk songs the native tongue was preserved throughout years of foreign oppression. For this reason, folk songs comprise an important part of all the Independence Day programs.

The Book of Festivals

*Vastla Päev, Shrove Tuesday.[1]

The Tuesday preceding Ash Wednesday

The last day before Lent is a gala occasion for children and young people, who joyously anticipate it for weeks in advance. It is customary for boys and girls to devote the entire day to riding down hill, for schools are closed and they have a holiday. Six, seven or more youngsters pile on a sled and coast from dawn until dark. At night, when they come home, their mothers have ready huge kettles of the traditional Shrove Tuesday soup, which is made from pigs' feet boiled with dried peas or lima beans. The fun is not over with eating the rich, steaming soup, for then children are entitled to play with the *vuriluu kont,* or bones of the pigs' feet. A hole is drilled in the middle of each bone and a stout doubled rope is inserted through the hole. When the contrivance is manipulated in a certain way it causes a terrific rattle, which delights the children and makes them feel that they are ending *Vastla Päev* with proper ceremony.

*Palve Päev, Day of Prayer.　　　*Sometime during Lent*

This Sunday is celebrated in all the churches as a time of special worship.

*Palmi Puude püha, Palm Tree Sunday.

The Sunday preceding Easter

The day commemorating Christ's triumphal entrance into Jerusalem is observed as a religious holiday. Although palms are used as decorations in the churches, they are not distributed to members of the congregation.

[1] Stars indicate movable feasts that depend on Easter. See table of Easter dates and movable feasts on pages 357–358.

Festivals of the Estonians

*SUUR NELJAPÄEV, Big Thursday.

The Thursday preceding Easter

By six o'clock in the evening all good housewives have their houses cleaned, the food prepared, and everything in readiness for the Easter holidays.

*SUUR REEDE, Good Friday.   *The Friday preceding Easter*

The village choirs, dressed in black, give recitals of Passion music. *Suur Reede* is purely a religious holiday. It is usual for everybody to attend church and take communion at the evening services.

*ÜLESTÔUSMISE PÜHAD, Easter Holidays.

Easter Sunday, Monday and Tuesday

Throughout Estonia pussywillows and branches of budding birch are typical Easter decorations. Eggs are colored with all kinds of natural dyes. Yellow is universally popular. Various lovely tones of this color are obtained by boiling the dried birch leaves which have been saved since autumn from the birch-twig whisks used in the bath houses. Boiled onion skins produce many soft mottled combinations, while moss, which either is found in the woods or else is pulled out from between the logs of country houses, produces pleasing shades of green. Young people enjoy the sport of knocking their eggs together, for the strongest egg wins the weak ones as prizes. The favorite Easter dinner consists of roast veal, roast potatoes and sauerkraut, with the occasional addition of blood sausage and dill pickle. Easter Monday is a gala day, devoted to concerts, parties and visits from friend to friend. Easter Tuesday usually is quiet, as tired merrymakers are returning and preparing for the business of the next day.

Jüri Päev, Saint George's Day. *April* 23

With the dawn of Saint George's Day, spring work starts on all the farms. New servants are hired and shepherds engaged. Seasonal farm workers hire themselves out from this day until *Mihkli Päev*, Saint Michael's Day, on September 29. This is the nameday of all Jüris. According to old custom, people try surreptitiously to tie the feet of men named Jüri, and refuse to undo the knots until their victims promise to treat with drinks.

Kevad püha, Bringing of the Spring. *May* 1

The celebration of *Kevad püha* depends largely upon the weather. If spring is early and the weather sufficiently warm, women don pink dresses and blouses and wear fresh flowers. Picnics are held in rural places and bonfires built on the heights. Doubtless these fires originally were intended to drive away winter spirits and welcome spring.

*Nelipühi, Pentecost. *The fiftieth day after Easter*

These early spring holidays are celebrated with music, excursions to the country and the decoration of houses and doors with fresh birch branches. If a relative is to be welcomed home on this day, the greens are interspersed with small Estonian flags. Dyed eggs are prepared for Pentecost as well as for Easter.

Jaani Laupäev, Saint John's Eve. *June* 23

Bonfires are built on the heights and great wooden swings constructed between stout trees, so that the people may carry out the ancient fertility rite of dancing about the fires and swinging high toward heaven. The tremendous bonfires, which are made from pitch-filled barrels and all kinds of resinous woods, burn for several hours. Young and old dance and sing and make merry by the brilliant light of the mounting flames. An old superstition exists that on this one night in the year the *sõnaialg,* a small fern-like plant, blooms in the depths of the forest, and that whoever finds the flower will get a sweetheart. It is customary, therefore, for boys and girls to wander through the woods seeking for the mystic flower of love.

JAANI PÄEV, Saint John's Day.   *June* 24

This day continues the festivities of the night before. On *Jaani Päev* it is customary in country places to make the traditional home-brew beer, which always is drunk on the festivals of Saint John, Christmas and the New Year. Selected rye and barley are soaked in water until the grain begins to germinate. After being thoroughly dried, it is ground, mixed with water until a thick paste is formed, and then browned in the oven. Hot water is poured over the mixture and hops are added. Then the liquid is put into barrels and strained through layers of straw. The resulting beverage is highly prized, especially when fresh. Men go about from farm to farm making merry and tasting one another's brew.

LAULUPIDU, Singing Festival.   *June 25—every fifth year*

Every fifth year (in 1938, 1943, 1948), Estonians hold their great national singing festival on Saint John's Day. Estonian representatives come to Tallinn from America, Latvia, Finland, Lithuania and other countries to participate in this festival of native folk music. Visiting choirs of many nationalities attend as delegates and learn to sing some of the native Estonian songs. All choir members dress in the folk costumes of their particular locality.

The Book of Festivals

SEATAPMISE PÄEV, Festival of Killing the Pigs.

Sometime in September

In rural districts the occasion of killing the pig is regarded as a family festival. Usually each village boasts a few experts in slaughtering animals. These men are in demand, as they know how to prepare the meat in traditional fashion. After the day's work the housewife has a fine meal—with plenty of vodka and *vere käkkid,* or "blood bread." This is a great delicacy made from blood combined with flour and cooked in boiling water. Often it is eaten hot. Sometimes it is sliced and fried in fat. In the evening, after everyone has eaten a tremendous meal, neighbors drop in and both young and old sing and dance far into the night.

MIHKLI PÄEV, Saint Michael's Day.

September 29

On this day, which marks the close of summer labor, the *suvilised,* or people in service, go home. School also opens on Saint Michael's Day.

USUPUHASTUS PÜHA, Reformation Day.

October 31

This anniversary commemorates the day, in 1517, when Martin Luther nailed his famous ninety-five theses to the door of Wittenberg Cathedral. The day is observed in all the Protestant churches.

VÄLIS-EESTI PÄEV, Overseas Union.

November 27

Estonians all over the world celebrate this day in commemoration of their national heritage. Speeches, folk dances, folk songs and great choral programs recall to Estonians, wherever they may be, the culture of the mother country.

Festivals of the Estonians

MARDI PÄEV, Martin's Day. *November* 29

This is a gala day for children, who as dusk falls don masks and grotesque costumes and go about in groups from door to door in the village. "Please let us in because Mardi's fingers and toes are cold," chant the children as they stop outside a farmhouse. If they are not received generously the boys and girls soon make their displeasure felt by singing highly uncomplimentary verses. Usually, however, farmers' wives prepare for the occasion and the children are invited into the fragrant kitchens where all kinds of goodies await their visit. The leader plays lively music on a mouth-organ while the other children perform a gleeful dance about the smiling housewife. The reward is shortly forthcoming, as the farmer's wife fills the children's bags with such delicacies as apples, nuts, cookies and raisin bread. Turnips are a much-coveted gift, as they represent one of the few Estonian winter vegetables. Then there is *viljandi kama* (a food particularly famous in the Viljandi county), which always is reserved for this and other festive occasions. *Viljandi kama* is a kind of meal comprised of about fifteen different grains and dried vegetables (such as rye, peas, lima beans and wheat). The ingredients are ground together and mixed with sour milk, sugar and cream. This meal is regarded as Estonia's national fare. On Martin's Day well-to-do housewives give children bags of *viljandi kama,* to prove to the neighbors that their farm is prosperous and raises many different crops. Young people often travel for miles over the countryside to places where they are certain to be rewarded with this or other special treats.

JÕULU LAUPÄEV, Christmas Eve. *December* 24

Even those who are not habitual church-goers attend Christmas Eve services. In rural districts farmers pack the sleighs snugly with straw and bundle in the whole family, from the

107

smallest child to the oldest grandmother. The church is decorated with lighted candles and a fragrant Christmas tree. After coming home through the frosty air everybody is ready to do full justice to the sumptuous holiday dinner, for which the housewife has prepared many weeks in advance. The typical feast consists of roasted pig's head, *veri vorstid,* or blood sausages (made by mixing thickened barley with blood, adding ground salt pork, and boiling), turnips sliced thickly and cut into quarters, and the inevitable potatoes. Potatoes are considered a great delicacy in Estonia, which is so noted for this fine vegetable that it earned the name of the "Potato Republic" at the time of its independence. A special wheat flour raisin bread, which resembles coffee cake, is served at this season, as well as delicious salad made from wild cranberries cooked with apples. For dessert there is the typical cranberry soup, which is thickened with potato starch, sweetened with sugar and served with cream. Of course, there is plenty of good vodka to add cheer to the festive meal, because Estonians consider their vodka—which is made from potatoes—the finest and purest in the world. After eating and drinking, exchanging reminiscences and singing old folk songs, both adults and children play games and enjoy the goodies hanging on the Christmas tree. The tree ornaments are simple and effective, as well as tempting to the palate. There are shining red winter apples, gilded nuts and toothsome candies, which are made from sugar and starch and wrapped artistically in colored papers decorated with bright pictures. In cities and larger towns the trees are lighted with colored candles, but in some rural districts effective hand-dipped tapers still are used. These candles are made by immersing a lamb's wool thread in hot sheep's fat.

JõULUD, Christmas.   *December 25*

Christmas is a family holiday, spent quietly at home.

After morning church services each family returns home to eat dinner and observe the holy season. In many homes parents do not allow the children to play, but insist upon prayers and carol singing for the rest of the day.

Teine püha, Second Christmas Holiday. *December 26*

Young people celebrate this holiday with all kinds of merrymaking, such as big dinners, dances, parties, concerts and choral programs.

Kolmas püha, Third Christmas Holiday. *December 27*

People bid farewell to Christmas by calling informally from neighbor to neighbor, eating the holiday left-overs and drinking to one another's health.

Vana Aasta Õhtu, New Year's Eve. *December 31*

Older people and those who are religious go to church and take communion on this night. The younger generation generally indulges in parties and all kinds of festivities. Usually games are played and fortunes told. One favorite method of looking into the future is to melt lead and throw it into a bowl of cold water. The various shapes assumed by the hardening lead are said to predict coming events. Thus when the lead takes the shape of a ship, its owner will sail the seas during the next twelve months; a casket means that death will come to some member of the family; a ring is a sure sign of a wedding, while a heart points to a new admirer!

FESTIVALS OF THE FINNS

UUDENVUODEN PÄIVÄ, New Year's Day. *January* 1

After the morning church service, friends visit and wish one another a Happy New Year.

LOPPIAINEN, Epiphany. *January* 6

Epiphany, the last day of the Yuletide season, is celebrated with particular gaiety. People drive in sledges from village to village, visiting friends and relatives and attending dances and parties. Games are played and Christmas trees lighted for the last time, for the following day will see them dismantled and thrown away.

JOHAN LUDVIG RUNEBERGEN SYNTYMÄPÄIVÄ, Birthday of
Johan Ludvig Runeberg. *February* 5

This great festival honors Finland's national poet. Schools are closed. In Helsinki, shop windows display busts and pictures of Runeberg, which generally are placed against a blue background and surrounded by lilies-of-the-valley, blue and white being the colors of Finland's national flag. Rows of white candles, placed in the foreground of the windows, are lighted at night. Special ceremonies are observed at Runeberg's monument in the Esplanade. The statue is decorated with garlands of pine and spruce, hung between four great torches. In the evening the lighted torches flame brilliantly against the dark sky. Delegations of students lay wreaths of flowers at the foot of Runeberg's monument and sing the impressive national anthem, composed by the poet. Lighted candles burn in the windows of apartments and houses. This great festival of lights is symbolic of the nation's love for the celebrated poet, who died in 1877 and whose work—of classic simplicity and epic greatness —has gone far in interpreting Finland to other nations.

KALEVALAN PÄIVÄ, Kalevala Day.   *February* 28

This national holiday honors Elias Lönnroth who in 1835 published the first edition of the *Kalevala*, Finland's national epic. This work marked the turning point in Finnish literature, as heretofore little had been written in the language. Honors similar to those paid at Runeberg's monument are accorded to Lönnroth's statue.

*LASKIAISPÄIVÄ, Shrove Tuesday.[1]
                    The Tuesday preceding Ash Wednesday

All schools are closed on this day, so that children may follow the ancient custom of coasting and enjoying out-of-door sports. According to an old folk saying, the finer the coasting and the longer the hills one rides on *Laskiaispäivä*, the better the coming harvests will be. In olden times, women did not spin nor men plane on this day, for if the women spun it was said no flax would grow the following summer, and if farm animals trod on the chips made by the men's planes, their feet would become swollen and sore. Characteristic foods of the day

[1] Stars indicate movable feasts that depend on Easter. See table of Easter dates and movable feasts on pages 357–358.

are Finnish pea soup, and *blini,* or rich pancakes, served with caviar and *smetana,* a kind of sour milk. The typical dessert consists of delicious wheat buns, which are filled with almond paste, placed in deep dishes and eaten with hot milk.

*PALMUSUNNUNTAI, Palm Sunday.
The Sunday preceding Easter

On this day it is customary for boys and girls to go to the woods in search of pussywillows. When the season is backward and the snow deep, the young folk have to content themselves instead with branches of birch. These branches, decorated with gay feathers and gaudy paper flowers, are saved for the Easter Sunday ceremonies.

*PITKÄPERJANTAI, Long Friday, Good Friday.
The Friday preceding Easter

This is Finland's strictest church holiday, as well as the quietest day of the year. All stores and places of business are closed. All activities cease. Everyone is expected to attend church services. Altars and pulpits are draped in black, in commemoration of Christ's crucifixion. Communion is administered on this day.

*PÄÄSIÄISAATTO, Easter Eve. *The Saturday preceding Easter*

Banks and food shops are open for a short time in the morning. All other places of business are closed until the Tuesday following Easter. Easter Eve is a gay occasion, celebrated with family parties and a supper for which special holiday foods are prepared. The meal begins with many varieties of the delicious hors d'œuvres, for which every Finnish housewife is famed. Of course there are colored Easter eggs, and *mämmi,* a traditional dish of rye meal, which is mixed with water, malted or soured by heating over a slow fire, flavored, and baked in birch-bark baskets. *Mämmi* is served with thick rich cream.

*PÄÄSIÄISSUNNUNTAI, Easter.

The day is usually spent in visiting friends and attending elaborate dinners. Early in the morning boys and girls spank one another with pussywillow or birch switches until they receive rewards of Easter eggs.

*TOINEN PÄÄSIÄISPÄIVÄ, Easter Monday.
The Monday after Easter

The Easter festivities are continued on this day.

VAPUN AATTO, May Day Eve. *April* 30

May first, which symbolizes to the Finns the season of returning light, is observed by wearing new summer clothes and making merry in restaurants, cafés and hotels. In Helsinki, May Day Eve is an especially memorable occasion for young students of the State University, who may don their white student caps on this date and wear them until September 30. It is customary for students to carry their caps under their arms when they go to the hotels or restaurants where they expect to spend the evening. When the clock strikes twelve, the students put on their caps. Late in the evening, the boys and girls walk home, singing and gay, in the light of the long spring night.

VAPPU, May First. *May* 1

In Helsinki, groups of university students meet early in the morning and march up to the Kaisaniemi and Alppila summer restaurants. There they drink *sima,* a special kind of malt ale, and eat *struvoja,* delicious crullerlike cakes. The day is spent in singing and enjoying the country. The rest of the population strolls through parks and streets, carrying multi-colored balloons and birch whisks. The working people hold parades and have speeches and demonstrations in parks and public places.

*HELATORSTAI, Ascension Day. *The fortieth day after Easter*

This church festival is little observed except in Ritvala, a village of Sääksmäki parish. In this small community *Helka-juhlat* and *helkavirret* are given—special folk dances and songs which originated in pagan times.

J. V. SNELLMANIN SYNTYMÄPÄIVÄ, Birthday of J. V. Snellman.

May 12

On the anniversary of the birth, in 1806, of the great statesman, patriot and journalist who helped to further the nationalist movement in Finland, special honors are paid at Snellman's statue.

SUOMEN ARMEIAN LIPPUJUHLA, Flag Day of the Army.

May 16

This national holiday, commemorating Finland's freedom from Russia in 1917, is observed with military parades and demonstrations.

JUHANNUSAATTO, Saint John's Eve.   *June* 23

Housewives prepare for Finland's great midsummer festival with special housecleaning and the decorating of rooms and porches with freshly cut birch branches—symbols of new life and of rejoicing in nature. In advance of the holiday youths and men of every village prepare on the lake shores or on prominent eminences enormous bonfires, consisting of boards, fallen trees and old tar-barrels. In the evening these *kokko* fires are lighted as symbolic greetings of joy and renewed life to the folk in neighboring villages. The young people, dressed in national costume, dance about the lighted bonfires throughout the long, light midsummer night. According to old folk custom, girls go to the fields on *Juhannusaatto,* to gather wild flowers and grasses. These they fashion into fragrant bouquets and tuck them under their pillows at night. The men who appear as the maidens slumber are sure to be their future husbands! Cities are empty and lifeless on *Juhannusaatto,* because everyone who can celebrates the midsummer festival in the country.

JUHANNUSPÄIVÄ, Midsummer Day.   *June 24*

On this day the midsummer festivities and games continue.

SUOMEN LIPUN PÄIVÄ, Finnish Flag Day.

The Finnish flag, which has a blue cross on a white background, flutters from every public building and is seen in every house and apartment.

ADVENTTI, Advent Sunday.
                    The Sunday nearest to November 30

On this Sunday everyone goes to church to sing "Hosanna." Boys and girls who have attended confirmation classes celebrate their first communion. Generally the little girls dress in white. If they live in poor rural communities, however, their dresses are of more practical black, because the same garments probably will be worn on festive occasions for possibly several years.

Suomen Itsenäisyyspäivä, Independence Day.   *December 6*

This is the anniversary of the Finnish Declaration of Independence in 1917, when the country was freed from Russian rule. Throughout Finland, the day is celebrated with patriotic festivals, speeches and national music.

Jouluaatto, Christmas Eve.   *December 24*

In rural districts a rye sheaf is always set up in the farmyard for the wild birds, and an extra portion of food is given to all barnyard animals. Everyone in the family takes a *sauna* or steam bath and dresses in spotless holiday attire. Then the various members of the family gather about the long festive board. Someone lights the scores of candles on the Christmas tree, which is trimmed with intricate homemade toys of paper or wood, tempting gingerbread cookies, gilded walnuts and many colorful trifles. By flickering candlelight, the head of the household solemnly reads the Christmas prayer and sermon. Then, and then only, does the holiday meal begin. All kinds of hors d'œuvres, *lipeäkala,* the Christmas fish, *Joulukinkku,* the Christmas ham, rye and white bread, *torttuja,* a kind of plum cake, strong black coffee and the traditional rice pudding are features of the Finnish Yuletide feast. Somewhere in the tempting depths of the rice pudding an almond is hidden. This prize is eagerly sought for, because the boy or girl who finds it is sure to be married before the following Christmas. In the cities, where churches are more easily reached, people always attend services before participating in any of the holiday festivities. All traffic ceases at five o'clock, and crowds of people gather at the churches, where they place flowers and lighted candles on the graves of deceased members of the family.

JOULUPÄIVÄ, Christmas.   *December 25*

People rise early to attend the Christmas service held at five or six o'clock on Christmas morning. In rural sections families drive to church in sledges. Although the countryside is black in the early dawn, stars glimmering overhead and candles burning in farmhouse windows make the road shine white and straight beneath the swiftly moving hoofs of the sturdy Finnish ponies. Christmas Day is spent in feasting and visiting among friends and relatives.

UUDENVUODEN AATTO, New Year's Eve.   *December 31*

In Helsinki the New Year is formally greeted with a concert given from the steps of the *Suurkirkko,* or Great Church, which is located in the capital's imposing *Suurtori,* or Great Plaza. At midnight church bells peal forth and harbor ships give whistle salutes in welcome to the New Year. According to ancient folk custom, people throw melted tin into a bucket of water at the midnight hour, in order to read in the various forms assumed by the stiffening metal predictions of good or ill for the coming year.

FESTIVALS OF THE FRENCH

LE JOUR DE L'AN, LE JOUR DES ÉTRENNES, New Year's Day.

January 1

The first day of the year is characterized by family reunions, gay *étrennes*, or presents, and the exchange of greeting
cards. Early in the morning children give their fathers and
mothers little handmade gifts and wish them a *Bonne Année.*
Tradesfolk send their errand boys or girls to patrons with the
season's compliments and gifts representative of their trade.
The fish merchant, for example, may offer oysters, the baker a
brioche, the butcher a chicken, the dairyman a dozen eggs, and
so on. It is customary to give wine and *étrennes* of money to
those who bring the gifts. Servants and clerks generally are
allowed a double month's pay as a New Year's gift. *Bonbon-
nières* filled with chocolates or other sweets, flowers, and all
kinds of fresh and *glacés* fruits are the customary gifts exchanged among family and friends. The New Year's dinner is
an elaborate affair, attended by relatives from far and near. In
the afternoon men call on their women friends and younger
people on their elders. The streets present a festive air, with
their brilliantly lighted shop windows and crowds of eager holiday folk—laughing, exchanging greetings and hurrying to
meet friends. In the evening a dinner party usually is held at
the home of the "head of the house"—the eldest member of the
family. As the French "family" means all the relatives,

118

whether close or several times removed, these reunions are large
affairs which are greatly enjoyed by both old and young.

ÉPIPHANIE, Epiphany Eve. *January* 5

In small towns and villages of Normandy it is customary
for bands of poor boys and girls, carrying illumined Chinese
lanterns and empty baskets, to go from house to house on
Epiphany Eve. They sing traditional songs, begging the rich
to share their bounty with the destitute. In accordance with the
gracious custom of former days, householders give the singers
gifts of food and drink, money or clothes. In Provence and
some other parts of southern France, the children go out on
Epiphany Eve to meet the Three Kings. Sometimes they carry
offerings of cakes and figs for the hungry Magi and hay for their
weary camels. Even though the children fail to meet the Kings
on any of the roads, they may be sure to see the stately figures
of the Magi near the altar of the church, where the Epiphany
Mass is celebrated at night.

LE JOUR DES ROIS, Day of the Kings; FÊTE DES ROIS, Feast of
Epiphany. *January* 6

Le Jour des Rois is celebrated, especially in Normandy,
with parties for children and grown-ups. The *galette des rois,*
or cake of the Kings, is the crowning glory of an elaborate feast.
The cake, which is thin and round, is cut in the pantry, covered
with a white napkin and carried into the dining room on a small
table. The cake always is cut into one more piece than there are
guests, and this piece, which is intended for the first poor person
who comes to the door, is called *le part à Dieu,* God's share.
The youngest member of the company, who often hides under
the table, is asked to designate which piece of cake shall go to
each person. Great excitement prevails during the distribution

of the pieces, for, according to custom, a small china doll (in former days a bean) must be baked in the cake. The one finding the doll in his or her portion becomes a king or queen of the merry revel. The king or queen chooses a consort and together they rule the feast. Every move made by the royal couple is commented upon and imitated with mock ceremony by the entire company, who shout lustily, "The queen drinks," "The king laughs," "The queen drops her handkerchief," "The king sneezes." Throughout the night, festivities continue in the form of feasting, games, dancing, and all sorts of gay nonsense.

*MARDI GRAS, Shrove Tuesday, Carnival.[1]
The Tuesday preceding Ash Wednesday

Carnival is a period of boisterous hilarity, especially in southern France, where people masquerade the streets and indulge in all sorts of noisy pranks, such as parading, tooting tin horns, singing and pelting passers-by with confetti and flowers. In Nice, where the carnival assumes more picturesque proportions than elsewhere, an enormous effigy of King Carnival, surrounded by a train of clowns and buffoons, is formally presented with the keys of the city. King Carnival is seated on a throne, from which he rules the scene. Flower-decked cars and floats drive for hours along the wide *Promenade des Anglais.* As friends and acquaintances pass and repass, they pelt one another with missiles of flowers. In Paris and many other French cities butchers observe Carnival with the fête of the *Bœuf Gras,* or Fat Ox. A great ox, decked with garlands, flowers, festoons of green and floating ribbons, is led through the streets in procession. He is followed by a triumphal car in which rides a little lad known as the "King of the Butchers." The crowd pays

[1] Stars indicate movable feasts that depend on Easter. See table of Easter dates and movable feasts on pages 357–358.

tribute to the small king by blowing horns and throwing confetti, flowers and sweets. Brilliant parties, balls and other festivities mark the end of the pre-Lenten gaieties.

*MI-CARÊME, Mid-Lent. *The fourth Sunday in Lent*

The gloom of the Lenten season is broken by the mid-Lent festivities. In Paris the day is celebrated by the fête of the *blanchisseuses,* or laundresses. Washerwomen from each of the various metropolitan districts select a queen. Later a queen of queens is chosen from among these beautiful young women. The queen of queens elects a king, who sits beside her on a golden throne as she rides through the streets on a float. The district queens follow, each boasting a brilliant retinue of courtiers and ladies-in-waiting. At night the laundresses attend a colorful ball, presided over by the queen of queens.

*DIMANCHE DES RAMEAUX, Palm Sunday.
The Sunday preceding Easter

After attending morning Mass, at which blessed palms are received, everyone goes to the cemeteries to put the family tombs in order and decorate them for Easter.

*VENDREDI-SAINT, Good Friday. *The Friday preceding Easter*

Throughout France solemn high Masses are held to commemorate Christ's crucifixion. Since the church bells do not ring from Good Friday until Easter, mothers and nurses tell the children that "the bells have flown away to Rome."

*PÂQUES, Easter.

On Easter morning the children rush into the garden to

watch the bells "fly back from Rome." As the small folk scan
the sky for a glimpse of the returning bells, their elders scatter
bonbons on the ground. "You are too late to see the bells," declare the grown-ups. "See, they have already passed this way!
They have dropped sweets under your very noses." Easter is
the one Sunday in the year when everyone goes to church.
Candles blessed at the Easter service are carried home and
lighted only on special festivals, for an Easter taper must last
until the following *Pâques*. Everyone must wear something
new on Easter Sunday. The children receive little presents of
colored candy eggs and chocolate chickens.

*LUNDI DE PÂQUES, Easter Monday. *The Monday after Easter*

Continuation of the Easter holiday. Shops and places of
business are closed.

MOIS DE MARIE, Month of Mary. *Month of May*

Since May is *Mois de Marie,* the "month of Mary," services in her honor are held throughout the month. Altars are
decorated with blue and white, the colors of the Virgin. Processions, hymns to Mary and beautiful floral decorations characterize the worship of the Virgin in all parts of the country. First
Communion comes sometime during May and one sees many
charming processions of little solemn-eyed lads and of garland-
crowned girls, who wear white veils and dresses and often carry
diminutive white parasols.

PREMIER MAI, May Day. *May 1*

On this day it is considered lucky to wear *muguets*, lilies-
of-the-valley, received from friends. People say that any wish

one makes while wearing the flowers is bound to come true. Sprays of pressed lilies, accompanied by messages of love and affection, are sent to distant friends. In southern France the streets resound with shrill cries of flower-vendors, who hawk their fragrant wares and persuade passers-by to purchase lilies-of-the-valley for friends. Throughout France many workmen assert their freedom by taking May Day as a holiday, although it is not officially recognized as such by employers. The day is marked by speeches, parades and political demonstrations.

Fête de Jeanne d'Arc, Festival of Joan of Arc.
The second Sunday in May

This is a church festival, celebrated with special ceremony in Rouen and Orleans. Streets and houses are decorated with banners, garlands and pictures, in memory of the Maid of Orleans, who led the French forces to victory at Patay and brought about the coronation of Charles VII at Rheims, July 17, 1429.

Fête des Saintes Maries, Feast of the Holy Maries.
May 24–25

The small Provençal village of Les Saintes-Maries-de-la-Mer is the annual destination of thousands of devout pilgrims. Here gypsies pay tribute to Sarah, the Egyptian handmaid of Mary Jacoby and Mary Salome, who, according to legend, were set adrift from Syria anc shipwrecked off the Provençal coast. Tradition says that the three holy women died at Les Saintes-Maries. The relics of Saint Sarah, patroness of gypsies, are deeply venerated by gypsies of southern France, who try to worship at her shrine at least once during their lives. Solemn services are held in the fifteenth century church of Les Saintes-Maries, where the reputed remains of Saint Sarah and the two

Maries are preserved. An impressive part of the service is the adoration of the flower-decked reliquary of the Maries, which at a dramatic moment is lowered slowly through a door in the ceiling of the church. On the second day of the festival a colorful procession goes to the sea, where the painted wooden "Bark of the Saints" is blessed with great reverence. The Bark contains a silver urn, said to hold the bones of the saints. Games and exhibitions of horsemanship end the great annual *Fête des Saintes Maries*.

*Pentecôte, Pentecost, Whitsuntide.

The fortieth day after Easter

All city people try to spend these early spring holidays in the country. Picnics, excursions and outings of all kinds are planned at this time.

*Fête-Dieu, Corpus Christi.

The Thursday following Trinity Sunday

This great church festival, celebrated in honor of the Blessed Sacrament, is observed throughout France. Gorgeously robed priests, followed by choir and laymen, carry the Eucharist through the streets under a canopy richly embroidered in gold. In some towns and villages the path of the Eucharist procession is covered with a thick carpet of rose petals. Prizes are offered for the most beautifully decorated houses. Often flowers are pinned to sheets, and hung against walls or the sides of the buildings. *Reposoirs,* or small altars, are built at the crossroads. These shrines are covered with altar cloths and decorated with flowers, garlands and greens. Canopies of interwoven boughs give them the appearance of woodland chapels. The priest makes the village rounds and blesses the various shrines.

Festivals of the French

FEUX DE LA SAINT JEAN, Saint John's Eve.   *June* 23

In Burgundy, Brittany and some other parts of France the
ancient pagan fire-festival of midsummer still is observed with
lighted bonfires on Saint John's Eve. In many sections of
Brittany the ceremony retains much of the religious solemnity
of olden days. In Finistère bonfires are built whenever possible near a chapel dedicated to Saint John. Everyone in the
parish brings fuel for the fire—a log, a stout branch, a bundle
of slender faggots. The priest kindles the pile at the close of
the vesper services. After singing hymns and chanting prayers,
the young folk dance about the fires. Some of the embers are
carried home as a talisman against fire, lightning and disease.
In Upper Brittany the Saint John's fires are built around tall
poles, set on the hilltops. A lad named Jean or a maiden named
Jeanne provides a bouquet or wreath for the pole and kindles the
bonfire. The young people sing and dance about the great fire,
as it burns. Later they leap over the dying ashes, with a wish
that crops may grow as high as they jump.

LA RETRAITE AUX FLAMBEAUX, The Night Watch.   *July* 13

The Eve of the anniversary of the Fall of the Bastille, at
the outbreak of the Revolution of 1789, is celebrated with colorful processions of torch-bearers, soldiers and bands. The city
lights are darkened as the procession marches through the
streets. Flaming torches, Chinese lanterns swinging from long
poles, stirring martial music and patriotic songs fire the enthusiasm of spectators, who follow the procession throughout
the city. The festival ends at the house of some prominent
citizen, who provides drinks for the torch- and lantern-bearers.
Singing and gaiety continue far into the night.

QUATORZE JUILLET, FÊTE NATIONALE, Independence Day.
July 14

Throughout France the anniversary of the Fall of the Bastille in 1789 is observed with speeches, processions, national music and official dinners. In Paris the day begins with firing the cannon a hundred times. The *Fête Nationale* is celebrated with fireworks, free performances for the poor at the state theatres, music and street dancing in memory of the *Carmagnole,* which the Paris populace danced when taking the Bastille.

LE PARDON DE SAINTE ANNE D'AURAY, Pardon of Saint Anne
d'Auray.
July 25, 26

This famous festival of Auray, Brittany, is celebrated in honor of Saint Anne, the mother of the Virgin Mary. According to a seventeenth century legend, Saint Anne appeared in a vision to a peasant named Yves Nicolazie, and commanded him to interest pious folk in rebuilding her ruined chapel. The peasant reported what he had seen to the bishop, who believed him. Soon after, a broken effigy of the saint was discovered in a field. Believers from far and near brought offerings, that it might be enshrined. The church at Auray was built and later became a place of pilgrimage for worshipers from many parts of France. Annually thousands of devout Christians fast and ascend on their knees the *Scala-Santa,* or sacred stairway, which leads to the chapel enclosing Saint Anne's statue. Bretons believe that if they burn their candles at the shrine, Saint Anne will bless household and crops and ships at sea. The Pardon of Saint Anne is one of the most picturesque of all French festivals, as the Breton peasants—both men and women—attend in the rich and beautiful costumes for which their *Département* is famed.

ASSOMPTION, Assumption of the Virgin Mary.   *August* 15

This church holiday is widely observed as an occasion for making excursions into the country.

TOUSSAINT, All Saints' Day.   *November* 1

Also a church holiday, this is celebrated with joyous services in memory of all the saints who are glorified.

JOUR DES MORTS, All Souls' Day.   *November* 2

On the *Jour des Morts,* which is dedicated to prayers for the dead who are not yet glorified, cemeteries are visited and the graves decorated with artificial flowers and wreaths of immortelles.   The church services are gloomy and funereal.   In Brittany, boys play many hideous practical jokes in the cemeteries.   They often frighten visitors by rattling human bones in empty pails, or by putting lighted candles inside human skulls and placing them in dark corners of the graveyard.   Native tales abound which tell of the evil likely to befall those who tamper with the bones of the dead.

SAINT MARTIN DE TOURS, Saint Martin of Tours.   *November* 11

This festival of Tours honors the fourth century patron of the city and the guardian of vine-growers, tavern-keepers and beggars, marks the anniversary of the translation of the saint's relics, and is observed with special services at his shrine in the cathedral.   In some parts of France there is a traditional holiday dinner which includes roast goose, many rich foods, and the first new wine.   *Faire la Saint Martin* is the term the French give to feasting at this time of year.   The festival is celebrated locally on July 4 in some parts of France.

JOUR DE L'ARMISTICE, Armistice Day. *November* 11

Every town throughout France remembers its war heroes with special church services, military parades and the decoration of the monuments of those who died in the World War. In Paris impressive ceremonies are held at the grave of the Unknown Soldier. The *Anciens Combattants,* or war veterans, hold banquets and reunions on this day.

SAINTE CATHERINE, Saint Catherine. *November* 25

On this day, all over France unmarried girls of twenty-five *coiffent Sainte Catherine*—don little white paper caps in honor of Saint Catherine and pay gay tribute to the patron saint of old maids. The girls choose a queen, who also wears a cap, and ceremoniously escort her through the city streets. *Coiffer Sainte Catherine,* "to don Saint Catherine's bonnet," is an expression used to warn girls that they are likely to become spinsters. In Paris the *midinettes,* or sewing girls, hold an annual procession along the *Rue de la Paix.*

SAINTE BARBE, Saint Barbara. *December* 4

In some parts of France Saint Barbara's Day marks the beginning of the Christmas season. On Saint Barbara's Eve in southern France, especially in Provence, wheat grains are soaked in water, placed in dishes and set to germinate in the warm chimney corner or a sunny window. According to old folk belief, if the Saint Barbara's grain grows fast, crops will do well in the coming year. If, on the contrary, it withers and dies, the crops will be ruined. The "Barbara's grain" is carefully tended by the children, who on Christmas Eve place it near the *crèche,* as a living symbol of the coming harvest.

Festivals of the French

Saint Nicolas, Saint Nicholas.   *December* 6

According to ancient French legend, the Virgin once gave Lorraine to Saint Nicholas as a reward. Consequently, the good saint became the special patron of that province, which he visits each year. Sometimes representatives of the saint, dressed in the bishop's regalia, walk through the streets and bring presents for the children. On Saint Nicholas' Eve in Lorraine and some other parts of France, children hang their stockings near the fire and retire with a prayer that the saint will remember them.

"Saint Nicolas, mon bon patron,
Envoyez-moi quelqu'chose de bon,"

is an old French rhyme. The good things children anticipate are toys and gay bonbons; the bad they fear, especially if they have been naughty during the year, is a stout rod of chastisement. Saint Nicholas is a stern disciplinarian, and he remembers how children have behaved during the past twelve months. As a reminder of his watchfulness, small ribbon-tied bunches of birch twigs accompany the gifts left for even good boys and girls.

Veille de Noël, Christmas Eve.   *December* 24

On Christmas Eve the children arrange the *crèche,* or miniature nativity scene, which is made with small figures representing the Christ Child, Joseph and Mary, the Magi and the shepherds set against a charming background of moss, stones and small branches. At midnight the church bells joyously announce the birth of Christ and the hour of Christmas Mass. In Paris cathedrals the service is magnificent, while in rural districts the ceremony is observed with naïve simplicity. The beautiful *crèche,* artistically lighted with burning tapers, the singing of century-old provincial carols, incense, the pealing of many bells—all combine to make this service the most colorful of the year. After midnight Mass everyone attends *Réveillon*, a meal which includes *pâté de foie gras,* blood sausage and plenty of good native wine. On the following day the newspapers always report the number of kilometers of blood sausage people have eaten at *Réveillon*. In southern France many survivals of ancient mystery plays still are found in the village churches. On Christmas Eve children carefully set their wooden *sabots,* or shoes, before the fireplace, for *le petit Noël* or *le petit Jésus* will stop before dawn to fill waiting shoes with nuts and sweets, sometimes even with longed-for toys. In some parts of the country carol-singers, holding lighted tapers and reverently carrying a little *crèche,* go from house to house in the community. The lads sing old songs of Christ's birth and receive small money gifts.

NoËL, Christmas. *December 25*

Christmas is a time for family dinners, reunions and parties, not a period for merrymaking and exchanging gifts. Oysters, roast goose or turkey with chestnut and pork filling, *bombe glacée,* and an abundance of fine wine are among the delicacies characteristic of the Christmas feast.

FESTIVALS OF THE GERMANS

Neujahr, New Year's Day.   *January* 1

According to old German folk tradition, the first day of the year must be lived as one would like to live during the next twelve months. The housewife puts the home in order; everybody wears at least one new garment; no money is spent, but the coins in one's pocket are shaken "for luck." No unpleasant work is begun, doctor and chemist are avoided and everyone keeps on good terms with his neighbor! With a start such as this, the peasant thinks the New Year will be happy and prosperous. The exchange of greeting cards is universal at the beginning of the year. Presents rarely are given, with the exception of money remembrances to the postman, janitor and others who have served the family during the year.

Dreikönigsfest, Festival of the Three Kings.   *January* 6

The Christmas tree is lighted for the last time, as Epiphany marks the end of the Yuletide season. In Upper Bavaria peasant lads, wearing wooden masks and cracking long whips, symbolically drive from the village *Frau Percht,* the mysterious witch who wanders about harming mortals on the "Twelve Days" between Christmas and Epiphany. Good spirits, represented by a fantastically-garbed couple, then dance before the houses, bringing (so folk say) good luck and blessings to all

131

the village. In Catholic Germany, particularly in western and southern sections of the country, salt and chalk are consecrated in the churches. People chalk over their doors the initials of the Three Kings, to prevent evil from entering their homes. "Caspar, Melchior, Balthasar, protect us this year from all danger of fire and flood" is the legend peasants from the Bavarian Forest write above the lintel. In this same section of the country an Epiphany cake is eaten. A bean or a coin is hidden in the pastry and whoever finds either token becomes king of the feast. In many places processions of the "kings" go about singing old folk songs and asking for alms. The kings wear gold paper crowns and carry large cardboard stars. One of the carolers' favorite songs is, that the Three Holy Kings, with their star, like to eat and to drink, but they don't like to pay for what they get!

*FASTNACHT, Ash Wednesday Eve, Carnival.[1]
The Tuesday preceding Ash Wednesday*

Fastnacht is celebrated with masquerades and carnival processions that vary in character and spirit according to locality. Many of the carnivals of the Rhine district originated in religious rites and are characterized by adherence to sacred tradition. In Mayence, companies of guards pitch camp along the city thoroughfares, especially in the vicinity of the cathedral, and act as a bodyguard to Prince Carnival—a fairly recent addition to the old festival. In Cologne, Prince Carnival holds sway over a Fool's Court. He is attended by councilors who wear high peaked caps and badges of the Order of Fools. The Sparks, as Prince Carnival's bodyguard is called, carry wooden muskets over their shoulders and are resplendent in the uniforms of old Cologne's City Guards. Probably some of the most

[1] Stars indicate movable feasts that depend on Easter. See table of Easter dates and movable feasts on pages 357–358.

charming carnival celebrations are to be found in Eastern Saxony, where a symbolic battle is fought between representatives of Winter and Spring. Winter always is vanquished and Spring is welcomed with laughter, merrymaking and song. In many localities this type of carnival celebration is held later than *Fastnacht*. Eisenach, which has observed the battle of the seasons since 1286, "wins the summer" by burning Winter in effigy after his defeat by Dame Sun. In Munich the Shrovetide festival is characterized by the splendor and pageantry of the Middle Ages. Ancient guild dances are performed by actors dressed in costumes of former days, while historical floats and ceremonies portray much of the picturesqueness of Munich's past. Among the traditional foods eaten at this season are eggs and pretzels and the famous "Berlin pancakes," which are popular among all classes.

*GRÜNDONNERSTAG, Maundy Thursday.

The Thursday preceding Easter

In Saxony tradition says that green salad should be eaten on this day. Whoever neglects this duty is in danger of "becoming a donkey"! A certain kind of cottage-cheese dish is another favorite food of the season.

*OSTERN, Easter.

Apart from the religious significance of the season, Easter is primarily a children's festival. The special rites of the day center largely about eggs, fire and water. According to ancient legend, the Easter rabbit brings the eggs, which he hides in strange places. In many parts of Germany, especially in certain Swabian villages, little "rabbit gardens" are built for the Easter bunny. In the Deister, in Hannover, he leaves his eggs in carefully prepared nests of moss. When skies are fair, the

Easter hare prefers to hide his eggs in gardens and out-of-door nooks, but in stormy weather he visits curious corners in the house. The bunny leaves a great variety of treasures, ranging all the way from colored hens' eggs to elaborate satin-covered affairs which contain exciting little presents of perfume, handkerchiefs or sweets. Eggs play an important rôle in all the Easter games. Throughout northwestern Germany peasants hold formal contests to see who can devour the most eggs. *Eierlesen,* or egg gathering, and *Eierschieben,* egg rolling, are two of the most popular sports of the season. The egg-gathering contests require remarkable agility and skill. Eggs are placed at given intervals along a racing track. Boys with baskets run down the line, trying to see who can gather the eggs most rapidly. In the Black Forest and many other parts of Germany, the contestants ride on horseback or bicycles. Egg-rolling contests are enjoyed chiefly by children, who roll their eggs downhill. The child whose egg goes the greatest distance is the winner. In many parts of northern Germany, as in the Harz, the Rhineland, Oldenburg and Westphalia, bonfires are built on the heights, probably as a survival of ancient sacrificial rites. In some places young people go about singing rhymes and begging for contributions of fuel or money for the Easter fires. Usually the fires are tremendous piles made from tar-soaked barrels, old tree roots and limbs. In Luegde, a village of Westphalia, the usual bonfire is varied by binding twigs and straw to a wheel, lighting and rolling it into the valley. Wherever the wheel touches the ground it is thought to carry special blessings to the land. Water, as well as fire, is important in Easter rites. In the Harz, in Thuringia and in many other places girls go at sunrise to the river banks to dip up the "Easter water." If the girls perform the ceremony without uttering a word and then bathe in the water, they will be blessed with beauty throughout the year! Easter is a great holiday for shop and factory workers, who don knapsacks and go hiking in the country.

Festivals of the Germans

TAG DEN NATIONALEN ARBEIT, Day of German Labor.   *May* 1

Although many beautiful old May Day folk customs are observed in rural Germany, the first of May is the Day of German Labor.   Throughout the land, workmen and employers, together with highest government officials, take part in celebrations that symbolize the unity of the German people, in contrast to the class strife existing in many other countries.

*HIMMELFAHRTSTAG, Ascension Day.
                              The fortieth day after Easter

Ascension Day is a great out-of-door festival, which is celebrated by picnics and open air parties.   Many picturesque local customs also exist.   The Middle German villages of Fienstadt, Goedewitz, Salzmuende, Zoernitz, Gorsleben and Krimpe, of the Mansfeld Lake district, celebrate Ascension Day with the traditional drinking of "Ascension beer."   According to thirteenth century documents possessed by these hamlets, the inhabitants are commanded to drink on this day in memory of the Countess Elizabeth, who, in olden times, relieved them from the payment of tithes.

*PFINGSTEN, Pentecost.   *The fiftieth day after Easter*

Many picturesque customs are observed on this great spring holiday, which everybody tries to spend in the country.   In cities as well as villages, houses and doorways are decorated with branches of tender birch.   Shepherds from near Schramberg, in the Black Forest, assemble on this day on the Fohrenbuehl Hill, to do lively business in buying and selling cowbells.   Bells of different sizes and tones are tested and tried out, both singly and together, for it is every shepherd's ideal to acquire a harmonious set of bells.   After finishing the business of the day, the shepherds take partners and dance the *Hammeltanz,* a traditional rustic dance, which is performed about a sheep. A staff is handed back and forth between the dancers. Whoever happens to be holding the staff when a final bell sounds, receives the sheep as a prize. In some places in the Harz, noted for the raising of songbirds, members of the various *Finkenklubs,* or finch clubs, enter their birds in singing contests. The cage of the winning bird is decorated with garlands. Later in the day townsfolk gather to sing the old folk songs of their district. In Kroetzting, in Bavaria, a Pentecost Bride and Bridegroom are chosen at the close of a colorful procession of some two hundred horsemen, who perform the annual *Pfingstritt,* or Pentecostal Ride, for which the village is noted. The horsemen, led by the priests and carrying church banners and crosses, make a pilgrimage to the Steinbuehl church in the Zeller valley. In Deidesheim, in the Rhenish Palatinate, a buck goat annually is auctioned off at Pentecost. The custom originated with Kaiser Rupprecht, who commanded that the city of Lambrecht each year should provide a buck, as tribute for use of the Deidesheim forest and pasture lands. The buck, which had to be auctioned, was sold for the first time in 1404. Pentecost is a great holiday for Berliners, who make it the occasion for family picnics and parties in the open. Often people migrate from the city at dawn, breakfast at some country tavern and spend the rest of the day roaming through fields and meadows. Men's glee clubs and societies ride to the country in wagons decorated with greens and flowers.

SOMMERSONNENWENDE, Summer Solstice.   *June* 23

Bands of boys, girls and young people march singing to hills or open places, where they build enormous bonfires in honor of the summer solstice. After a picnic meal eaten in the early summer twilight, the *Johannisfeuer,* or Saint John's fire, is lighted. Then the young people sing old folk ballads and dance about the fire. The more hardy lads leap through the flames, while young betrothed couples join hands and try to jump together over the fire. If they succeed, folk say they never will part!

BARTHOLOMÄUSTAG, Saint Bartholomew's Day.   *August* 24

The day of Saint Bartholomew, patron of husbandmen, is observed in Markgoreningen and some other Swabian towns, with a festival known as the Shepherds' Race. This celebration is typically Swabian. After morning church services and a colorful procession, the sports of the day begin. Barefooted shepherds and shepherdesses have a race. The two winners— a man and a woman—are crowned with metal crowns and presented with prizes of large mutton roasts. The race is followed by other pastoral festivities, such as a shepherd dance and a water-carriers' race. After drinking to the victors with the first wine of the year, a great banquet is held in honor of the shepherds and shepherdesses.

OKTOBERFEST, October Festival.

Late September to early October

In Munich the famous October Festival celebrates the annual season of buying and selling, feasting, merrymaking and drinking. The *Theresienwiese,* a field in the environs of Munich, becomes a huge tenting ground for men and women, old and young, who gather to enjoy the delights of the season. Roller coasters, merry-go-rounds, side shows and innumerable booths that sell sweets, foodstuffs, household articles and other merchandise, provide entertainment for the hundreds of eager visitors. People hold great feasting bouts at which they roast animals over open fires and drink quantities of Bavarian beer.

LEONHARDIRITT, Leonard's Ride.   *November* 6

This very old autumn procession is widely observed in different parts of Bavaria, where Saint Leonard is patron of cattle. One of the most picturesque processions is held annually at the little village of Toelz-on-Isar. Peasants in native costume ride into town in *Truhenwagen,* chest wagons, which are gaily decorated with scenes from Saint Leonard's life. The horses' manes, tails and harnesses are ornamented with ribbons, flowers and sprays of green. Each wagon is accompanied by an outrider, carrying a colorful banner. Members of the clergy and town council ride in a wagon drawn by great white horses. The picturesque procession makes its way up the steep Calvary Hill where the church is situated. After going about the church the priest reads an open-air Mass. Later the procession returns to town, where it finally disbands, to the accompaniment of singing and the cracking of whips. In some places cattle participate in the procession.

MARTINSFEST, Saint Martin's Festival.   *November* 10

Martinsfest is a double festival, which honors both Saint Martin and Martin Luther. Saint Martin, the fourth century friend of children and the poor, is especially revered along the Lower Rhine. One of the most picturesque festivals takes place in Düsseldorf, where huge torchlight processions of children go through the streets. Many of the participants carry hollowed-out pumpkin lanterns, illumined from within with lighted candles. Saint Martin, followed by hundreds of children, rides through the streets in person. The rites of Saint Martin probably originated as an early thanksgiving festival in honor of Freya, goddess of plenty, who guarded the harvests of the ancient Germans. Just as German Catholic communities honor Saint Martin at this season, so Protestant groups, especially in such sections as Thuringia, celebrate Martin Luther's birthday with the picturesque rites. In Erfurt, where Martin Luther attended the university, thousands of children with lighted lanterns form a picturesque procession, which finally marches up to the Plaza in front of the cathedral and the Severi Church. There the children form with their lanterns the "Luther rose," or the escutcheon of Martin Luther.

SAINT NICÓLAUS, Eve of Saint Nicholas.   *December* 6

German Yuletide festivities begin with Saint Nicholas' Eve, when in many small towns and rural districts the good saint puts in an appearance and makes his annual calls on children. If boys and girls are good, he promises them sweets and toys. But if they are bad, he flourishes a bundle of birch rods, or presents them with a little cluster of twigs, which are either real or of candy. Usually Saint Nicholas is nothing more than an advance Christmas messenger who looks into the children's behavior. The holiday gifts are not received until Christmas, with the arrival of the *Weihnachtsmann,* the Christmas man, or of *Christ Kindle* himself, the Christ Child, who wanders across the snow with blessings and presents for old and young.

HEILIGABEND, Christmas Eve.   *December* 24

For weeks before the holidays the public squares of towns and villages are thronged with people who buy and sell at the holiday fairs. Probably the ancient Hamburg *Dom* is one of the most unique Christmas fairs, not only in Germany, but in the world. In olden days this market was held in the open square before the *Dom* or cathedral, from which it derived its name. Today it occupies the *Heiligengeistfeld* or Holy Ghost Field, in the center of town. The *Dom* is like the Munich Fair, but on a larger scale. It has booths filled with tempting toys, sugared gingerbreads and holiday sweets, as well as all the useless trifles which invariably attract the human eye. The *Dom* opens in November and continues until shortly before Christmas. Christmas is the gayest holiday of the German calendar and the *Weihnachtsbaum* or Christmas tree, with its lighted candles, gilded nuts, red shining apples and dancing, raisin-eyed gingerbread men, is the symbol of the German Yuletide. The real holiday begins with Christmas Eve church services, which are followed by festivities and family gatherings. In most parts of Germany the trimming of the Christmas tree is done on the twenty-fourth, although in some places people do it whenever convenient during the days preceding. Usually the rite is performed in the utmost secrecy by the heads of the household, who are the only persons having access to the room in which the tree is kept. Presents for each member of the household, including the domestics, and *bunte Teller,* plates filled with apples, nuts, *Pfefferkuchen* and other goodies, are grouped under and around the tree. When the tree is lighted and everything is ready for the *Bescherung,* or distribution of the presents, all the members of the family are summoned to the room. After singing Christmas carols, which usually include *O Tannenbaum* and *Stille Nacht,* everybody looks for the packages marked with his or her name. The rest of the evening is spent in merrymaking.

WEIHNACHTEN, Christmas.   *December 25*

   Roast goose and *Christstollen,* long loaves of bread bursting with nuts, raisins, citron and dried fruits, *Lebkuchen, Pfefferkuchen,* marzipan, and scores of other tempting dainties are important among the holiday foods. Berliners eat carp at Christmas. Whoever finds roe with his fish is happy, for he will find money in the coming year! Christmas usually is spent as a quiet home day with relatives and friends. Many of the younger generation are breaking away from the old tradition of Christmas as a family day, and are seeking to revive the holiday as the pagan festival of the winter solstice. The young people spend the day in the country, where they build fires in the open and perform ceremonial dances and songs in honor of the sun god's return to earth. This festival is termed *Wintersonnen-wende,* or winter solstice. Many old folk superstitions are held regarding the "Twelve Nights" between Christmas and Epiphany. Peasants often forecast weather for the twelve months by the "onion calendar." They cut an onion into twelve slices and sprinkle each portion with salt. The wetness or dryness of coming months is predicted according to the degree of moisture found on each of the twelve slices.

ALLERKINDER TAG, Holy Innocents' Day. *December* 28

On the anniversary of Herod's slaughter of Bethlehem's children, boys and girls of Thuringia and some other parts of Germany go about the streets with switches and boughs of green. They spank passers-by with their rods and demand little gifts of coins. In some parts of the country the custom is called "whipping with fresh greens." In ancient days the whipping probably was intended as an early spring rite for expelling demons and evil spirits.

SYLVESTERABEND, Saint Sylvester's Eve. *December* 31

This is a merry night all over Germany. Food plays an important part in the celebrations held in different sections of the country. Even in fashionable metropolitan restaurants people think it "lucky" to eat the traditional Saint Sylvester's carp, and to keep a few of the shining scales as a New Year charm. In many places the traditional Sylvester punch, a fine hot toddy consisting of red wine flavored with cinnamon and sugar, is served with *Pfannkuchen,* or doughnuts. On this night people from Baden eat a dried pea soup, said to bring luck to the partakers. Along the lower Rhine there are many special New Year's Eve foods, such as the *Nöujoer,* or "little New Year" cakes, which are baked in the form of spiral wreaths. Sometimes the same dough is fashioned into pretzel or circle forms. *Ballbaüschen,* a cake made with currants and raisins, is much esteemed in Bergisch-Land and Wuppertal. Regardless of locality or the kind of fare enjoyed on the last night of the year, tradition demands that a little of each kind of food be left on the plates until after midnight, to insure a well-stocked larder for the next twelve months. New Year's Eve shooting parties are popular in the Bavarian Alps, especially at Berchtesgaden. The indiscriminate shooting of firearms which used to be prevalent in many parts of Germany, originated in the old folk belief that the prowling demons and devils of New Year's Eve must be routed with tremendous noise. The last night of the old year is regarded as a propitious time to look into the future. Consequently, "lead-pouring" parties are popular among the young people, who drop a little melted lead into cold water and read fortunes for the coming year from the shapes it assumes. In the lower Rhine districts card games are the popular pastime of the season. The games continue until midnight. As church bells ring and sirens blow everybody throws down the cards and shouts the old-time greeting, *"Prosit Neujahr!"* In some parts of Germany processions of children go from house to house singing "star songs." In return for their carols householders give presents of nuts, apples, *Pfefferkuchen* and coins.

FESTIVALS OF THE GREEKS

Too Ayeeoo Vasileeoo, Saint Basil's Day; Protochroneea, New Year's Day. *January 1*

Special Masses for the New Year are held in the churches. In many cities of the United States the Greek consul or other important government representative makes an address and extends greetings and good wishes to members of the community. Parents give presents of money to their children either on Saint Basil's day, or the Eve preceding. The ancient custom of "cutting the *peta*" (*basilópitta*) or New Year cake is observed by Greek families in the United States and elsewhere no less than in Europe. The *basilópitta*, meaning cake of Basil, originally was made in honor of the fourth century Bishop of Caesarea, whose death-day the Greek Church celebrates. The cake is round, flat and thin. Within its toothsome depths is hidden a coin, destined to bring good luck to the finder. The smallest denomination custom allows is a drachma, a silver piece equivalent to an American quarter. In wealthy families gold coins are used. In Greece the *basilópitta* is made with great ceremony by the mistress of the house. Even the cutting follows traditional rules. The first piece of cake always is set aside for the Lord Christ, the second for the Holy Virgin, the third for Saint Basil, the fourth for the home, the fifth for the head of the house, the sixth for the mistress, and the remaining pieces for the different members of the family. Saint Basil's, like many other saints' days, is important as a nameday. The relatives and friends of a person named Basil visit and offer congratulations. The guests are served wine, pastries, coffee and sweets.

PARAMONEE TON THEOPHANEEON, Epiphany Eve. *January 5*

Special services are held in the churches. The priest, accompanied by his ministrants, blesses the homes with holy water.

TA AYEEA THEOPHANEEA, Epiphany, Blessing of the Waters.
January 6

Epiphany is observed (in the United States as well as in Greece) with special church services at which the Blessing of the Waters takes place. Worshipers kiss the cross and drink from the blessed water. Bottles of holy water are carried home and placed near the ikons. In Tarpon Springs, Florida, the annual ceremony of Blessing the Waters rivals in pomp and splendor the Epiphany rites of Greece. The priest, followed by a stately procession of worshipers and accompanied by federal, state and church dignitaries, carries a golden crucifix to the harbor. After giving his benediction, he throws the crucifix into the waters, from which divers later recover it. In New York and many other cities in the United States the priest still leads his congregation to a stream or river, where he performs the traditional service. In every port town of Greece, Epiphany is observed with ceremonial rites which make it one of the country's greatest church days. On Epiphany as well as Christmas, some Greek housewives make *teganítes,* a kind of fancy unsweetened bread, which is fashioned into all kinds of geometrical shapes—triangles, figures-of-eight or circles—and fried in boiling oil. These golden-brown bread-cakes are delicious, especially when eaten with cheese.

Festivals of the Greeks

Too Ayeeoo Antoniou, Saint Anthony.   *January* 17

A church holiday in honor of Saint Anthony, the third century Egyptian monk who was the father of monastic asceticism.

Too Ayeeoo Athanassiou, Saint Athanasius.   *January* 18

At this church festival Saint Athanasius, the fourth century patriarch of Alexandria, who fought against the heresies of Arian and founded Greek orthodoxy, is honored with special ceremonies.

Ton Treeon Eerarchon, Day of the Three Archbishops.
      January 30

This anniversary commemorates the work of the three fourth century archbishops, Basil the Great, Gregory the Theologian and John Chrysostom. Greek schools observe the day with special exercises, both because the three archbishops were opposed to the heresies of Arian, and because they struggled to retain the classic Greek tradition in a period when many of the early Christians were opposed to all literature of non-Christian origin.

Tees Ypapantees, Presentation of the Infant Christ in the
      Temple.   *February* 2

This festival marks the anniversary of the Virgin Mary's presentation of Christ in the Temple on the fortieth day after his birth.

The Book of Festivals

*PSYCHOSAVATO, Decoration Day.[1] *The Saturday preceding the Saturday before Carnival—or nine days before Carnival*

This day, like the forty-ninth day after Easter, is dedicated to the memory of the dead. Each family gives the names of its deceased members to the priest, who remembers them in prayer. Wheat is boiled, taken to the church to be blessed and then distributed to the congregation, in memory of the souls of the departed. The graves are decorated with flowers and lighted candles.

*APOCREO, Carnival. *The Sunday before the beginning of Lent*

This is the last day of indulgence and merrymaking before Lent begins. On this day and throughout *Tyrinee,* as the preceding week is called, cheese, eggs, milk, fish and everything but meat may be eaten.

*MEGHALEE TESSARAKOSTEE, Beginning of Lent.
The Monday after Carnival

ELLENIKEE ANEXARTEESIA, Independence Day.   *March* 25

If March 25 does not fall on Sunday, Greeks in the United States usually celebrate the anniversary of their freedom from the Turks, in 1821, on the Sunday following. Special services are held in the churches. All Greek societies observe the occasion with patriotic programs, dances, plays and addresses by prominent Greeks and Americans. When Calvin Coolidge was governor of Massachusetts he instituted the present gracious custom of raising the Greek flag over the Boston State House on this anniversary.

[1]Stars indicate movable feasts that depend on Easter. See table of Eastern Orthodox Easter dates and movable feasts on pages 370–371.

146

Festivals of the Greeks

*TON VAEEON, Palm Sunday.   *The Sunday preceding Easter*

In Greece the joyous service that commemorates Christ's triumphal entry into Jerusalem is characterized by waving branches of laurel, symbolic of honor and victory. In the United States and other countries where laurel is not obtainable, the custom often is modified by the use of palms.

*MEGHALEE PEMPTEE, Holy Thursday.
The Thursday preceding Easter

In Greece the annual ceremony of the Washing of Feet is observed in some monasteries and churches. In the United States there is a special church service.

*MEGHALEE PARASKEVEE, Holy Friday.
The Friday preceding Easter

On this most impressive festival of the holy season, a funeral service is held in memory of the mourning at Christ's burial. The crucifix is carried to the center of the church, where the body of Christ is removed and placed in a symbolic flower-decked sepulchre. The *epitáphios,* as the replica of the tomb is called, is raised on the shoulders of four men and solemnly taken about the sanctuary. In cities of large Greek population, as, for example, New York City, Lowell, Massachusetts, and many other places, the *epitáphios* is carried through the streets. Worshipers, chanting and holding lighted tapers, follow in procession. In Greece the ceremony is even more impressive. Military bands playing a funeral march precede the bier. Soldiers and worshipers follow with lighted candles. When the *epitáphios* is returned to the church the flowers are removed and distributed among the congregation.

147

*MEGHALO SAVATO, Holy Saturday.

The Saturday preceding Easter

The Holy Saturday service begins late Saturday night and continues until three or four o'clock Sunday morning. At midnight, the reputed hour of Christ's resurrection, the church is made dark. The priest lights a single candle at the altar and invites the worshipers to kindle their tapers from his. "Come and get light from the Eternal Light," he chants, "and glorify Christ who was raised from the dead." The people carry their "new lights" in joyous procession. Then they take the tapers home and use them to kindle the ikon lamps.

*TO AYEEON PASCHA, Easter.

After the Easter morning service friends and relatives greet one another by knocking together red eggs—red symbolizing joy—and uttering the traditional greetings, "Christ is risen," and "He is risen indeed." Then the eggs are exchanged. Easter is the day for great family reunions. Directly after the early morning service a special dish prepared from lamb's heart and liver is eaten. Other foods typical of the holiday feast are whole roast lamb with potatoes, chocolates and all kinds of sweets, including special cakes known as *baklavá* and *kourambiédes*. *Christópsomon*, "bread of Christ," is baked at this season. *Christópsomon* consists of round loaves of bread marked in the center with a Greek cross and decorated with red Easter eggs.

*THEFTERA TOO PASCHA, Easter Monday, Second Day of Easter.

The Monday after Easter

Continuation of feasting and merrymaking.

Festivals of the Greeks

ZOODOCHOS PEGE, Life-Bearing Spring.

The Friday after Easter

This church festival commemorates Leo's discovery of the miraculous spring that restored health to the infirm. According to tradition, before Leo became emperor he once found a sick man lying in a meadow. Leo determined to take the man to Constantinople where he could receive care. On the journey to the city the man begged for water. Since the grass round about was green, Leo thought a spring might be hidden in the vicinity. His search proved fruitless, however, and Leo was about to give up in despair when he heard a voice saying, "Leo the King, a spring is nearby. Look for it." Again Leo searched without success and again the voice repeated, "There at thy feet is a spring. Look for it." Leo looked down and lo! he found the spring. The sick man drank of the water and became well. When Leo was crowned Emperor of Constantinople, he built the Church of the Holy Virgin, the Life-Bearing Spring, on the spot where the miracle occurred.

TOO AYEEOO YEORGEEOO, Saint George's Day. *April 23*

Church services mark the anniversary of the martyrdom of Saint George, in 303 A.D. This is a great nameday in Greece, and one especially celebrated because of King George.

PROTOMAYEA, First Day of May. *April 30*

On May Day Eve young people go to the woods to pick wild flowers, which they fashion into wreaths. The garlands are hung outside, above the doors, where they remain until the end of May. On June 23, the Eve of Saint John, the wreaths are burned with great ceremony.

149

ANTHESTERIA, Day of Flowers.   *May* 1

May Day customs are fast dying out in large towns and cities. In rural districts, however, schools are closed and teachers take their pupils to the woods for a holiday. As in the days of ancient Greece, boys and girls dance and sing in honor of the spring. In 1936 the Greek community of Chicago made an attempt to revive this festival.

TON AYEEON CONSTANTINOO KE ELENEES, Saints Constantine
        and Helena.   *May* 21

This is a church festival in honor of the Emperor Constantine and his mother Saint Helena, who according to tradition went to Jerusalem in her seventy-ninth year and discovered the Holy Cross and the tomb of Christ.

*TEES ANALEEPSEOS, Ascension Day.
                           The fortieth day after Easter

This festival is celebrated by special Masses. Ascension Day usually marks the official opening of the swimming season.

*PSYCHOSAVATO, Decoration Day.
                        The forty-ninth day after Easter

People visit the cemeteries and decorate the graves with wreaths and flowers.

*PENTEEKOSTEE, Pentecost.   *The fiftieth day after Easter*

This church anniversary commemorates the descent of the Holy Ghost on the Apostles, after Christ's ascension.

150

Festivals of the Greeks

To Yenethlion too Prodromoo, Birthday of Saint John the Baptist.   *June* 24

In some parts of Greece bonfires are built on the heights on Saint John's Eve. The wreaths made on the first of May are burned in the flames.

Petroo ke Pavloo ton Apostolon, Saints Peter and Paul.
June 29

This is a church holiday in honor of the apostles Peter and Paul.

Ee Synaxis ton Dodeca Apostolon, Twelve Apostles.
June 30

This holy day honors the twelve Apostles who were sent forth to preach the gospel.

Ayeeon Anargyran Cosma ke Damianou, Saints Cosma and Damiano.   *July* 1

This church holiday honors the memory of the two Roman Christian physicians, who died in 284 A.D. Saints Cosma and Damiano gave their services to the poor. The only payment they asked was that those who were cured should believe in Christ.

Too Propheetoo Eelia, Saint Elijah.   *July* 20

A church festival in memory of Elijah, the Great Hebrew prophet of the ninth century B.C., who was fed miraculously by ravens at the stream Cherith, succored by the widow of Zarepath and finally translated to heaven in a chariot of fire.

Too Aveeoo Pantelamon, Saint Panteleimon.   *July 27*

The name Panteleimon, meaning "I pity everyone and offer my services," describes the life of the physician-saint, who was born in Nicomedia, Asia Minor, of a Christian mother. Saint Panteleimon died in 305 A.D.

Metamorphosis too Soteros, Transfiguration.   *August 6*

The anniversary of the transfiguration of Christ on Mount Tabor is observed by special church services. In the little Chapel of the Transfiguration, situated on the highest peak of Mount Athos in Greece, monks and penitents keep the vigil of the Transfiguration throughout the night.

Koimesis tees Theotokou, Assumption of the Virgin.

August 15

This church holiday marks the anniversary of the Virgin's ascent to heaven.

Apotomee tees Timias Kephalees too Prodromoo, The Beheading of John the Baptist.   *August 29*

This day of strict fast commemorates Herod's beheading of John the Baptist.

Yenethlion tees Theotokou, Birthday of the Holy Virgin.
September 8

A church holiday that is observed with special services.

Ee Ypsosis too Timiou Stavrou, Exaltation of the Cross.
September 14

This day of fasting was observed by both Greek and Latin

churches as early as the fifth and sixth centuries. When Saint Helena, mother of Constantine the Great, discovered the Holy Cross in Jerusalem, in 325 A.D., it was elevated upon the *ambon* and all the people cried out *"Kyrie eleison,"* "Lord have pity upon us." The cross remained in Jerusalem until 614, when the Persians occupied Palestine. It then was carried to Persia with the conquerors. In 628, when Herakleios of Constantinople defeated the Persians, he regained the cross and took it to Constantinople. The following year he returned the sacred relic to Jerusalem. The barefooted Emperor bore the cross in a *litanee,* or procession, in which the entire population of the city participated. On September 14, 629, the cross was elevated to its previous position on the *ambon.* Following Holy Cross Day all the great Greek fairs are opened. Stalls are erected in towns and villages, and peasants gather from remote places to buy and sell livestock and various kinds of wares.

Too Ayeeoo Deemeetrioo, Saint Demetrius.   *October 26*

After Saint George, Saint Demetrius is the most popular military hero of the Greek Church. According to legend the saint was arrested for preaching the gospel and, in the year 290, was pierced by a lance while in his cell.

Ton Taxiarchon Michaeel ke Gavrieel, Saints Michael and Gabriel.   *November 8*

A church festival, observed with special services in honor of the two archangels.

Ta Eesodia tees Theotokou, Presentation of the Virgin.

November 21

Special church services commemorate the Virgin's presentation in the Temple at three years of age.

AYEEAS EKATERINES, Saint Catherine.   *November* 25

This day is in honor of Saint Catherine, who was martyred in 305 A.D. during the persecutions of the Emperor Valerian.

APOSTOLOS ANDREAS, Saint Andrew.   *November* 30

The church honors with special services Andrew, the first apostle to be called by Christ. Saint Andrew was martyred in Patras, Greece, where he was crucified head downward.

TOO AYEEOO NIKOLAOO, Saint Nicholas.   *December* 6

On this day Saint Nicholas, patron of ships and mariners, is honored by all seamen. Every Greek ship, from the smallest fishing sloop to the largest sailing vessel, carries an ikon of Saint Nicholas, before which a light is burned and prayers are said for the safety of the ship.

TOO AYEEOO SPYRIDONOS, Saint Spyridon.   *December* 12

The fourth century archbishop of Tremithus, Cyprus, is venerated as one of the great wonder workers of the Greek Church. His day is especially observed in Corfu, where the saint's relics are worshiped by devout pilgrims.

PARAMONEE TON CHREESTOOGENNON, Christmas Eve.
December 24

Calanda singers—boys who carol of Christ's birth—go from door to door in the village and are rewarded with gifts of coins. When people are not generous, the singers often add amusing verses regarding the stinginess of the householders.

Festivals of the Greeks

CHREESTOOGENNA, Christmas. *December 25*

This is a great day for family reunions, parties and merry-making. In some parts of the country Greek mothers again make their famous *teganítes* or fried cakes, while the children watch in wide-eyed wonder and shiver over tales of the *Kallikanzaroi*. According to old folk belief, these half-human and half-monster beings wander about on the twelve days between Christmas Eve and Epiphany and attempt to work mischief among human beings.

EE SYNAXIS TEES THEOTOKOU, Holy Virgin and the Three Wise Men. *December 26*

Church services celebrate the story of the miraculous birth and of the Magi, who brought gifts to the Infant Jesus.

TOO AYEEOO STEPHANOU, Saint Stephen's Day. *December 27*

Special services are held in honor of the Archdeacon Stephen, the first Christian martyr.

PARAMONEE TOO AYEEOO VASILEEOO, Saint Basil's Eve, New Year's Eve. *December 31*

Calanda singers go from house to house on this night, singing of Saint Basil and collecting gifts of money. Sometimes the boys carry replicas of the Church of Sophia (symbolic of the national dream of recapturing Constantinople), or of Saint Basil's ship (symbolic of Greece's maritime interests). Men, women and children play cards for money. Poker and other gambling games are equally popular.

FESTIVALS OF THE HINDUS

IT is said that two-thirds of the three hundred and fifty million inhabitants of India are Hindus.[1] For this reason only Hindu festivals are included in the following pages. It would be almost impossible to make any accurate list of Indian holidays as such, since each province has its own festivals, which are celebrated in strict accordance with local customs and religious rites (see the Hindu calendar, page 359).

Another serious difficulty which stands in the way of making a fixed holiday list is the fact that the dates of the various Indian festivals are regulated according to lunar calculations, and that different calendars are used in different parts of the country. The year 1937, for example, was the 1344th year of the Bengalese calendar. Entirely different systems of reckoning time exist in many of the other provinces. Although the Central Government has adopted the western as the Indian civil calendar, it allows each province to celebrate native holidays in conformity with local needs.

Besides the many widely observed Hindu festivals, India boasts numerous religious fairs which are celebrated with great solemnity at such holy centers as Benares, Puri, Allahabad, Hardwar, Pandharpur, Gaya and Dwarka. These fairs usually are held at the time of eclipses of the sun or moon and are attended annually by tens of thousands of devout pilgrims.

[1] The other principal religious groups represented in the country are the Mohammedans, Christians and Buddhists.

Festivals of the Hindus

Characteristic of the remarkable religious tolerance existing in India today is the fact that the holidays of Hindus and Mohammedans, Parsees and Christians, Jews and other religious groups generally are observed side by side, without conflict or interference either by state authorities, or by leaders of the various sects.[2] This spirit of tolerance is beautifully expressed through the teachings of the *Bhagavat-Gītā:*

"As all rivers have the same source—the water underground—and as they follow different courses through different lands, but seek the ocean as their ultimate goal, so all religions have the goal of leading man to God. . . . If you worship me in your own way—with a flower, with the burning of incense or the pouring out of water—any of these gifts, when offered with true sincerity, and in the form of prayer and worship, will reach my throne."[3]

BAISAKHI, Hindu New Year (on the first day of *Baisakha*).

April–May (Baisakha)

Bathing in the Ganges and other holy waters is considered propitious on this day. Many folk beliefs exist regarding this ceremony, which is thought to avert evil influences. Hindus visit the temples, where, at evening services, the calendar of the New Year is read. The day is spent in feasting, merrymaking and in wearing gala clothes. Gifts are exchanged and prayers offered to the family gods.

[2] Religious riots sometimes occur, however, when religious processions of Hindus pass near Moslem mosques, because Moslems object to music near their places of worship. Similarly, Hindus are likely to riot when Moslems sacrifice cows near Hindu temples. The cow is sacred in Hindu worship and therefore public slaughter of this animal is regarded as desecration.

[3] Freely rendered from the Sanskrit by Taraknath Das. The *Bhagavat-Gītā*, the "Song of the Blessèd One," probably ranks among the greatest of India's sacred writings.

SAVITRI-VRATA, Savitri Vow.　　　*May–June (Jyaishtha)*

This day, in honor of the legendary Savitri, whose piety
and devotion restored her husband's life, is celebrated by Hindu
women.　Women whose husbands are alive fast and pray for
loyalty and power to save them from death, while those who
have lost their husbands beg to be delivered from the miseries of
widowhood in a future existence.　Women observe the *vrata,* or
vow, annually, usually over a fourteen-year period.　Wives usually offer special prayers, anoint their husbands' foreheads with
sandalwood paste and give them presents of food and flowers.
The festival is held in memory of the brave princess Savitri[4]
who loved her husband Satyavan so faithfully that she refused
to leave him, even when Yama, King of Death, led away his
soul.　Savitri's courage and persistence finally caused Yama to
relent and give back Satyavan to his wife.

ARANYA SHASHTI, Festival of Shashti.

Shashti, the god who dwells in the forest, is the deity who
is invoked by women wishing offspring.　Consequently Rajputanan women perform certain ceremonies on this day, in the
hope of being blessed with children.　In Bengal, sons-in-law are
welcomed into the family and presents are given.

JAGANNATH, RATHA YATRA, Car Procession.

　　　June–July (Asarha)

The procession of the car of the god Jagannath, or Vishnu,
is a universal Indian holy day, which is observed with special
ceremony at Puri.　To the pious Hindu, there is no caste before

---

[4] The story of Savitri is charmingly told by Margaret Noble (the Sister
Nivedita) in *Cradle Tales of Hinduism.* New York, Longmans, 1907. "Savitri,
Indian Alcestis," p. 53–66.

God. Consequently, caste distinction is not observed in the matter of food, which may be partaken of by anyone within the temple that is consecrated to Vishnu. The gorgeously arrayed images of Krishna, Balarama and Subhadra are brought out from the sanctuary and carried in procession before the eyes of devout worshipers.

NAGA PANCHAMI, Worship of the Serpent God.

July–August (Sravana)

This ancient Bengalese festival is dedicated to the pro-pitiation of Naga, chief of the serpent race. In East Bengal, where there are many snakes, the festival is observed throughout the month. Although *Naga Panchami* falls within the dreary rainy season, it is an especially joyous occasion. Offerings of milk, grain and other foods are made to snakes, and plants are strewn over the thresholds to prevent reptiles from entering the homes of men. The evening ceremonies are devoted to reading from Hindu mythology, singing folk songs and dancing native dances.

RAKHI, Festival to Pledge Protection. *July–August (Sravana)*

This festival celebrates the binding on of *rakhis,* or brace-lets, made of strands of silk, cotton, gold thread or colored cloth. Sisters still bestow bracelets on their brothers, in memory of the Rajputanan princess of several centuries ago, who, when in grave danger, sent a portion of her silken bracelet to Sultan Babar, the Mohammedan Emperor at Delhi. The Emperor, upon learning that the Hindu practice of sending *rakhis* signi-fied a woman's need for brotherly help and protection, imme-diately rendered aid to the princess. In this way the Mohamme-dan emperor became "brother" to the Hindu princess he had adopted as "sister." Like the knights of medieval days, it was customary in India for men who had received *rakhis* to risk their lives, whenever necessary, to help their "sisters" and rescue them from danger.

JANAM (or JANMA) ASHTAMI, Birthday Festival of Krishna.
August–September (Bhadra)

The anniversary of Krishna's birth is also a day of special worship for Devaki, his mother. Ceremonies symbolic of Krishna's birth are performed, and little clay figures of him as an infant are swung in cradles and worshiped. Since Krishna is reputed to have spent his youth among herdsmen, the festival is observed with special ceremonies by men of this calling.

ANANT CHATURDASI, Eternal Anniversary of the Fourteenth Day of the Month Bhaedra. *August–September (Bhadra)*

This is a festival observed principally by women, who believe that unending merit will result from fulfilling certain sacred vows, such as fasting, feeding the Brahmans and taking ceremonial baths.

PITRA PASKSHA AND AMAVASYA, Feast of the Dead.
September–October (Asvina)

A two-week festival honors the dead, whose spirits are said to return at this season. All who have lost their fathers hold memorial services and offer special food and drink to the souls of the deceased. This ceremony usually is discharged by the eldest son of the family. Gaya, which is situated on the bank of the Phalgu River, is the scene of special offerings and religious fairs, since this city is considered particularly sacred to paternal spirits.

Festivals of the Hindus

DURGA PUJA, Festival of the Goddess Durga.

September–October (Asvina)

This greatest of Indian festivals is in honor of Durga, daughter of the Himalaya Mountains and wife of Siva. Reverence is paid to Durga as the Divine Mother, the personification of Energy. In Bengal, where the religious aspect of the festival is observed with great solemnity, the goddess Durga is invoked on the first day and worshiped on three successive days. On the fifth day the image of Durga is thrown into the water. After the ceremony children pay respect to their parents. Friends and neighbors settle quarrels and ask forgiveness. Everyone dons his best clothes and an air of general gaiety and goodwill prevails in each community. Families hold joyful annual reunions at this season. In northern India, where the festival is known as *Dasahara,* various scenes from the life of Rama are enacted. According to sacred mythology, Rama worshiped Durga before and after his successful struggle against Ravana, Ceylon's ten-headed demon king, who had captured Sita, Rama's wife.

LAKSHMI PUJA, Festival of the Goddess of Fortune.

September–October (Asvina)

In Bengal, immediately after the festival of Durga Puja, Lakshmi, goddess of fortune, is worshiped. During this festival lights shine from every house and no one sleeps.

DIWALI, Festival of Illuminations.

October–November (Kartika)

Diwali, which falls at the time of the autumn equinox, is celebrated throughout India as a kind of harvest festival. In Bengal the festival is marked by feasting and family reunions.

The houses are gaily illumined with myriads of small lamps. In Bengal, the festival is called *Kali Puja,* in honor of the goddess who represents Primeval Energy, symbolizes Destruction, the Creative Power of Siva, the Absolute. Kali Puja destroys the evil forces of nature as well as the wicked propensities of men. The goddess also protects the virtuous and gives shelter to her devotees. Her day is observed with fireworks and illuminations. In mountainous regions this is the occasion for burning all accumulations of old rubbish.

BHRATRI DWITYA, Festival of Brothers.

According to Hindu mythology, Yama, god of death, takes holiday on this occasion to attend the feast of his sister Yamuna, the river goddess. In memory of this event sisters and brothers perform an impressive annual ceremony. The sister anoints her brother's forehead with sandalwood paste and prays that as Yama, god of death, is deathless, so may her brother, also, be deathless. The sister then announces the happy occasion by blowing a conch shell. She gives her brother gifts of spices, food and clothes. Should a brother be away from home on his festival, the sister makes a special mark for him on the wall.

GANESHA CHATURTHI, Festival of the Elephant God.
January–February (Magha)

This holiday honors Ganesha, the elephant-headed god of success, who is invoked before each new undertaking. Elaborate images of the god are carried in procession and later are cast into the water, with the worshipers' prayers and good wishes.

Festivals of the Hindus

BASANT PANCHAMI, Festival of Spring and of Saraswati, Goddess of Learning.   *January–February (Magha)*

This festival is celebrated throughout India in honor of Saraswati, goddess of learning, who comes each year in the spring. In Bengal, Saraswati is worshiped with particularly impressive ceremonies by students in schools and universities.

SHEORATRI, Night of Siva.   *February–March (Phalguna)*

This religious festival is in honor of Siva. Vigil and fasting on this night are thought to bring blessings in the next world, to even the meanest outcaste. The occasion is celebrated with great fervor in Benares, a center of Siva worship.

HOLI, Vernal Fire Festival.   *February–March (Phalguna)*

The Hindu vernal fire festival occurs at the full moon of Phalguna. Except in Madras, the holiday is observed with the burning of bonfires in every town and village. Dancing, singing and ceremonial rites are performed about the fires. In Bengal the festival is associated with incidents in the life of Krishna. Everybody dons new clothes. As people throng the streets in gay dresses, young lads and students armed with syringes containing various kinds of dye, secretly hide on balconies or roofs. Suddenly taking aim at an unsuspecting friend or relative in the street below, the boys discharge a shot of crimson, yellow or green dye on the sleeves or back of some new garment. The game is both merry and lively. Nobody minds being drenched with dye, as the splotches of color only testify to a person's popularity! Crimson, the color of joy, predominates during this festival of gladness.

The Book of Festivals

RAMA-NAVAMI, Festival of Rama.   *March-April (Chaitra)*

This festival marks a period of rejoicing in honor of the god Rama. Passages from the *Ramayana*, India's great medieval epic on the life of Rama and of Sita, his devoted wife, are read in the temples, and special dances are held for the great hero-god.

FESTIVALS OF THE HUNGARIANS

UJÉV NAPJA, New Year's Day.   *January* 1

Chimney sweeps with brooms go from house to house, singing New Year songs and receiving gifts of money. According
to ancient custom, one must try to break twigs from the brooms
without being detected by the sweeps, who often shut their eyes
and pretend not to see what is going on. People tie the tiny
branches together with ribbons and keep them "for luck"
throughout the coming year. The traditional *pièce de résistance*
for dinner is a young roast pig, with an apple or a four-leaf
clover in its mouth, which is said to bring good luck when eaten
on this day.

VIZKERESZT, Blessing of the Water.   *January* 6

In the churches the priest sanctifies and mixes salt and
water, with which he blesses his parishioners. In small villages
he goes from house to house, followed by his ministrants. Each
household is blessed with the holy water and each door marked
with the initials G, M, B, in memory of the three Wise Men,
Gáspár, Menyhért and *Boldizsár*. In some parts of Hungary,
boys masquerading as the Three Kings make the village rounds.
They sing of the shepherds and the miraculous birth, and receive food and coins in return. Sometimes groups of white-clad
girls, led by a girl representing an old hag, take the place of the
singing "kings."

FARSANG, Carnival.   *January 6 to Ash Wednesday*

During this gayest season of the year most of the weddings are celebrated, the most brilliant parties, balls and entertainments held, and the richest foods eaten. On Shrove Tuesday, in some parts of the country, villagers perform the symbolic burying of King Marrow Bone, who represents the indulgences of life. Prince Cibere, so named from the sour bran soup eaten during Lent, commences his forty-day reign on Ash Wednesday.

GYERTYASZENTELŐ BOLDOG ASSZONY, Blessing the Candle of the Happy Woman, Purification of the Virgin.

February 2

Every family has a candle blessed in church. These candles are carefully preserved as talismans against sickness, storm and death.

BALÁZS NAPJA, Saint Blase and GERGELY NAPJA, Saint Gregory.   *February 3 and March 12, respectively*

These saints are patrons of schools and learning. Saint Blase, whose day is observed only by Catholics, also is patron against diseases of the throat. On his anniversary people have their throats blessed in the churches. On the days of these two saints, children dressed like soldiers and armed with wooden swords go singing through the village streets as the saints' "armies." According to legend, Saint Blase's soldiers and Saint Gregory's knights persuaded unwilling scholars to love the alphabet and learn to write. The children keep up the old tradition by reclaiming would-be truants. Sometimes they collect sums of money for their schoolmasters' support. Like brave Hussars of old, the children dance, but instead of praising a soldier's life they praise those who love to learn.

Festivals of the Hungarians

ANNIVERSARY OF THE BLOODLESS REVOLUTION.   *March* 15

In 1848, Magyar independence was proclaimed under the brilliant leadership of Louis Kossuth and Alexander Petőfi. Political prisoners were freed and the press was seized and used for the first time in the cause of freedom. Petőfi's famous poem, *Talpra Magyar* (Rise, Magyar), which appeared at this time, is recited on the fifteenth of every March, in memory of Hungary's first attempt to free herself from Austrian rule.

*VIRÁG VASÁRNAP, Palm Sunday.[1]

The Sunday preceding Easter

Religious processions in memory of Christ's triumphal entry into Jerusalem are a feature of the church services. Pussywillows are blessed in church and later carried home, where they are kept in a holy corner. In some villages Prince Cibere, represented by an ugly effigy of straw or rags, is burned, drowned or thrown out of the village. With this ceremony peasants believe that sickness and trouble are banished from their midst and spring enters the village.

*ZÖLD CSÜTÖRTÖK, Green Thursday, Holy Thursday.

The Thursday preceding Easter

In churches the traditional foot-washing ceremony takes place. In homes, the first green vegetable of the year—usually spinach—is served for dinner.

*NAGYPÉNTEK, Good Friday.   *The Friday preceding Easter*

By Good Friday village houses must be scoured and white-

---

[1] Stars indicate movable feasts that depend on Easter. See table of Easter dates and movable feasts on pages 357–358.

washed, the Easter baking done and the eggs painted, in readiness for the Easter season. "Even the raven washes her son on Good Friday," says an old folk ballad. The peasant cleanses his soul through confession and puts on clean garments. The cooking is done in advance, as no fire is permitted until the ringing of the first bell on Holy Saturday.

*NAGYSZOMBAT, Holy Saturday.

The Saturday preceding Easter

"The bells come back from Rome" on this day, according to an old folk saying. People go from church to church to "resurrect the Christ." After the ringing of the bells, fast is broken and each household celebrates its Easter Eve supper.

*HUSVÉT, Easter.

Hungarian peasants carry baskets of meat, eggs and homemade bread to be blessed in church, a custom observed also by Hungarians in the United States. The Easter dinner, which is eaten after church, is one of the greatest feasts of the year. In Catholic communities this is the first big meal after long weeks of fasting, as meat has been eaten sparingly during Lent.

*HUSVÉT HÉTFŐJE, Easter Monday, "Ducking Monday."

The Monday after Easter

In olden times it was customary for village boys to duck the girls in streams or fountains on Easter Monday. Nowadays the boys sprinkle the girls with perfumed water, that they, like the flowers, "may not wither away." The victims pay for their sprinkling with gifts of eggs and flowers. The girls invite their tormentors to a meal of new bread, fresh cakes and wine, which they themselves prepare and serve.

Festivals of the Hungarians

SZENT GYÖRGY NAPJA, Saint George's Day.   *April 23*

Farmers engage their servants on Saint George's Day and pay them on Saint Michael's Day. Summer clothes are received on Saint George's Day, winter ones on Saint Michael's. It is customary to celebrate the occasion with picnics, at which tender roast pork is eaten as the chief luxury.

SZENT MÁRK NAPJA, Saint Mark's Day; BUZA-SZENTELŐ,
Blessing of the Wheat.   *April 25*

Processions go to the wheat fields to bless the future bread. Each person returns to the village carrying a spear of wheat, which has been blessed "so fog shall not strangle, hail shall not destroy, storm shall not trample, fire shall not consume the only hope of the people." In Calvinist communities fresh bread is offered to God with a prayer of thanksgiving for the prospering of the wheat crop.

FÜLÖP ÉS JAKAB NAPJA, Day of Saints Philip and James.
May 1

According to the ancient custom, village lads plant a May tree before their sweethearts' doors. The branches are stripped from the trees and the leafy crowns decorated with gay ribbons and scarfs. Whenever the May tree is planted before a church, it recalls the legend of the virgin who helped the Apostles Philip and James convert the Scythians. The virgin, who was accused of impurity for assisting the Apostles, stuck her staff into the ground and prayed God to prove her innocence. Hungarians regard the subsequent miracle of the budding of the staff as the origin of their May tree.

The Book of Festivals

*ÁLDOZÓ CSÜTÖRTÖK, Ascension, Absolution or Communion
Thursday.   *The fortieth day after Easter*

On this day the boys and girls attend their first communion.
In rural sections of the country the three days preceding Ascension are called "Visiting the Crosses." Processions go from hamlet to hamlet, visiting the village crosses and offering prayers.

*PÜNKÖSD VASÁRNAPJA, Whitsunday; PIROS PÜNKÖSD, Red
Whitsun.   *The fiftieth day after Easter*

"As short as the Kingdom of Whitsun" is a popular Hungarian saying, since Whitsuntide is but a two-day festival and the "king" reigns only from Sunday to Monday! In some places village girls choose a little white-clad maiden as their Whitsun queen. They take her from house to house, singing symbolic songs of the queen and her red-rose wreath. At last they lift the little queen by the arms, saying, "May your hemp grow as high as this." The singers generally are rewarded with goodies. In some sections of Hungary a Whitsun king is elected, while in others the queen has attendants who represent the four Evangelists.

*ÚRNAPJA, Corpus Christi, Day of God.
    The Thursday after Trinity Sunday

This great festival is in honor of the Eucharist. Four altars built outside the churches are decorated with flowers and boughs of green. To the accompaniment of music and the tolling of bells, the priest leads his people in prayer before the altars. The village processions consist of nuns, students, white-clad children and peasants in festival dress.

Festivals of the Hungarians

SZENT IVÁN NAPJA, Saint Ivan's Day; KERESZTELŐ SZENT JÁNOS NAPJA, Saint John the Baptist's Day; VIRÁG-SZENTELŐ SZENT JÁNOS, Feast of Flowery Saint John.

June 24

Originally this was the festival of the summer solstice. The day now is dedicated to singing and dancing in the open, jumping over Saint Ivan's fires and telling stories of long ago. Custom decrees that should a mother lose her child during the year, she must eat no fresh fruit until Saint Ivan's Day.

PÉTER ÉS PÁL NAPJA, Day of Saints Peter and Paul, "Saints of the Quarrel." *June 29*

All over Hungary harvesting is begun on this day and the priest blesses fields and crops.

ARATÁSI ÜNNEP, Harvest Festival. *Sometime in June*

When the last wheat is harvested in the fields, the workers make a beautiful wreath of grain and wild flowers. They carry the wreath to the master's house, where, amid shouting and rejoicing, they fasten it to the door. The master invites the harvesters to sing, dance and make merry at a great feast prepared in their honor.

ANNA NAPJA, Day of Saint Anna. *July 26*

The festival in honor of the Virgin Mary's mother is regarded as Hungary's "Mother's Day." All work is set aside and everyone devotes the day to enjoyment. Among the rich, brilliant "Anna balls" are held. Among peasants, folk dancing and merrymaking are in evidence everywhere. Great "Anna fairs" are held at the churches, both in Hungary and among

171

Hungarian communities in the United States. All kinds of trinkets, scarfs, sweets and toys are sold. Music, dancing and eating make Saint Anna's Day a gala occasion in the calendar.

NAGYBOLDOG ASSZONY NAPJA, Assumption of the Virgin Mary.
August 15

This is a great church day, both in Hungary and in the United States. According to legend, Saint Stephen, Hungary's first Christian king, on this day placed his country under the patronage of the Blessed Virgin.

SZENT ISTVÁN NAPJA, Saint Stephen's Day.   *August* 20

This greatest of all Hungarian national festivals is dedicated to Saint Stephen, Hungary's king (1001–1038), who converted his people to Christianity. The anniversary is celebrated by church processions in which the Sacred Hand of Saint Stephen, in its gold and glass reliquary, is borne aloft from the Chapel of the Royal Palace to the Coronation Church. Church dignitaries, military and civil notables, Hungarian peasants in native costume and military bands, all form a part of the impressive procession, which still retains the glory of medieval days. Sporting events, music, folk dances and performances of old folk plays give added national interest to the event. In the United States, "Saint Stephen fairs" are features of the celebration.

SZENT MIHÁLY NAPJA, Saint Michael's Day.   *September* 29

On this day servants receive their pay and their winter clothing.

Festivals of the Hungarians

ANNIVERSARY OF THE EXECUTION OF ALL THE MARTYRS OF THE
HUNGARIAN REVOLUTION, 1849.   *October 6*

REFORMÁCZIO NAPJA, Reformation Day.   *October 31*

On October 31, 1517, Martin Luther nailed to the door of
the Wittenberg Cathedral the ninety-five theses, in which he
accused the Church of abuses. The anniversary is celebrated by
services in all the Protestant churches.

SZÜRET, Grape Gathering.   *Toward the end of October*

This event marks the gay ending of the yearly farm work.
Since wine is the national drink of the Hungarian people, there
is great rejoicing when the grapes finally are gathered. After
the day's labor the workers fashion an enormous "bouquet" of
grapes. They carry it to the farmer's house to the accompaniment of laughter, song and the gay fiddling of gypsy musicians.
The girls wear white dresses and bright wreaths of field flowers.
When the farmer's house is reached, the workers suspend the
bunch of grapes from the ceiling and accept his invitation to eat
and make merry over the grape harvest.

MINDENSZENTEK NAPJA, All Saints' Day.   *November 1*

In the United States, as in Hungary, peasants go to the
cemeteries to decorate the graves with flowers and lighted
candles.

HALOTTAK NAPJA, All Souls' Day.   *November 2*

This day also is spent in the cemeteries, where people visit
from grave to grave and commune with the spirits of friends
and relatives.

173

The Book of Festivals

SZENT ANDRÁS NAPJA, Saint Andrew's Day.   *November* 30

On this day young people delight in all kinds of fortune-telling games. A favorite method of divination is to pour melted lead into a glass of cold water through the handle of a key. The form assumed by the lead foretells the occupation of a maiden's future husband! Dumplings are a popular food on this day, since "fortunes," written on small pieces of paper, are hidden within each bit of dough.

MIKULÁS NAPJA, Saint Nicholas' Day.   *December* 6

This is a great holiday for the children, who leave their shoes outside the window for Saint Nicholas to fill. If the children have been good throughout the year, the gifts consist of candy; if bad, a switch or a tiny toy devil represents the saint's offering. Saint Nicholas appears in person to lecture the children on conduct and morals.

LUCA NAPJA, Saint Lucia's Day.   *December* 13

As on Saint Andrew's Day, fortunes are told and omens read. Bands of *Kotylók* (cacklers), or fortune-telling lads, go from house to house singing ancient fertility chants. The *Kotylók* wish for hens and geese, for many eggs and bountiful blessings. If the mistress of the house welcomes the singers and gives them the traditional presents of dried pears, blessings are sure to follow. Otherwise she must beware, lest she have but one chicken and that one be blind!

DISZNÓTOR, The Killing of the Pigs.
Sometime during November or December

This is a family holiday to celebrate the slaughter of the

174

pigs. After the work is done, the mistress of the house prepares a dinner for all who have helped. Rich pork-marrow soup with thin noodles, stuffed cabbage, headcheese, many kinds of sausage and wine comprise the traditional meal.

KARÁCSONY VIGILIÁJA, Christmas Eve, Adam and Eve Day.
December 24

The day before Christmas is called Adam and Eve Day. On Christmas Eve, the tree is lighted and the family supper prepared. Throughout Hungary the meal is essentially the same, consisting of fish and *mákos bobajka,* or poppy-seed dumplings. After supper the Christmas presents are distributed, children play with their new toys, and old carols are sung. At midnight everybody attends services at the church.

KARÁCSONY, Christmas.
December 25

In addition to the usual dinner of wild game, roast meat, stuffed cabbage and hare, there are all kinds of poppy-seed dumplings, poppy-seed and nut cakes and choice little pastries with poppy-seed fillings. The day is spent in feasting, merry-making, and visiting.

VÉRTANÚ SZENT ISTVÁN NAPJA, Day of Saint Stephen the
Martyr. *December* 26

The third day of Christmas is celebrated in the United States, as in Hungary, with eating, drinking, visiting and continuation of the holiday festivities.

APRÓSZENTEK NAPJA, Little Saints' Day, Whipping of the
Innocents. *December* 28

This is the festival of all the minor saints, who have no

175

special days of their own. According to ancient folk custom, men and boys whip the women and girls with switches made of willow twigs, or beribboned birch branches. The victim of the switching is said to become healthy, beautiful and free from carbuncles!

SVILVESZTER ESTE, Saint Sylvester's Eve. *December* 31

According to old folk superstition a pig must be touched "for luck" on Saint Sylvester's Eve. In the principal restaurants and cafés of Budapest a live pig is set loose at midnight. As the creature runs squealing across the floor, everybody tumbles after, trying to touch it, so luck may "hold" in the coming year.

FESTIVALS OF THE ITALIANS

"WE have revived and fostered all those traditional manifestations which lighten the heart and make the mind healthy," said Signor Mussolini speaking of the National Leisure Hours Institution, which to a remarkable degree is cherishing Italy's heritage of popular festivals, folk costumes, songs and dances. Few countries are so rich in folk life as Italy, and few have fostered their peasant traditions with greater intelligence and skill.

It is peculiarly difficult to write about Italian festivals, since each mountain hamlet and coast village possesses characteristic celebrations that are worthy of note. Each community observes with grandiose splendor the day of its patron saint. Each locality has its own festal customs and dances which have been preserved intact through countless generations. All large towns and cities, on the other hand, are famed for the picturesque festivals that are also known and celebrated in every country where Italian people live.

The feast days and holidays described in the following pages are typical of their kind. Although space limitations make it impossible to include many important feast days, those that are given represent different parts of Italy and diverse types of peasant culture.

The Book of Festivals

Capo d'Anno, New Year's Day.   *January* 1

The beginning of the New Year is celebrated with parties, visits and all kinds of holiday festivities. It is customary on this day for children to receive *strenna*, or money gifts from their parents. At Capri groups of dancers meet in the spacious *Piazza di Capri* and hold contests of the Capri *Tarantella*. At Santa Agata dei Goti dramatic presentations featuring the "Story of the Blue Knight" are enacted on the public *piazza*. At Aregno, Como, the Sacred Mysteries are performed to celebrate the New Year festival.

La Vigilia dell'Epifania, Epiphany Eve.   *January* 5

In many parts of Italy children receive gifts at Epiphany, in memory of the presents the Magi brought the Christ Child. *La Befana,* the little old woman whose name doubtless is abbreviated from *Epifania,* is the gift bearer in many sections of the country, especially in the North. According to legend, *la Befana* was sweeping her house when the Kings came by with offerings for *Gesú Bambino*. When *la Befana* was asked to accompany them, she gruffly replied that she was too busy with her work. Later, however, when her sweeping was done, the old woman started out toward Bethlehem. She lost her way and could not find the Child, for whom she still searches. Each year *la Befana* passes through Italy, and each year she leaves pretty gifts for children who are good and bits of charcoal for those who are naughty. In Rome the Feast of the Epiphany is celebrated annually in the *Piazza Navona,* where toys dangle invitingly from hundreds of gaily decorated stalls. The *piazza* is thronged with children, young laughing mothers, bent old men and withered grandmothers, moving from stall to stall, gossiping, bargaining, buying toys for the children and exchanging greetings. Everyone buys at least one tin horn or trumpet or perhaps a homely little clay figure which is painted brightly and fitted with a shrill whistle. The crowd surges back and forth through the square, laughing, jostling, whistling and blowing, until all Rome seems mad and the air shrieks with deafening sound. Processions of youths march around, blowing on large cardboard trumpets. At Montona, Pola, boys and men carrying a rotating illumined star go from house to house singing traditional Epiphany songs. At Varenna, Como, men dressed like the Three Kings and their attendants go through the countryside, carrying torches and giving gifts to the needy. In some sections of the country bonfires are kindled on Epiphany Eve. The people dance about the fires and predict good or bad weather for the coming year, according to the direction in which the smoke blows.

EPIFANIA, Epiphany.   *January 6*

A quaint old custom called the "Clothing of the Child Jesus" still persists at Niscemi, Caltanissetta, where a poor parish child is carried naked to the church and there dressed to represent the Infant Jesus. Finally a procession of priests and worshipers takes the child home, to the joyous accompaniment of bagpipe music. The parishioners offer all kinds of gifts.

CARNEVALE, Carnival.   *January 17 to Ash Wednesday*

Carnevale always begins on January 17 and continues until Ash Wednesday. The ceremonies of the last three days of the carnival are the gayest, especially those of *Martedì Grasso,* or Shrove Tuesday. Throughout Italy the occasion is celebrated with splendid pageants, masquerades, dancing, music and all kinds of merrymaking. The Parade of the Months is a feature of the carnival at Cambria and a number of other Italian towns and villages. Allegorical figures, representing the twelve months, pay homage to the "King," who is accompanied by four harlequins. The Months sing traditional verses to the King. The procession moves from place to place, and the harlequins are crowned as members of the King's retinue. The ceremony ends with a great banquet for the participants. In Istria the performance is somewhat similar, except that the Twelve Months are accompanied by the Old Year instead of the King. The Months are attended by various persons representing the important saints of the Istrian calendar. On *Martedì Grasso* King Carnival makes his annual appearance in Venice, where he is treated with traditional ceremony. Here, as always, he is represented as a fat man, for eating and drinking are characteristic of the pre-Lenten period. His straw body is filled with firecrackers. His reign is merry but brief, as he is burned at midnight in the *Piazza San Marco*. The festival of the *Polentone* is celebrated at Ponti, Alessandria, on the last Friday in *Carnevale*. An enormous dish of *polenta*, weighing about six hundred kilograms, and an omelet containing a thousand eggs, are made by famous cooks of the town. Later these foods, together with native wine, are distributed free to the populace. Merrymakers, costumed and masked, sing songs in honor of the tasty *polenta* and parade through the town in decorated wagons.

LA CANDELORA, Candlemas.   *February 2*

A church festival celebrating the purification of the Virgin Mary after Jesus' birth.

SANT' AGATA, Saint Agnes.   *February 5*

Saint Agnes, patroness against fire and diseases of the breast, is honored with special reverence at Catania, where her relics are preserved. This third century Sicilian saint is reputed to have suffered many sorts of torture—including the amputation of her breasts—rather than yield herself to Quintianus, King of Sicily. In Catania her festival begins on the first of February and continues for five days. Barefoot processions of the faithful, who carry the saint's urn through the streets, poetry contests, fireworks, band music and confetti, all make this one of the most picturesque Sicilian festas. *Candelore,* or enormous tapers, are tied together, and placed on platforms which are carved with scenes from Saint Agnes' life. Eight or more men carry these platforms to the homes of the various citizens who have contributed to the preservation of this traditional feature of the festival. At every stop the *candelore* are greeted with cheers and popular demonstrations.

SAN GIUSEPPE, Saint Joseph.   *March* 19

The anniversary of Saint Joseph, husband of Mary, is widely observed as a day of feasting, merrymaking and sharing with the poor and unfortunate. Preparations for the feast start in advance. The people of a given village often prepare a "table of Saint Joseph" as a thank-offering for deliverance from drought, heat, disease or other disaster. Everybody contributes his or her share to the enterprise in the form of money, candles, flowers or food. The women bake pastry, prepare elaborate macaroni dishes, vegetables, and breads representing a scepter, beard, crown or cross. A long community table is spread with finest linen and set with the various foods. People representing Joseph, Mary and Jesus are selected as guests of honor. The other guests are preferably the orphans, widows, beggars and village poor. After morning Mass the guests form in procession and are blessed by the priest, who then sanctifies the feast. Cheers of *"Viva la tavola di San Giuseppe,"* are uttered by the poor as the food, first blessed by the child representing Jesus, is passed from one to another. Each person is given something to carry home. In the evening the group again meets to sing and hear stories about Saint Joseph. This feast of Saint Joseph is observed widely among Italians in the United States and other countries.

ANNIVERSARIO DELLA FONDAZIONE DEI FASCI, Anniversary of the Founding of Fascism.   *March* 23

The founding of Fascism, in 1915, is celebrated with patriotic speeches, the reviewing of Italian troops, national music and public demonstrations.

ANNUNZIAZIONE DI MARIA VERGINE, Annunciation of the Virgin Mary.   *March* 25

This is a church holiday in memory of the Angel Gabriel's announcement to the Virgin Mary.

*MEZZA QUARESIMA, Mid-Lent.[1]   *The fourth Sunday in Lent*

Just as *Carnevale* always is represented as a fat man, so *Quaresima*, or Lent, always is depicted as a lean old woman. In *negli Abruzzi* and other parts of Italy, where she appears as a tow figure pierced with seven feathers, she is suspended from a rope stretched from one side of the street to the other. On each Saturday in Lent the people pluck out a feather, since each represents one of the seven weeks of Lent. On Holy Saturday, the last Saturday before Lent, villagers burn a string of chestnuts to symbolize sending "Lent and its meagre fare to the devil." Children often have seven-legged pasteboard figures of Lent as toys. At *Mezza Quaresima* the image is cut in two and half the body removed.

[1] Stars indicate movable feasts that depend on Easter. See table of Easter dates and movable feasts on pages 357–358.

Festivals of the Italians

*DOMENICA DELLA PASSIONE, Passion Sunday.

The Sunday preceding Palm Sunday

On the Sunday preceding Palm Sunday all the crosses in the churches are shrouded in black and violet draperies. They are not removed until the *Sciolta della gloria,* the midday Mass of Holy Saturday.

*DOMENICA DELLE PALME, Palm Sunday.

The Sunday preceding Easter

For many generations the little village of San Remo on the Genoese riviera has enjoyed the privilege of supplying all the palms that are used on Palm Sunday in Saint Peter's Church in Rome. The palms distributed to the poor are plain, while those sold from the basilica steps to well-to-do worshipers are elaborately woven and artistically decorated with roses, lilies and other flowers. Following the blessing and distribution of the palms is an impressive ceremony which dramatizes the opening and closing of the gates when Christ entered Jerusalem. The procession of worshipers, carrying palms and singing joyous hymns, makes a "triumphal march" through the basilica and then about the portico. The doors, which at first are closed behind the faithful, are dramatically opened at the knock of one of the priests. The procession then makes its way to the high altar, where Mass is said.

*GIOVEDÌ SANTO, Holy Thursday.

The Thursday preceding Easter

The Thursday before Easter is observed in many places with processions of worshipers who carry plastic representations of the various episodes in Christ's Passion. Music and rich illuminations make these processions both dramatic and picturesque. In many places the Last Supper is enacted at the altar

183

by twelve needy parish men. The Ceremony of Foot Washing is performed by one of the priests, and finally each of the men is presented with a loaf of bread and gift of money. In Naples, as in many other large cities, Holy Thursday is the quietest day of the year. The *Via Toledo,* one of the busiest streets in the city, is closed to traffic and the peace which pervades the thoroughfare is so complete that it seems to partake of the spirit of the sanctuary. On Holy Thursday the "sepulchre of Christ" is prepared in the churches for the services of the following day.

*VENERDÌ SANTO, Good Friday.   *The Friday preceding Easter*

In many towns and villages processions wind through the streets with a bier on which lies a symbolic figure of the dead Christ. The bier is followed by cloaked and hooded worshipers, young lads carrying candles attached to long poles, and men bearing the cross, spear, crown of thorns, hammer, nails and other Passion symbols. Angels holding the stained grave-clothes, the sorrowing Virgin and funeral music all add realism and pathos to these processions. Following the afternoon service, which is called *l'agonia,* worshipers visit from church to church to see the reproductions of the sepulchre.

*SABATO SANTO, Holy Saturday.
              The Saturday preceding Easter

The antiphonal singing of the priests makes the services of this day singularly beautiful. The clergy, singing outside the closed doors of the church, are not admitted until they knock. Within, the church is gloomy and desolate. Black and purple draperies have hung over altar and crosses since Passion Sunday. Bells have not rung since Holy Thursday. With the singing of the *Gloria,* however, the entire church suddenly comes to life. Shrouds drop, revealing the figure of the risen

Christ. Bells ring, lamps flare into brightness. Animation and gladness are substituted for darkness and sorrow. In Rome and many other places it is customary on this day for the priest to bless houses and shops with holy water.

*LA PASQUA, Easter.

In many towns and villages sacred dramas commemorating various episodes in the Easter story or tales of historical or Biblical interest are held in the *piazzas*. People don their gayest attire, eat, drink and rejoice in the passing of Lent and the glory of the risen Christ. The traditional foods of the season include *capretto* and *agnello,* lamb and kid. Pastries called *corona di nove,* which are baked in circles and decorated with Easter eggs, are favorites with the children. Among Italians in the United States the same kind of dough is fashioned into rabbits instead of circles. There are also many sorts of elaborate small cakes, and a kind of potcheese cake, known as *pastiere,* which consists of unsweetened noodles, citron and other ingredients and is covered on the outside with a lattice-work of sweetened noodles.

NATALE DI ROMA, Birthday of Rome. *April 21*

The anniversary of the traditional founding of Rome in 753 B.C. is observed as a national holiday, with historical dramas, music and patriotic speeches.

CALENDIMAGGIO, Maytime of the Maidens. *April 30*

In Modena a charming annual festival takes place on May Day Eve, when youths of the town sing May songs and greetings under the village windows. One of the finest musicians is engaged to sing to the sweethearts of the others. The boys vie with one another in composing greetings. On the Sunday following the serenading it is customary for the boys to appear with empty baskets, which the different families fill generously with all kinds of delicious foods. *Calendimaggio*, May Day, has lost most of the beauty of the original pagan spring festival. Horse races, firework exhibitions and various kinds of lotteries and competitions are held in many parts of the country.

*CORPUS DOMINI, Corpus Christi.

The Thursday following Trinity Sunday

The great church festival in honor of the institution of the Eucharist is celebrated with splendor throughout Italy. Among the most picturesque ceremonies of the season are the beautiful mosaic flower carpets, which are made in accordance with old tradition. The villages of Genzano and Villa Orotava are especially famed for their carpets and decorations. At Genzano the procession of clergy and worshipers walks up hill, from the square to the church, over a marvelous flower carpet which often consists of geometrical patterns, armorial designs, the Angel of Peace, or other elaborate motifs. At Villa Orotava the carpets are equally beautiful and even more sumptuous, since they often consist of multi-colored flower petals set in a background of dark green. At Brindisi a novel feature of the festival is the richly caparisoned white horse which the archbishop rides at the head of the Eucharistic procession.

COMMEMORAZIONE DELLO STATUTO ALBERTINO, Constitution Day. *The first Sunday in June*

The first Sunday in June is observed in commemoration of the adoption of the Constitution of 1861. The holiday is celebrated with parades, music and speeches. Soldiers receive extra pay on this occasion.

Festivals of the Italians

SANT' ANTONIO DI PADOVA, Saint Anthony.   *June* 13

Saint Anthony, patron of Padua and of animals, is especially honored in Rome, at the Franciscan church dedicated to his name. Horses and mules, and their harnesses and trappings as well, are blessed by the priests and sprinkled with holy water.

FESTA DEL PALIO, Festival of the Palio.   *July* 2

Palio is the name given to the picturesque horse race which the Sienese hold twice a year—on July 2 and August 16 (the day following Assumption)—in honor of the Virgin Mary. The *Palio,* which has been observed since the fourteenth century, retains many of its medieval features. Each of the seventeen city wards selects a jockey and his attendants. With gorgeous banners and in medieval costumes, they form a procession which triumphantly carries the *Palio,* or standard of the Virgin, through the city streets. The chief event of the festival is a horse race, run in the large *Piazza del Campo.* The jockeys ride bareback, each one holding a stinging ox-sinew *nerbo,* or whip, which he is permitted to use on his opponent as well as on his own horse. The end of the race is announced with the firing of cannon. Revelry and merrymaking continue until dawn, and the victorious jockey is fêted and honored with feasting and song.

VISITAZIONE, Visitation of the Virgin Mary.   *July* 2

A church holiday commemorates Mary's visit to Elizabeth before the birth of Jesus.

SANTA ROSALIA, Saint Rosalia.   *July* 5–15

According to legend, Saint Rosalia, who died in 1160,

187

forsook the world and lived in a cave on Monte Pellegrino, near Palermo. In 1625 the saint's reputed relics were found and taken to the church at Palermo. At the same time the Black Death, which was raging in the city, ceased and Saint Rosalia therefore was made patroness of Palermo. In former times the festival was celebrated with a procession featuring an enormous triumphal car, decorated with scenes from the saint's life. Since the burning of the car in 1924, the anniversary has been observed with races, fireworks and elaborate processions.

LA MADONNA DEL CARMINE, Festival of the Madonna of Carmine. *July* 16

In Naples, where *la Madonna del Carmine* is patroness, her festival is celebrated with dances, singing and all kinds of revelry. Magnificent fireworks and illuminations are special features of the celebration. Italians in the United States observe the day with great ceremony. In New York City, the Italian community is illuminated with festoons of green, white and red electric lights. Pushcarts loaded with sweets, fruits, strings of chestnuts and all kinds of little cakes and delicacies line the streets, which are thronged with worshipers, fortune-tellers and sightseers. Candles of all sizes, brightly decorated wax replicas of parts of the human body, are sold at booths near the church. Elaborate services are held in the Church of the Madonna of Carmine, where sufferers from various ailments offer representations of the diseased portions of their bodies and pray for restoration of health.

SAN ROCCO, Saint Roche. *August* 16

This day, in honor of the patron of the sick and plague-stricken, is celebrated with great ceremony throughout Italy. In Florence there is a flower festival with various picturesque features, such as a fourteenth century historical costume procession, races and competitions. In Realmonte the saint's poverty is recalled by a procession of ragged folk who carry about a shabby picture of the saint. Musicians accompany the strangely garbed band, which finally goes to church for the Mass of Saint Roche.

NASCITA DI MARIA VERGINE, Birthday of the Virgin Mary.

September 8

A church holiday and a great nameday for all the Marias, who receive presents on this occasion.

GIORNO DEI SANTI, All Saints' Day.   *November* 1

A church holiday on which prayers are said for all the saints, but especially for the patron and family saints.

GIORNO DEI MORTI, All Souls' Day.   *November* 2

Sicilian children believe that the souls of the family dead return on this night with presents of sweets, toys and new clothes, taken from rich shopkeepers. These gifts are given to "good" children who have prayed for the *morti*, the souls of the departed. Sometimes the *morti* leave their gifts in the children's shoes, which are placed outside doors and windows.

NASCITA DI SUA MAESTÀ VITTORIO EMANUELE III, Birthday of
     His Majesty Victor Emmanuel III.   *November* 11

This day is observed throughout the country with special music, parades and patriotic exercises.

SAN MARTINO, Saint Martin.   *November* 11

From Venice in the north to Sicily in the south, it is customary to taste new wine on Saint Martin's Day. According to ancient legend, Saint Martin shared his cloak with a poor drunkard who stumbled and fell. The festival, consequently, is celebrated freely by all lovers of wine. At Caltagirone Falls, where the day is particularly observed, large quantities of wine are consumed by the villagers and the saint's image is carried in colorful procession through all the town's byways and alleys.

SAN NICOLA, Saint Nicholas.   *December* 6

The festival in honor of this fourth century Archbishop of Myra is celebrated with special pomp at Bari, where thousands of people make annual pilgrimage to the saint's tomb. It is customary for sailors to carry Saint Nicholas' image through the streets of the town in solemn procession. Then they place the statue on a vessel decorated with flowers and banners, and take it far out to sea. Hundreds of small craft, crowded with worshipers, follow the image, which at night is restored to its shrine. Bonfires and fireworks, solemn litanies and chants in honor of Saint Nicholas mark the occasion as one of the great festivals of the year.

L'IMMACOLATA, Festival of the Immaculate Conception.
                                               December 8

Each town and village has its traditional manner of celebrating this festival, which is based on the doctrine that the Virgin Mary was conceived without original sin. At Sommatino, *vampate,* or huge bonfires, are lighted in the square before the church. At Nicotera, Catanzaro, sailors reverently carry the statue of the Virgin along the water front. One of the most elaborate ceremonials takes place at Bagnoli Irpino, where the Virgin's image, surrounded by children who represent angels and warriors, is carried through the streets on an elaborately decorated wagon.

SANTA LUCIA, Saint Lucy.   *December* 13

This festival, honoring the fourth century saint who was said to have cut out her eyes because their beauty attracted a heathen nobleman, is particularly celebrated among the Sicilians. Saint Lucy is the patroness of Syracuse. In some parts of Sicily *cuccia,* or cooked wheat, is eaten on this day. In the village of Montedoro, Saint Lucy's Eve, the festival of lights, is observed with a torch procession and bonfires in the streets. The image of the saint, represented as holding a dish on which lie her eyes, is carried at the end of the long procession which marches to the center of the *piazza.* There all the torches are thrown on a great pile of straw which blazes high in honor of the saint. Possibly the fact that this festival falls on the shortest day of the year has something to do with its association with bonfires and many lights.

LA VIGILIA, Christmas Eve.   *December* 24

The *presepio,* or miniature representation of the manger, is the holiday symbol found in every Italian home. Long before Christmas little clay figures of the Holy Family, the angels, shepherds and kings, are on sale in every market and village fair. The settings for the manger are built at home, either with cardboard, moss and bits of twig, or with more professional properties. Sometimes the backgrounds are very elaborate, depicting as they do the sacred grotto, the tavern, the shepherds' huts and glittering pools, all set in a charming Italian landscape. The figures of the Magi journey across the countryside with their camels and precious gifts. Angels, suspended from invisible wires, seem to sing halleluiahs, and ragged shepherds kneel before the tiny pink-cheeked Babe with their gifts of flowers and fleecy lambs. Adults as well as children delight in these mangers, which usually are very artistic. In Southern Italy, especially in *negli Abruzzi* and *nelle Calabrie, zampognari,* or itinerant pipers, come to the homes through the *novena* (the nine days preceding Christmas), and sing pastoral hymns in honor of the Christ Child. On Christmas Eve, when the tapers are lighted, the children surprise their elders by reciting little verses before the *presepio.* The *cenone,* or Christmas Eve supper, consists largely of fish prepared in many elaborate ways. Eels stewed in wine are a favorite delicacy of the season. In Rome and some other parts of the country the *panettone,* a delicious currant loaf, not only accompanies the holiday meal but is given to relatives and friends. In the evening everyone attends Christmas Mass and worships before the life-sized figures of the Holy Family. In rural districts peasants often lay humble offerings of fruits, nuts or vegetables at the Christ Child's feet. At Irpino the image of the Babe is carried in solemn procession before the eyes of devout worshipers. The music of bagpipe and flute, the rough white sheepskins worn by many of the participants and the presence of shepherds from the hills, all add rustic charm and simplicity to the Christ Child's festival.

Il Natale, Christmas.   *December 25*

Christmas Day is a sacred holiday celebrated with solemn religious ceremonies in all the churches. In the Franciscan church of Ara Coeli in Rome, the famous *Bambino,* or image of the Christ Child, is laid in the *presepio.* Many legends have grown up about the *Bambino,* which wears a jewel-incrusted crown and is thought to possess miraculous healing powers. At Epiphany the *Bambino* is taken from the church and held aloft as the priest blesses the city of Rome from the top of the long flight of steps leading to the sanctuary.

SAN STEFANO, Saint Stephen.   *December 26*

In Baiano the festival in honor of the first Christian martyr is celebrated by chopping down the *maio*, a fine strong chestnut tree, and setting it up in the church *piazza*. Woodcutters and young men hew down the tree, which is taken to the *piazza* in a specially constructed bullock cart. Amid music, rejoicing and the clergy's blessing, the martyr's tree is set in a deep hole and covered with wood, which is supplied by devout townsfolk. To the accompaniment of rifle shots, the *maio* finally is ignited. Later the ashes are sold for charitable purposes. On Saint Stephen's Day it is customary to eat boiled or roasted chestnuts.

FESTIVALS OF THE JAPANESE

F—one of four great national holidays.
N—national holiday.
P—popular festival, observed widely by the people.
S—special holiday, observed only in certain circles.

(F) OSHOGATSU, New Year's Day.   *January* 1

The Imperial Household officially opens the New Year by performing at the Imperial Sanctuary the religious rite of *Shihohai*, or "worshiping in four directions." The Emperor prays for divine blessing on the Empire and for peace and prosperity during the year. Throughout the Empire all executive offices observe solemn New Year ceremonies. Japanese homes are cleaned and prepared, far in advance, for this great holiday of the year. House entrances are scrubbed and sprinkled with purifying salt. Gateways are decorated with branches of pine and bamboo, which symbolize respectively prosperity and adjustability. Above the gates are hung *shimenawa*, or ropes of twisted rice straw, symbolic of strong ties. These picturesque ropes are decorated with oranges, signifying "roundness and smoothness." Inside the houses sprays of pine, plum and bamboo are arranged artistically, like miniature plants. Large thick rice cakes, sometimes graduated in size and laid one upon the other, with an orange on top, are favorite offerings for the Kitchen God and other household deities. Early in the morning people rise, take the "first cleansing" of the year, and make offerings, before the ancestral tablets and family shrines, of pink and white rice cakes, rice cakes with oranges, and various kinds of fruit. After these early devotions everybody partakes of *ozoni,* a favorite soup, with rice cakes floating on top. Other foods are beans, symbolizing good health, fish roe for prosperity and plentiful offspring, dried squid for happiness, and rice cakes. Calling begins at an early hour. Men exchange cups of wine and the traditional greeting, "May your New Year be happy. Thank you for your kindness during the past year and may your good will continue throughout the year that is to come." In the afternoon the young people often go out, the boys to fly their new kites and the girls to play battledore and shuttlecock. Cards and gifts are exchanged among friends and relatives. During the first three days of the New Year, shops and places of business are closed and streets are almost deserted.

(S) SHIGOTO HAJIME, Beginning of Work.   *January 2*

Since good beginnings are important, work properly begun on this day is thought significant to its happy continuation throughout the year. To celebrate joyous beginnings, young children are given their first lessons in writing, workmen begin to use their tools, Geisha girls play their *samisens* for the first time, and wholesale houses ceremoniously deliver the first orders of the year.

(N) GENSHI-SAI.   *January 3*

This national holiday marks the beginning of the year's first Court functions. Ceremonies at the Imperial Sanctuary are attended by the Emperor, all members of the imperial family, high government officials and the Japanese peerage.

(N) SHINNEN ENKAI, New Year Party.   *January* 5

At the Homei Hall of the Imperial Palace, the Emperor and Empress hold the first banquet in honor of the princes of the blood, ministers of state, members of the imperial household, foreign officials and other dignitaries of rank.

(P) SETSUBUN, Change of Season, Bean-Throwing Night.

February 3 *or* 4

According to the old lunar calendar, these days mark the official ending of winter and the beginning of spring. Custom decrees that people shall scatter as many beans through their houses as there are years in their lives. This ceremony, which is called *mamemaki,* is symbolic of driving out evil spirits and calling in good luck. The rite is observed not only in homes but also in shrines and temples. Often professional actors and wrestlers perform the office of bean-throwers.

(F) KIGENSETSU, Anniversary of the Accession of Emperor
    Jimmu.   *February* 11

This great national holiday commemorates the accession to the throne of Jimmu Tenno, first Emperor of Japan, in the year 660 B.C. The holiday is observed with elaborate ceremonies in every city, town and village throughout Japan. The celebration is most elaborate in Tokyo, however, where fitting rites are performed at the Imperial Sanctuary. A Court luncheon is given for high officials, fireworks are displayed, and speeches made on Japan's place among the nations.

(P) HINA-NO-SEKKU, Girls' Doll Festival.   *March* 3

This festival is dedicated to girls. As the peach blossoms

bloom at about this season, the day sometimes is known as the Peach Festival. In every home the best room is given over to an exhibition of dolls, many of which are heirlooms of great magnificence. The dolls and their belongings, such as furniture, chests, dishes and toilet articles and clothes are arranged artistically on decorated platforms or shelves. Little girls, daintily arrayed in their best kimonos, receive their friends and serve refreshments according to the formal rules of Japanese etiquette. Offerings of vegetables and fruits are made to the dolls, which represent many historical characters as well as the Emperor, the Empress, lords and ladies-in-waiting, court musicians and servants.

(S) CHIKYU SETSU, The Empress' Birthday.　　*March* 6

Throughout Japan this day is observed by special exercises in girls' schools and by meetings of women's organizations and societies.

(S) RIKUGUN-KINENBI, Japanese Army Commemoration Day.
March 10

This solemn anniversary commemorates the sufferings of the soldiers who fought and died in the Russo-Japanese War. The day is observed with speeches and formal gatherings.

(N) SHUNKI KOREI-SAI, Festival of the Vernal Equinox.
March 21

On this great spring festival, schools and places of business are closed. The day is devoted to worship of the imperial ancestors and ancestresses at the Imperial Sanctuary.

The Book of Festivals

^(P) VIEWING OF THE CHERRY BLOSSOMS.   *Month of April*

Throughout Japan festivals and gala events are held
during April, when the cherry blossoms bloom. Between the
fifteenth and twenty-fifth of the month, the *Kan-Wo-Gyokai,* or
Imperial Party for Viewing the Cherry Blossoms, is held in the
palace grounds in Tokyo. City folk go to parks to enjoy the
beauty of the cherry blossoms. Parties of flower-lovers pack
picnic lunches and make expeditions to countryside or mountains, in order to see the beautiful trees in their greatest per-
fection.

^(N) JIMMU-TENNO-SAI, Anniversary of the Death of Emperor
Jimmu.   *April 3*

The anniversary of the death of Emperor Jimmu, Japan's
first Emperor and great national leader, who ruled the country
for seventy-six years, is commemorated with special ceremonies.
The reigning Emperor observes the occasion with rites before
the Imperial Sanctuary.

^(F) TENCHŌ SETSU, Birthday of the Reigning Emperor.
                                                    April 29

The birthday of the Emperor Hirohito, the 124th ruler of
Japan, is observed with offerings and prayers to the imperial
ancestors and appropriate services at the Imperial Shrine. The
Emperor reviews the army at the Yoyogi Parade Ground in
Tokyo, and gives a state banquet for the chief dignitaries of the
Empire. The day is widely celebrated throughout the country.
Services in the Emperor's honor are held in every school in
Japan.

198

Festivals of the Japanese

(P) TANGO-NO-SEKKU, Boys' Festival, Carp-Flying Day.

May 5

This day, which is dedicated to the boys of Japan, is observed by all families blessed with male heirs. In many parts of Japan, especially in rural districts, tall poles are set up near the houses. Large red and black paper or cloth carps, with wide mouths and with bodies often measuring several yards long, are suspended from the poles. When inflated with air, the carps fly out strongly in the wind. They remind young lads that they must be as strong as the carp when he climbs the waterfall. In the guest rooms of the houses there are exhibitions of dolls, which represent the Empire's national heroes, princes and warriors. This ancient festival originated in a desire to foster courage and endurance in the little boys of Japan.

(S) KAIGUN-KINENBI, Navy Memorial Day.

May 27

This anniversary commemorates the victory of the Japanese over the Russians, in 1904, in the Battle of Tsushima. The day is devoted to memorial services in honor of those who lost their lives in the great naval encounter.

(P) TANABATA-MATSURI, Feast of Tanabata.

July 7

An old lunar festival still observed in many rural communities. On this one night of the year, the Weaver of the star Vega joins her lover, the Cowherd of the star Altair, who dwells on the other side of the "Heavenly River," as the Milky Way is called. In olden days Japanese girls prayed on the Seventh Day of the Seventh Moon for skill in weaving and other handicrafts. Today they hold in their schools special exhibitions of weaving, sewing, embroidery, poem writing and other feminine arts. It is customary to deco-

199

rate many of the doors with gay strips of paper inscribed with poems in honor of the Weaver and Cowherd lovers.

(P) O-BON, Feast of Lanterns. *July* 13–15

This is the Japanese Feast of the Dead. People visit the cemeteries, where they clean and put the graves in order. Then they light gay paper lanterns and build bonfires to symbolize lighting the spirits' footsteps on their way back to earth. Under the golden light of gently swaying lanterns, peasant folk in temple compounds and elsewhere perform *Bon Odori,* a characteristic dance of the *Bon* season.

(N) SHUKI-KOREI-SAI, Festival of the Autumnal Equinox. *September* 23

This national holiday and Shinto festival is held in commemoration of the imperial ancestors. Appropriate ceremonies are performed at the Imperial Palace.

(N) KANNAMÉ-SAI, Harvest Festival. *October* 17

This national festival honors the new grain, which the Emperor offers at the Shrine of Isé to the Sun Goddess and the other imperial ancestors. Special services are held before the Imperial Sanctuary.

(F) MEIJI SETSU, Birthday of Meiji Tenno. *November* 3

The Emperor Meiji, who ruled Japan from 1864–1911, is honored by this festival. The birthday of the Emperor who abolished feudalism in Japan, raised the common man's standard of living and caused Japan to be recognized as a great world power is celebrated with the closing of schools and places of business. The week in which the holiday falls is set aside as national athletic week.

 (N) NIINAME-SAI, Festival of Niiname-Sai. *November* 23

On this second national harvest festival, the Emperor partakes of new grain and offers a portion to the Sun Goddess and the other imperial ancestors. Both the Emperor and his subjects rejoice and give thanks for the bounty of the harvest.

(N) TAISHŌ TENNŌ-SAI, Anniversary of the Death of Emperor Taisho. *December* 25

This national holiday honors Emperor Taisho, son of the great Meiji and father of the present Emperor.

(P) ŌMISOKA, The Last Day of the Year. *December* 31

This is the great accounting time of the year. Custom decrees that the man who closes his debts satisfactorily may bring the year to a propitious close by eating noodles at his evening meal. The Japanese regard the noodle, which is very long, as a symbol of long life and continued prosperity throughout the next twelve months.

FESTIVALS OF THE JEWS

"BY their festivals ye shall know them" might be written of the Jewish people, who have developed elaborate ceremonials for almost every occasion in life. Throughout the ages, the ancient Jewish rites have served not only as a means of expressing religious sentiment but also of preserving the spiritual traditions of the Hebrew race. Although Judaism, like all other faiths, has its various dogmatic teachings and sectarian divisions, it lays deeper emphasis on character than on doctrine, and on living than on believing. Whether the modern Jew is Orthodox or Liberal, whether he belongs to one group or another, fundamentally he obeys but one command, "Ye shall be holy, for I, the Lord your God, am holy."

Holiness, to the pious Jew, means to live life with regard to its inner sanctity. Holiness means to invest everyday experiences with spiritual dignity. Holiness means to transform the very bread that feeds the body into symbolic fare that feeds the soul.

The Sabbath, or Seventh Day of the Week, which commences with the lighting of candles shortly before sunset on Sabbath Eve or Friday night, ushers the weekly rest day into Jewish homes. After greeting the Sabbath, which is represented as a Bride, the parents invoke God's blessing on the children. The father, the head of the family, or possibly an honored guest, recites the *Kiddush,* or sanctification ritual over the cup of wine, and blesses the *hallas,* or twisted loaves. The best linen and silver, gay flowers and holiday attire make the Sabbath observance an occasion anticipated by each member of the family. The day itself is primarily a period of rest and relaxation. It is characterized by cessation from the strenuous occupations of the week and a consideration of spiritual values.

Through his festivals and holy days the Jew gives tangible expression to his religious tradition. In order to understand this tradition, even slightly, it is necessary to consider the character of the Jewish calendar and the symbolic significance of the days it includes.

ROSH HASHANAH, New Year, Feast of Trumpets. *Tishri* 1[1]

Jewish tradition regards this high holy day as the birthday of creation. *Rosh Hashanah* is also a day of memorial, which not only recalls personal acts but reviews events occurring since the beginning of time. Synagogue services express hope for the restoration of Zion and feature the story of Abraham's intended sacrifice of Isaac. The blowing of the *shofar,* or ram's horn trumpet, brings to mind God's providence. In the homes, special prayers for a sweet year are pronounced over an apple dipped in honey. Round smooth loaves of bread symbolize a wish for a smooth and prosperous New Year. Orthodox Jews observe this festival for two days.

FAST OF GEDALIAH. *Tishri* 3

This minor fast commemorates the murder of Gedaliah, the Jewish prince whom Nebuchadnezzar appointed to govern Palestine.

YOM KIPPUR, Day of Atonement. *Tishri* 10

The ten days beginning with *Rosh Hashanah* and ending

[1] See table of Jewish holidays and fasts, pages 365–367, for the corresponding dates in the Gregorian calendar.

with *Yom Kippur* are called Days of Penitence. *Yom Kippur,* the culmination of the penitential period, is the most sacred day of the Jewish year. It is observed by services in the synagogues, by fasting and by prayers for forgiveness. Memorial services for the dead are held on this day. In homes and in the synagogues lights are kept burning as a symbol of the immortality of the souls of the departed.

Succoth, Feast of Tabernacles, Feast of Ingathering.

Tishri 15

This eight-day festival commemorates the rejoicing of an agricultural people in the ingathering of the autumn harvest. Since God watched over the Israelites when they dwelt in frail tabernacles in the wilderness, the modern Jew builds a *succah,* or hut, in memory of that fact. The men cover the *succah* with green boughs, "so the stars can shine through the roof." "Open *succah*" prevails during the festival, when friends, relatives, rich and poor are invited to share the hospitality of the household. In the ceremonial observance of the festival the Four Species: *Ethrog* (a citron); *Lulab* (a shoot of a palm tree in its folded state before the leaves are spread); *Hadassah* (three twigs of myrtle) and the *Aravah* (two willow branches) are employed in accordance with the Biblical injunction given in Leviticus 23:40.

Shemini Atzereth, Eighth Day of the Feast of Tabernacles.

Tishri 22

The chief feature of the synagogue service is a prayer for rain. Memorial services are held for the dead.

Simchat Torah, Rejoicing of the Law.   *Tishri* 23

This festival symbolizes the Jew's rejoicing over the Torah

204

and the end of the harvest. On each Sabbath during the year a portion of the Torah Pentateuch is read in the synagogue. On *Simchat Torah* the last part is read. The scroll of the Torah then is rerolled and the first portion of Genesis read. In this way the infinity of the Torah is symbolized. Hymns, religious folk songs and processions with the Torah characterize the synagogue services.

ROSH HODESH, New Moon.[2]   *Heshvan* I

ROSH HODESH, New Moon.   *Kislev* I

CHANUCAH, Feast of Lights, Feast of Dedication.   *Kislev* 25

The festival of *Chanucah* commemorates the rededication of the Temple in the year 164 B.C., after the armies of Judah Maccabee, surnamed "The Hammer," had routed the forces of Antiochus IV. The miraculous relighting of the perpetual light in the Temple is observed today by kindling candles in synagogues and homes. While the *Chanucah* lights are burning —one is kindled on the first evening and one more on each of the succeeding seven days of the festival—games are played, parties held, gifts exchanged and *Chanucah* plays and entertainments featured. This is one of the most popular festivals of the Jewish calendar.

ROSH HODESH, New Moon.   *Tebet* I

FAST OF TEBET.   *Tebet* 10

This minor fast commemorates the beginning of the siege of Jerusalem under Nebuchadnezzar in 605 B.C.

[2] For explanation of rites of *Rosh Hodesh* see the Jewish calendar, page 365.

Rosh Hodesh, New Moon.   *Shebat* 1

Hamishah Assar Bi-Shebat, New Year for Trees, Arbor Day.
Shebat 15

In ancient times the Jewish farmer set out trees on this day and blessed the standing orchards. It was customary to plant a tree for every newborn child—a cedar for a boy and a cypress or pine for a girl. Sometimes branches from these trees formed the marriage canopies for the young bridegroom and bride. When the colonists returned to Palestine, about half a century ago, they reclaimed the barren land with trees. Today children of modern Palestine celebrate *Hamishah Assar Bi-Shebat* with outdoor games and tree planting. In other lands, Jews observe the festival by eating oranges, figs, dates, raisins, pomegranates and other fruits that grow in the Jewish Homeland.

Rosh Hodesh, New Moon.   *Adar* 1

Ta'anith Esther, Fast of Esther.   *Adar* 13

This day is observed as a fast in commemoration of Esther's three days of fasting and prayer before she pleaded with King Ahasuerus to save her people. According to the Book of Esther, Haman set aside this time for the slaughter of the Jews in the Persian dominions.

Purim, Feast of Lots.   *Adar* 14

Purim is so called because Haman cast lots for a lucky day on which to slaughter his Jewish foes. *Purim* is the Jewish carnival, a day of feasting and gladness, of gifts to relatives and presents to the poor. This is the one festival when everyone is expected to make merry. Small honey and poppy-seed-filled cakes called *Hamantaschen,* or Haman's ears, and *Bub,* a dish of large lima beans, are served. *Bub* symbolizes the coarse meals Esther ate in the king's palace, where she refused heathen fare. Children armed with clappers and horns masquerade from house to house, singing and reciting comic verses. Parties, balls and historic plays are characteristic entertainments. The Biblical book of Esther is read in the synagogues.

ROSH HODESH, New Moon. *Nissan* 1

PESACH, Passover. *Nissan* 15

The *Pesach,* or "passing over," derives its name from the Biblical account of the Death Angel who passed over Jewish homes when he slew the first-born Egyptian sons. *Pesach* also is called the Feast of Unleavened Bread, because all leaven-made foods are prohibited at this season. In the weeks preceding *Pesach* homes are cleaned so as to remove all leaven, and the traditional Passover dishes are prepared. Throughout the festival the Jews relive—through Scripture readings, parables, religious chants and eating symbolic foods—virtually the entire Egyptian episode of their history. In Palestine only one *Seder* night is observed and the Passover continues only seven days. Orthodox Jews, however, observe the *Seder* for two successive nights and the festival for eight days.

ROSH HODESH, New Moon. *Iyar* 1

LAG BA'OMER, Thirty-third Day of the Counting of the Omer. *Iyar* 18

Lag Ba'Omer also is called the "Scholars' Feast," since

legend says that a plague which had raged among Akiba's followers ceased on this day. The festival commemorates the final desperate resistance of Bar Cochba and Akiba to reestablish Jewish national independence against the Romans, in the year 135 A.D. It is said that the manna that fed the Israelites in the wilderness fell for the first time on this day. The festival marks, moreover, the death of Rabbi Simeon ben Johai, who is the hero of *Lag Ba'Omer*. Children of Jerusalem visit Rabbi Simeon's tomb and spend the day out of doors. During the forty-nine days of the Counting of the Omer, marriages, dances and festivities are restricted. On the day of *Lag Ba'Omer* these restrictions are lifted.

ROSH HODESH, New Moon. *Sivan* 1

SHABUOTH, Feast of Weeks. *Sivan* 6

This day is also called Pentecost, because it occurs on the "fiftieth day" after the first day of Passover. Originally it was an ancient agricultural festival marked by the offering of first-fruits in the Temple. After the destruction of the latter, the day assumed historic significance and became associated with the giving of the Law. Reform Jews observe the festival for one day. As it commemorates the Revelation on Mount Sinai, they have their children confirmed on this day. Both synagogues and homes are decorated with flowers and greens. The traditional foods of the season are dairy products (since milk is plentiful in Palestine at this time) and honey, reminiscent of the sweetness of the Torah which was given to Israel on *Shabuoth*.

ROSH HODESH, New Moon. *Tammuz* 1

FAST OF TAMMUZ. *Tammuz* 17

This is a minor fast which commemorates the breach made in the wall of Jerusalem by Nebuchadnezzar.

ROSH HODESH, New Moon. *Ab* 1

TISH'AH B'AB, Fast of Ab. *Ab* 9

This fast day is the anniversary of the fall of Jerusalem and the destruction of both the first and second Temples. The first Temple was destroyed by King Nebuchadnezzar the Babylonian, in 586 B.C., and the second by Titus the Roman, in 70 A.D. *Tish'ah b'Ab* is regarded as the great day of mourning.

ROSH HODESH, New Moon. *Elul* 1

FESTIVALS OF THE LATVIANS

JAUNA GADA DIENA, New Year's Day. *January 1*

Both morning and afternoon services are held in the churches. The day is spent quietly, the afternoon being devoted to calling among officials, friends and relatives.

ZVAIGZNES DIENA, Epiphany. *January 6*

On this day, which marks the end of the holiday season, Christmas trees are dismantled.

*PŪPOLU SVĒTDIENA, Palm Sunday.[1]

The Sunday preceding Easter

Pussywillows instead of palms are distributed in the churches. According to ancient folk custom, parents and children switch one another early in the morning with willow branches. Originally this rite probably was intended to renew life and vigor in the early spring.

*ZAĻĀ CETURTDIENA, Green Thursday, Holy Thursday.

The Thursday preceding Easter

Every household is busy on this day, which is the time for

---

[1] Stars indicate movable feasts that depend on Easter. See table of Easter dates and movable feasts on pages 357–358.

decorating the Easter eggs. Many of the eggs are painted in traditional designs by a process not unlike batik dyeing. Natural substitutes such as onion skins, tree barks and roots are used to color the eggs, as commercial dyes are common only in the cities. On Green Thursday homes usually are decorated with the first flowers of early spring.

*LIELĀ LŪDZAMĀ DIENA, Great Friday, Good Friday.
                              The Friday preceding Easter

No work is done on this day and schools and places of business are closed. On Great Friday, and throughout the week, churches are draped in black and communion is administered at morning and evening services.

*KLUSĀ SESTDIENA, Quiet Saturday.
                              The Saturday preceding Easter

Church services are universally attended in the evening. Organ recitals and special music are features of the services. No parties, dinners or amusements are allowed on this day.

*LIELDIEŃAS SVĒTDIENA, Easter Sunday.

After morning worship in the churches everybody devotes the remainder of this day and the two days following, to having a gay time. Everywhere parties and dinners are held for relatives and friends. Easter eggs and boiled ham usually are served at the holiday meal. Nobody forgets to wish his neighbor "Happy Easter," nor to exchange charmingly decorated eggs when calling on acquaintances. It is customary to give trifling gifts, such as handkerchiefs, perfumes, tiny soap eggs and Easter bunnies. For children and young people the day is a festive event. Easter eggs are hunted among the garden bushes and in out-of-the-way nooks. Chocolate bunnies and colored candies are among the gifts brought by the Easter hare. Young people play all kinds of egg games in courtyards and gardens. Chief among the Easter sports are the egg-rolling contests. Colored eggs are rolled, one by one, down an inclined plane. As long as the eggs roll to the right, they go to the first player. When they swerve to the left, however, they become the second player's property. Swinging is another character-istic Easter sport. Large platforms are suspended from the trees by four stout ropes. A boy and a girl stand facing each other on the platform. Someone pushes the couple off. They swing faster and faster, and the higher they swing the more precarious the position on the platform becomes. This custom of greeting the spring with swinging is very ancient and prob-ably was regarded originally as a festal rite for making crops grow.

*LIELDIENAS OTRIE SVĒTKI, Easter Monday.
                    The first day after Easter

    Second day of Easter.

*LIELDIENAS TREŠIE SVĒTKI, Easter Tuesday.
                    The second day after Easter

    Third day of Easter.

*DEBESBRAUKŠANAS DIENA, Ascension Day.
                    The fortieth day after Easter

    This church holiday, which commemorates Christ's ascent to heaven forty days after his resurrection, is celebrated by special services.

Festivals of the Latvians

TAUTAS APVIENOŠANAS DIENA, National Unity Day.   *May* 15

This is the anniversary of the reorganization of the Latvian government by President Karlis Ulmanis.   The day is celebrated with speeches and public demonstrations.

*VASARAS SVĒTKI, Whitsunday, Pentecost.
                    The fiftieth day after Easter

Houses are decorated with spring flowers and young birch branches, and the first outings to the country are made on this day.

ZĀĻU VAKARS, Herb Evening, Saint John's Eve, Midsummer Eve.   *June* 23

This is the beginning of the three-day midsummer festival, *Līgo Svētki,* which is the most characteristic of all Latvian celebrations.   On Saint John's Eve boys and girls meet in the village squares where, according to ancient custom, the boys chase the girls and beat them soundly with cattail switches.   Then the young people gather flowers and herbs and fashion beautiful wreaths of cornflowers, water lilies and fragrant grasses.   These wreaths are used in the ceremonies of the following day.   Every Latvian community has scores of traditional *Līgo* songs, which are practiced on this night.   The songs often take the form of singing contests in praise or blame of the various men in the neighborhood who are named Janis (or John), for *Līgo Svētki* is the great John nameday feast.   One group of singers praises a certain Janis for the prosperity of his farm and livestock, while another points out that weeds are growing in his garden, his barnyard is littered with rubbish and his servants slothful.   These songs serve as hints to the careless that everything must be in readiness for the guests who will arrive on the following night.

213

JĀŅU VAKARS, Saint John's Night.   *June* 24

Armed with their flowers and wreaths, the boys and girls
go from farm to farm in the neighborhood, singing traditional
songs and seeking for a man named Janis. Since Janis is a
common name in Latvia the singers do not often have far to go.
Arrived at the home of a Janis, the young people sing about his
cattle, his food and his crops—for they can see his cattle are fat,
his food plentiful and his fields rich, and they, poor folk, thirst
and hunger for a mug of ale and a bit of cheese. Of course
Janis and his wife, who are expecting their visitors, now throw
open the doors and give them hearty welcome. After ceremoniously placing wreaths on the head of Janis, his mother and
his wife, the singers partake of ale and cheese and make merry
with the family. Bonfires are built. Boys and girls dance
about the fires and jump over them, for, according to ancient
folk belief, the grain will grow as high as one can leap over the
Saint John fires. *Līgo* torches are waved aloft and the singing
and merrymaking continue throughout the night. The most
typical folk dances of this season are the *Trīspāru deja*, the
Jandaliņš, the *Āčkups* and the *Sudmaliņas*. In some parts of
Latvia, arches made from birch branches and field flowers are
placed before the village houses. Beneath these fragrant canopies garlanded lads and maidens perform the gracious ceremonies of the *Līgo* feast. In cities and towns every apartment
is decorated with birch branches, in welcome to the *Līgo* season.

JĀŅU DIENA, Saint John's Day.   *June* 25

Eating, drinking, dancing and other festivities continue on
this day. The swimming season opens with *Līgo Svētki*.

TICĪBAS ATJAUNOŠANAS SVĒTKI, Reformation Day. *October* 31

This is the anniversary of the day in 1517 when Martin

Luther nailed to the door of Wittenberg Cathedral his ninety-five theses, accusing the Church of abuses. Since Latvia is strongly Lutheran, the day is observed with services in all the Protestant churches.

Mārtiņu Vakars, Saint Martin's Eve.   *November* 10

This family feast is celebrated in honor of Saint Martin of Tours, the fourth century patron of beggars, vine growers and tavern keepers. Since *Martini* falls at the end of the harvest, the festival partakes of many of the elements of a harvest celebration. The traditional supper consists of roast goose and sauerkraut. Families hold reunions on this night, which is the occasion for merrymaking and gaiety in every home.

Mārtiņu Diena, Saint Martin's Day.   *November* 11

The festivities of the previous night continue throughout the day.

Latvijas Valsts Pasludinašana, Independence Day, Foundation Day.   *November* 18

This is the anniversary of the founding of the Latvian Republic in 1918, from territories formerly belonging to the Russian Empire. The day is celebrated with public festivals and processions, as well as with speeches, dinners, concerts and parties. Government officials visit the cemeteries to pay fitting tribute to the war heroes who gave their lives for Latvian freedom.

Ziemas Svētku Vakars, Christmas Eve.   *December* 24

Church services are attended in the late afternoon. With

the appearance of the first star, the cloth is laid for the festival meal and the family gathers to celebrate Christ's birth. Roast pork, goose and boar's head are served, together with *piradzini,* or little meat-filled pastries. After dinner the candles on the Christmas tree are lighted. Since the tree is the only Latvian Christmas decoration, it is made particularly lovely with gilded walnuts, artificial snow, tinsel, small red apples, bright bonbons, and colored twinkling candles on every branch and twig. After singing old-time hymns and carols, each member of the family greets his neighbor with a wish for a happy Christmas. Then the real gaiety of the evening begins. The Christmas presents, which have been piled beneath the tree, are distributed and opened. The merrymaking and excitement continue far into the night and throughout the two days following.

Ziemas Svētku Diena, Christmas Day. *December* 25

Gifts and cards are exchanged between friends and relatives. Parties, festivities and calling make this a joyous season for old and young.

Otrie Ziemas Svētki, Second Day of Christmas. *December* 26

Visiting, feasting, dancing and other festivities continue throughout the day and night.

Jaungada Vakars, New Year's Eve. *December* 31

Suckling pig in aspic, *piradzini* and dried fruit compote are among the traditional foods served on New Year's Eve and New Year's Day. No matter what happens, an unscaled and uncleaned fish, symbolic of good luck and plenty of money, holds place of honor on every Latvian table. The evening is celebrated with boisterous gaiety in the homes, which are the scene of family parties and reunions. Eating, drinking and laughter characterize the ceremony of welcoming another year. At the hour of midnight trumpets are blown from church towers, chimes are rung and pistols fired.

FESTIVALS OF THE LITHUANIANS

Naujų Metų Diena, New Year's Day. *January* 1

The first day of the New Year is spent in merrymaking and participating in out-of-door sports, such as skating and sledding.

Trijų Karalių Šventė, Feast of the Three Kings. *January* 6

Three crosses and the initials of the Magi Kings are chalked on the doors of houses and barns. In some parts of the country two men, representing a bear and a goat, make the village rounds. The first is dressed in pease-straw and the second in oats-straw. The men stop before the different houses, where they dance and perform antics in imitation of the animals they dramatize. The "bear" and the "goat" are given money gifts in return for their entertainment.

Nepriklausomybės Šventė, Independence Day. *February* 16

The anniversary of the founding of the Lithuanian Republic in 1918, from territories formerly belonging to Russia, is celebrated throughout the country with speeches, lectures, patriotic parades and concerts of national music.

Festivals of the Lithuanians

*Užgavenės, Shrove Tuesday.[1]

The Tuesday before Ash Wednesday

Special parties, masquerade balls and banquets characterize the last day before Lent.

Šventas Kazimieras, Saint Casimir. *March 4*

The anniversary of the death of the youthful Casimir, patron saint of Lithuania, is celebrated with special church services. The body of the fifteenth century saint who devoted his life to prayer and good works is buried in the city of Vilnius.

Pavasario Šventė, Feast of Spring. *March 16*

The ancient festival that was celebrated in early times as the first day of the year still is observed in certain districts with ceremonies of casting out winter's effigy and welcoming spring. Winter, symbolic to the peasant of death and disease, is represented as a hideous figure, stuffed with straw and old rags.

*Velykos, Easter.

Everybody dons holiday dress and attends morning church services. Then friends and neighbors exchange the season's greetings. *Margučiai*, or Easter eggs, colored and decorated well in advance of the holiday, are given as gifts, bartered and used in various types of Easter games.

[1] Stars indicate movable feasts that depend on Easter. See table of Easter dates and movable feasts on pages 357–358.

The Book of Festivals

*VELYKŲ ANTRA DIENA, Easter Monday.

The Monday after Easter

The second day of Easter is celebrated by visits, dances, banquets and all kinds of festivities.

*SEKMINĖS, Pentecost.   *The fiftieth day after Easter*

Servants and hired help usually decorate houses and farm animals with garlands and festoons of green, in recognition of the festival of early spring.

*DIEVO KŪNAS, Corpus Christi.

The Thursday following Trinity Sunday

The festival of the Eucharist is observed with colorful ceremonies and religious processions that vary according to the sections of the country.

ŠVENTO JONO NAKTIS, Saint John's Eve, Midsummer Eve.

June 23

As in olden times, young people still dance and sing about the Saint John's fires, which blaze from every height. Many superstitions exist regarding the supernatural events occurring on this night. Peasants say that witches and hail, diseases of animals and ravages by storm may be controlled by driving cattle through the ashes of the Saint John's bonfires. Superstition says that a small green bush known as *dievmedis,* or God's tree (artemisium aboratanum), blooms miraculously on this night. If a person succeeds in finding and plucking the flower before it is snatched by lurking spirits of darkness, he will be blessed with God's wisdom and knowledge to find hidden treasures.

220

Festivals of the Lithuanians

VAINIKINAS, Feast of July, The Binding of Wreaths.

Sometime during July

Young people still celebrate *Vainikinas,* the ancient Lithuanian summer festival, by going at dusk to the woods and picking flowers and branches of green. Laughing and singing they weave wreaths and garlands with which they adorn themselves. Slender twin birches or lime trees are twined together to form an arch. Two by two the girls and boys march through the arch. Whenever two girls meet two lads in their march, they kiss and sing traditional lines invoking a goddess' blessing on lads and maidens who meet as sweethearts.

NUBAIGAI, Harvest Festival.   *Sometime during the Autumn*

Throughout Lithuania the end of the harvest is celebrated with picturesque rites. The last sheaf of grain left in the fields is called the *Boba,* or Old Woman. *"Boba* sits in the corn," say the reapers. In some places *Boba,* dressed like a woman, is carried triumphantly to the farmer, on the last wagon to leave the field. At the master's house *Boba* receives a drenching—probably as a rain charm—and then everyone takes her for at least a single round of dancing. In some places the custom is slightly varied. The reaper who cuts down the last sheaf with his scythe is said to have "cut off *Boba's* head." The farmer then gives him a money gift, and the wife empties a jugful of water over his head. In other sections of the country, reapers fashion a wreath from ears of corn. Then the workers form in a procession, led by the prettiest girl, who places the wreath on a plate and covers it with linen. Singing ancient harvest songs, the procession goes to the farmer's home, and offers the garland to the master, who thanks the reapers and gives the girls gifts such as bright kerchiefs or pretty necklaces. The girl who presents the wreath, however, receives a more costly remembrance.

The chief reaper makes a speech to the master, who invites the workers to make merry and partake of an abundant meal. Dancing, feasting, drinking and games continue far into the night.

VILNIAUS GEDULO DIENA, Day of Mourning.   *October* 9

Throughout the country Solemn High Mass is celebrated on this day as a protest against the Polish occupation of the Vilnius district since 1920. Vilnius, the ancient stronghold of Lithuanian culture, was founded in 1323 by Gediminas, son of Liutavaras, one of the country's distinguished rulers.

VĒLINĒS, All Souls' Day.   *November* 2

Vėlinės, one of Lithuania's most ancient pagan festivals, is celebrated with prayers and the chanting of *raudos,* or songs for the souls of the dead. In former days the feast lasted over a four-week period. Everybody took large quantities of food and drink to the hillside cemeteries and prepared a tempting feast. After the living had eaten bountifully they left food for the hungry souls. Only the priests watched over the graves at night, singing funeral hymns and dancing the death dance. In the morning, when the people returned to the cemeteries, they thought the ghosts had eaten, since the food left for the spirits always was gone!

KŪČIOS, Christmas Eve.   *December* 24

With the appearance of the first star, families gather to celebrate *Kūčia,* the traditional Christmas Eve supper. Brightly colored, paper-thin *plotkeles,* or wafers, are broken and eaten by each member of the household as symbol of the season of "Peace on earth, good will to all men." Wishes for a happy Christmas are exchanged. A bit of hay placed beneath the tablecloth recalls the manger birth. Great loaves of bread sprinkled over with black poppy-seeds and stamped with figures of the Christ Child occupy the place of honor on the table. The first course, which consists of fish soup, is followed by all kinds of good foods, such as cabbage, fried and boiled fish, sauerkraut and an immense pike, which is accompanied by a rich brown gravy. At last the *kisielius* appears—a kind of *blanc mange* made from cream of oats and served with sugar and cream. Many sorts of wine go with the meal, which ends in merrymaking and rejoicing.

KALĒDOS, Christmas. *December* 25

Everybody is up early in order to attend Christmas Mass. After church, the remainder of the day usually is spent quietly at home, although dances sometimes are held in the evening.

ŠVENTO STEPONAS, Saint Stephen. *December* 26

The day following Christmas is one of the gayest in the year. Friends and relatives visit one another, all kinds of parties, dances and other festivities are held, and universal gaiety prevails among rich and poor, old and young.

NEKALTŲJŲ ŠVENTĖ, Holy Innocents' Day. *December* 28

Crude peasant plays, enacted from village to village, dramatize the story of Herod and his order to kill the little children of Bethlehem.

223

Naujų Metų Išvakarės, New Year's Eve.   *December* 31

   This is the great party night of the year. Groups of men
and women masked and dressed in fancy costumes, visit from
neighbor to neighbor. They eat *šaltanosidi,* a kind of holiday
bun, drink wine and dance. After a brief time of merrymaking,
the guests move on to the next home, taking along the people
who have just entertained them. As the evening progresses,
the parties grow larger and larger, until, toward dawn, very
long processions of torch-lighted sleds are seen skimming over
country roads from one hospitable home to another.

FESTIVALS OF THE MEXICANS

Día de los Reyes Magos, Day of the Wise Men.   *January 6*

Children stuff their shoes with hay and place them on the balconies, in anticipation of the coming of the Wise Men, whose horses are thought to eat the hay while the Wise Men leave sweets and pretty toys. The *pastorcitas,* children representing little shepherdesses, go about singing that they are on the way to Bethlehem and are seeking the Infant Christ. At night everybody gives a party, at which a *rosca de reyes,* a crown-shaped cake, is served in honor of the Three Kings. A little doll, representing the Infant Christ, is baked in the cake. The guest finding the image is expected to give a party to all the others on *Día de la Candelaria,* Candlemas Day.

San Antonio Abad, Saint Anthony the Abbot.   *January 17*

On this day *San Antonio Abad,* guardian of domestic animals, is invoked to protect the family beasts from disaster, disease and bad behavior. Oxen, burros, horses and other beasts of burden are rubbed down and decorated with ribbons and garlands of flowers. Sheep, dogs, cats, chickens, even parrots and other birds are numbered among the strange guests brought to the parish churchyard. The priest sprinkles the creatures with holy water and blesses them. In some rural communities peons bring bags of worms and destructive insects, so the priest's blessing may keep them from harming vegetables and grain.

225

DÍA DE LA CANDELARIA, Candlemas.   *February 2*

On this day the representation of the Christ Child is raised from the *nacimiento,* or manger, where it was placed on Christmas Eve, is carefully clothed, and laid on a tray decorated with flowers. In some parts of Mexico the godfather and godmother of the last night of the *posada* give a party to the other guests; in other places it is customary for the person finding the Christ Child's image in the *rosca de reyes,* to give the party.

*MIÉRCOLES DE CENIZA, Wednesday of Ashes.[1]

The first day of Lent

On this day, which marks the beginning of Lent, people attend ten o'clock morning Mass. The priest makes a black charcoal cross on each worshiper's forehead. All gaiety is suppressed during Lent. No amusements are participated in, towns and villages are quiet, and even marriages are not celebrated. Many of the older women wear black. The tolling of the church bells reminds townsfolk of the season of prayer.

*DOMINGO DE PALMAS, Palm Sunday.

The Sunday preceding Easter

In some parts of Mexico, men, women and children present the appearance of moving gardens as they approach the churches, carrying the flowers, laurels and palms that are to receive the priest's blessing. The blessed plants, which are kept until the following year, are regarded as useful antidotes against sickness and evil spirits. In certain sections of the country, women gather in front of the churches and weave palm leaves into crosses of various shapes and sizes. Sometimes they

[1] Stars indicate movable feasts that depend on Easter. See table of Easter dates and movable feasts on pages 357–358.

are plain, sometimes decorated with poppies. After the crosses are blessed they are tied to the balconies of the houses.

*Jueves Santo, Holy Thursday.
                              The Thursday preceding Easter

The Last Supper and the washing of the disciples' feet are enacted in the churches. In certain parts of the country children "drive the devil out of town" by creating a terrific din with rattles swung violently enough to terrify a host of fiends. Sometimes the youngsters add color to the ceremony by attaching rattles to a grotesque effigy of the devil, which is dragged through the village with a deafening racket.

*Viernes Santo, Good Friday. *The Friday preceding Easter*

This is a day of gloom and mourning. The darkened churches and black draperies are oppressive reminders of death. An effigy of the body of Christ is placed in a coffin and carried in procession, between rows of devout worshipers. Later the coffin is returned to the church, where people pay tribute to the crucified Savior.

*Sábado de Gloria, Saturday of Glory.
                              The Saturday preceding Easter

On this day Judas Iscariot, the Betrayer, is hung and burned with great rejoicing. Street vendors do a brisk business in selling papier-mâché effigies of Judas. These figures range from one to five feet in height and cost anywhere from a few cents to several dollars. Sometimes the effigies designed for children are stuffed with candies and hung in the *patios* of private houses. Other figures are filled with straw and rags; all have firecrackers attached. Judas usually is made to look as horrible as possible. Sometimes he has a huge red nose and wears a high hat and frock coat. Coins, pasted upon his garments, represent the thirty pieces of silver for which he sold Christ. By ten o'clock Saturday morning everything is in readiness for Judas' execution. Effigies of the traitor are suspended from roofs, balconies, lamp-posts, trees, shop windows. As soon as the Mass of Glory is over, fuses are lighted. Church bells peal forth. With loud explosions the Judases are torn to shreds. The people in the plazas shout with glee. If the effigies happen to be filled with candies, the scene is so much the gayer, as everyone joins in the wild scramble for sweets. At noon the church choirs sing the *Gloria,* the black draperies are stripped from altars and doorways and the Easter festivities commence.

*Domingo de Resurrección, Easter.

The resurrection of Christ marks the gayest day in the Mexican year. Churches, streets and plazas vibrate with vivid color. Plays, bull fights, gala clothes, music and laughter present a strange contrast to the season of Lenten gloom. Little sugar lambs, decorated with garlands of bright paper flowers, are featured in many of the shop windows at this season.

Día de la Santa Cruz, Day of the Holy Cross.   *May 3*

In some parts of Mexico this day is observed by miners or masons. The latter construct crosses, decorate them elaborately, and set them up on the buildings where they are working. Then they set off fireworks and celebrate the occasion as a *fiesta.*

*Corpus Cristi.   *The Thursday after Trinity Sunday*

Street vendors sell enchanting little cornhusk mules with panniers bulging with candies and glazed fruits. *Huacales* is the name given to the containers of these delicacies.

Festivals of the Mexicans

DÍA DE SAN JUAN, Saint John's Day.   *June* 24

Saint John, the saint of the waters, is honored in every town and hamlet of the Republic. Since Saint John is said on this day to preside over all the waters, people adorn their fountains and wells with flowers, tapers and gay paper festoons, and wash in streams and rivers. At midnight they begin to bathe, to the gay music of the village band. People take along plenty of foodstuffs—savory chicken *tamales,* stuffed peppers, pork *tacos,* meats of all kinds, fancy cakes, fruits, milk and delectable sweets. They also have quantities of flowers, for it is customary to throw flowers among the bathers. In rural districts the festival is observed with bathing, eating, dancing and music. In Mexico City and other metropolitan centers the celebration takes place in the fashionable bath-houses. Diving and swimming contests, band music, flowers and general gaiety characterize the scene. Indian street vendors sell many-hued flowers and small cornhusk mules, which are decorated with flowers and loaded with sugar cane and candies. When it rains on Saint John's Day—as it often does—old people say, "Saint John weeps."

FIESTAS PATRIAS, Festival of Independence.   *September* 15

The anniversary of Mexico's independence, which is celebrated for the greater part of a week, comes to a dramatic climax on the night of September 15. In Mexico City, as in every small town and village, the streets are thronged with people. Hundreds of electric bulbs in red, white and green—the colors of the Mexican flag—are hung across the streets and about the *Zócalo,* the capital's great plaza. Confetti, gay decorations, band music, all add a festival spirit as the throngs of merrymakers breathlessly await the President's appearance at the annual eleven o'clock ceremonies. As the President steps out on the balcony of the National Palace he repeats the famous *Grito de*

Dolores, the call to freedom, with which Miguel Hidalgo y Cos-
tilla, the hero priest, incited the peasants to independence in
1810. As the stirring words ring out across the plaza, "Long
live our most Holy Mother of Guadalupe! Long live America!
Death to bad government!" the people cheer themselves hoarse
with shouts of *"Viva México!"* Fireworks, pistol shots and wild
cheers continue as the President rings the old Liberty Bell with
which the Cura Hidalgo called his people to battle more than a
century ago. In small communities throughout the Republic,
the *Fiestas Patrias* are celebrated in much the same way as in
the capital. The *Grito de Dolores* is uttered at exactly eleven
o'clock by presidents of all the different towns and villages.

Fiestas Patrias, Festival of Independence. *September* 16

The festivities of the night preceding continue with parades, music, dramatic presentations and patriotic demonstrations. In small towns and villages, girls and youths dance on
the plazas or promenade around the bandstand, according to
historic tradition. The girls, dressed in gay full skirts and
dark *rebozos,* walk two by two in one direction, while the youths,
in wide *sombreros,* white suits and bright blankets, walk in
couples in the opposite direction. As the young people pass and
repass they shyly look at one another and exchange many secret
signs. The evening ends with a magnificent display of fireworks of different colors and elaborate forms.

Día de Todos Santos, All Saints' Day. *November* 1

This festival is dedicated to the *difuntos chiquitos,* the
little dead ones. On this night parents hold festivals for the
souls of little children who have died. In many homes, tables
are prettily arranged with toys, skull candies, funeral cakes and
other foods which the children enjoy when living. The spirits

230

of the Little Dead Ones are believed to return to earth on this occasion.

Día de Muertos, Day of the Dead.   *November 2*

This day, which is dedicated to the *difuntos mayores,* or adult dead, is a national holiday, celebrated in many places throughout the week. In Mexico City and other large centers, crowds of people stream into the cemeteries long before sunrise. Some folk come afoot, some in conveyances, but all are laden with candles, flowers and offerings of food. The cemeteries present the appearance of picnic grounds. The food for the dead, which later is eaten by the living, consists of candies, cakes, breads and other delicacies, fashioned into grinning skulls and gruesome symbols of death. Poets and musicians vie with one another in writing and singing of death. Children play with and eat tiny chocolate hearses, sugar funeral wreaths and delectable candy coffins. Everybody laughs, jokes and makes gay holiday with death. In some places the Indians set up in the cemeteries *ofrendas,* or altars to the departed. They arrange the *ofrendas* artistically, with lighted candles, special foods, such as skull candies, breads baked in animal and human shapes, and all kinds of drinks. Whatever the person liked in life is offered at this time, for it is thought that spirits return to enjoy what is set before them by relatives and friends. Theatres and amusement places are crowded, since everybody, from the youngest to the oldest, witnesses the ancient Spanish drama of *Don Juan Tenorio,* the reckless and wicked lover who is dragged to hell by the father-ghost of a beautiful outraged lady. According to one version of the drama, Don Juan Tenorio was a profligate who betrayed his friend, the Marquis de la Mota, by attempting to seduce the latter's fiancée. Finally Don Juan killed the girl's father, who tried to intervene. Don Juan erected a statue for his victim, and then in a spirit of bravado prepared a great feast and invited the statue to be his guest. The stone image of the girl's father appeared at the feast, called Don Juan to account for his crimes, and dragged him to hell.

NUESTRA SEÑORA DE GUADALUPE, Our Lady of Guadalupe.
December 12

Although the day of Our Lady of Guadalupe, patron saint of Mexico, is celebrated in every town and village of the Republic, thousands of humble pilgrims go each year to worship at the famous Church of Guadalupe, outside Mexico City. According to legend, Our Lady appeared many years ago to Juan Diego, a poor Indian lad, and commanded him to tell the bishop to build her a shrine on the site of the present church. The bishop laughed at the boy's story and steadily refused to believe him, until the Virgin bade Juan Diego return with his mantle filled with the roses she miraculously had caused to grow on the barren cliffs. When the Indian opened his wrap to show the roses, the flowers had vanished, and in their stead was imprinted a picture of the Blessed Virgin! The bishop, at last convinced of the boy's vision, had the church built. Each year the story of Guadalupe is enacted in a puppet show, which is witnessed by thousands of devout pilgrims. The Indians bring offerings of flowers, candles, pigs, hens and eggs. Relics of Our Lady of Guadalupe are sold in the streets. Altars decorated with lighted tapers, flowers and images of the Virgin are set up in windows and patios. All Mexico comes to Guadalupe to worship and invoke blessings from their patron saint.

LAS POSADAS, The Posadas.
December 16–24

Posadas, meaning "lodging," is the name given to the nine days of Christmas celebration that commemorates the events in the journey Mary and Joseph took from Nazareth to Bethlehem.

Festivals of the Mexicans

Among the poor it is customary for friends and neighbors of a given tenement house or locality to club together in sharing the *posada* expenses, for Christmas, to the Mexican, is a community more than a family event. Among the well-to-do, *posadas* often are the occasions for brilliant dances and parties, from which the religious element is entirely lacking. The *posadas* are described as they are observed by humble Mexican peasants and middle-class folk: After dark, on the night of the sixteenth of December ceremonies begin with a procession led by two children. The children bear a small pine-decorated platform on which are replicas of Joseph and Mary, riding on a burro. The members of the company carry lighted tapers, and sing the "Litany of the Virgin" as they approach the door of the house or apartment assigned to the first *posada*. The participants chant an old traditional song in which they waken the master of the house and ask lodging for Mary. From within the dwelling the pilgrims are threatened with beatings unless they move on. Once more the group outside pleads for admittance. When the owner of the house finally learns who his guests are, he and his family jubilantly throw open the doors and bid them welcome. The pilgrims kneel about the *nacimiento*, a lifelike representation of the manger, which is lent to the host of the night. After songs of welcome, *Ave Marias* and a prayer, the children sing delightful little verses in which they beg for sweets. Then the fun begins. Refreshments are served and young and old dance in the patio. A *piñata*, a pottery container which is filled with sweets and toys and covered with paper so that it looks like a dancing girl, a grotesque bird, a clown or even a ship, is hung by a long rope from the ceiling or a tree in the patio. One by one the children are blindfolded, turned around, and instructed to strike the *piñata* with a stout stick. Usually many attempts are needed before the container is broken. At last, however, with whoops of delight, the children dive after the sweets, which have scattered in every direction.

233

NOCHE BUENA, Christmas Eve.   *December* 24

In some parts of Mexico the ninth day of the Holy Family's journey is marked by preparations for the Holy Child's birth. Shortly before midnight, nine *Ave Marias* are sung, together with a little verse to the Virgin, which says that the desired night has come and her confinement is approaching. Small children dressed as shepherds stand at either side of the *nacimiento,* or manger, while two guests, representing the godmother and godfather, pass between them with the Christ Child's figure. The members of the company kneel and sing a Litany, after which the Child is lulled to sleep with the cradle song *El rorro,* "Babe in Arms." At midnight the birth of Christ is announced with fireworks, the ringing of bells and blowing of whistles. Throngs of devout worshipers surge into the churches to attend the famous *Misa de Gallo,* or Mass of the Cock. In some parts of Mexico magnificent processions and pageants representing the story of Christ's birth are performed. Often the *posadas* are given in the churches.

NAVIDAD, Christmas.   *December* 25

The *Misa de Gallo* is followed by a big dinner at which all kinds of special foods are served. The feast ranges from lamb and wine for the poor to roasted suckling pig and other rich foods for well-to-do. *Buñuelos,* thin pancakes served with brown-sugar sauce, are a special feature of the Christmas Eve feast. Christmas Day is not observed with gift-giving or with special festivities.

DÍA DE LOS INOCENTES, The Day of Innocent Martyr Saints.
                    December 28

On this day it is customary for Mexican children to try to

fool people by borrowing money or some coveted trinket, which they replace later with a small toy, tiny doll or worthless bauble. The object thus sent is accompanied with a jingle to the effect that you, innocent little dove, have allowed yourself to be fooled, in spite of knowing that nothing ever should be lent on this day!

FESTIVALS OF THE MOHAMMEDANS

THE festivals listed on the following pages are observed widely by Mohammedans in Albania, Arabia, China, Egypt, India, Mesopotamia, Persia, Syria, Turkey[1] and other countries of large Moslem population. Since holiday observances differ widely, according to racial background and cultural heritage, only the main features of the celebrations are described. Definite dates cannot be given according to the Gregorian calendar. Mohammedan festivals, which are calculated according to the moon, vary from country to country and even from town to town in the same country.[2]

NEW YEAR. *First day of the First Moon, Muharram*

People exchange good wishes and lucky pennies. The coin which is obtained on some pretense, without making mention of the day, is considered luckiest of all.

[1] Since the establishment of the Turkish Republic many national and political holidays have been added in place of the Mohammedan holidays previously celebrated. At the present time, only two Mohammedan holidays, namely, *Sheker Baïram* and *Kourban Baïram,* are nationally celebrated. These festivals, like all others of modern Turkey, are observed according to the western calendar.

[2] See the Mohammedan calendar, pages 372–374.

Festivals of the Mohammedans

'ASHURA. *Approximately the tenth day of the First Moon,*
Muharram

According to Turkish Mohammedans this is the anniversary of Noah's departure from the Ark to Mount Ararat. *'Ashura,* from which the day is named, is a sweet porridge that Turkish Mohammedans make and give to their neighbors and to the poor. Housewives match their culinary skill with one another in preparing this sweet, which is made from boiled wheat, dried currants, grain and nuts. According to legend, Noah when on Mount Ararat made a similar porridge from the grains and other foods that remained in the bins of the Ark. The Persian Mohammedans make a yellow porridge called *zerdeh,* which consists of saffron and rice. Among the Persians the entire month of *Muharram* is consecrated to mourning the violent death of Hussein, son of Ali. The Passion Play which dramatizes the tragedy of Hussein is enacted by Persians and the Shi'a adherents.

MAULID, Birthday of Mohammed. *Approximately the eleventh*
day of the Third Moon, Rābī 'Awwal

Among the Egyptian Mohammedans the hours of prayer are announced by cannon. The galleries of the minarets, from which shine hundreds of twinkling lights, present a fairylike appearance. The minarets of large adjoining mosques often are connected by *mahia,* or strings of lamps, which are interspersed with sacred writings. Sweets are distributed to orphans and the poor. Music, the dancing of dervishes (in Egypt only) and the roasting of bullocks and sheep are features of the celebration among Moslems of many countries.

RAMAḌAN, The Mohammedan Lent.   *Ninth Moon*

Every day from early dawn to sunset is kept as a strict
fast. Food, drink, tobacco, snuff and other indulgences are forbidden. At sunset everyone feasts. After the evening meal
people attend the theatre, dance or participate in other amusements. Food is eaten before morning, previous to the fast
beginning at early dawn. According to Mohammed, "Dawn
begins when you can distinguish the black from the white
thread."

'ID-IL-FIṬR (in Arabia); SHEKER BAÏRAM (in Turkey), End of
Ramaḍan.   *First day of the Tenth Moon, Shawwal*

This three-day festival breaks the fast of Ramaḍan.
Everyone dons new garments and exchanges *mendel,* or handkerchiefs, and other gifts with children or friends. In accordance with Mohammed's injunction to dispense each year *zikat,*
or a fortieth of one's surplus wealth, the dependent poor of each
family are scrupulously cared for at this season. Everyone
calls upon his neighbor and wishes him a blessed *Baïram.* All
guests are offered sweets. In Constantinople the boats on the
Bosphorus are decorated with flags. Music and rejoicing are
evidenced by people of every station. In small towns and villages, fairs and carnivals mark the occasion as a gala event,
especially for children.

'IDE AḌHA (in Arabia), KOURBAN BAÏRAM (in Turkey), Feast
of Sacrifice. *Approximately the tenth day of the
Twelfth Moon, Dhu-l-Hijjah*

Since this festival commemorates the sacrifice of Abraham,
every family, according to its means, offers a ram or some other
animal. The creatures presented for sacrifice are festive in

238

appearance. The rams have gilded horns and are decked with flowers and colored ribbons. The meat of the slain animals is distributed among relatives, friends, neighbors, and poor people who come to the door, since the underlying ideal of the festival is to feed the unfortunate and share freely with those who have nothing. According to a popular Turkish legend, the animals so offered will help men, on Judgment Day, to cross *Srath*, the bridge that hangs between Paradise and Hell. The bridge is narrow and the path perilous, so the only way a soul may enter Paradise is by riding on the back of a sure-footed animal sacrificed on *Kourban Baïram*.

FESTIVALS OF THE
NETHERLANDERS

Nieuwjaarsdag, New Year's Day. *January* 1

On the first day of the year children scramble out of bed early and try to be first in shouting "Happy New Year" to relatives or neighbors as they enter the room. Bachelor uncles and grandfathers often give the children gifts of shining new *guldens* for their savings banks. In some places poor children go about in groups, knocking on the doors and wishing householders happiness and blessings throughout the year. The New Year is set aside as a day of visiting and well-wishing. Friends and relatives call upon one another and exchange the season's compliments.

Driekoningenavond, Three Kings' Eve. *January* 5

This holiday is the occasion for festivities and parties among old and young. A pastry-tart containing a bean always is served at evening gatherings. The person finding the bean is proclaimed king or queen of the party.

Festivals of the Netherlanders

*Vastenavond, Fast Evening, Shrove Tuesday Evening.[1]
The Tuesday before Ash Wednesday

Among Roman Catholics of Brabant the day preceding
Lent is observed with all kinds of merrymaking and festivity. In
the evening it is customary for everybody to eat *worstebrood*, a
special kind of bread. Outside, the loaf has the appearance of
ordinary bread. Inside, however, it contains a mixture of de-
liciously spiced sausage meat, the last to be enjoyed until after
Lent.

*Palm Zondag, Palm Sunday. *The Sunday preceding Easter*

At the morning service palms are distributed at the church
door. On this day children in some parts of Holland make garlands of green leaves and fasten them to long sticks. Throughout Holy Week they carry these wreaths from door to door in
the village. The children sing an old ditty about how it is now
Palm, Palm Paschen, but soon it will be Easter, and they must
have eggs, three making one *Paaschei,* or Easter egg. Few
housewives can resist this plea for eggs, and so by the end of the
week all the children have collected enough for their Easter
sports.

*Paschen, Paasch Zondag, Easter.

In ancient times Easter fires were kindled, either near the
village church or else on some hill or high place. People danced
about the fires and carried home bits of the charred wood to protect their houses from fire and other disasters. Today, in many
places, the old custom persists in highly modified form. On
Easter Eve groups of boys and girls go out with lighted Chinese

[1] Stars indicate movable feasts that depend on Easter. See table of Easter
dates and movable feasts on pages 357–358.

lanterns which are attached to long sticks. The children march through the village streets and are joined on every corner by more young people, all with colorful lanterns bobbing from slender poles. The procession gains in volume and the boys and girls begin singing old folk songs. When the market place is reached, they dance with the same joy and abandon as did their ancestors who danced about the Easter fires.

*PASCHEN, PAASCH MAANDAG, Easter Monday.
The Monday after Easter

Eiertikken is the name children of the Netherlands give their favorite game with Easter eggs. The children color with coffee grounds, beet juice, onion skins and other vegetable substances the eggs they have collected during the week. Then the boys and girls carry them to a broad green meadow, where the *eiertikken* is held. Each youngster matches his red, brown or yellow egg against the green, pink or blue egg of his neighbor. The trick is to break the shell of his opponent's egg, but not that of his own. The child able to do this successfully not only keeps his own egg but collects his neighbor's cracked one. Fun and laughter run high and the winner of the *eiertikken* is proud indeed to prove his skill as champion egg breaker. Another Easter game, which was as popular in sixteenth and seventeenth century Holland as in modern times, is called the *eiergaren*. On Easter Monday the townsfolk assemble in the main street of the village. A tub of water, in which an enormous apple floats, is placed in the middle of the road. The village innkeeper usually provides the twenty-five eggs needed for this game. He brings them from the tavern in a large basket and places them one by one on the road, at intervals of about twelve feet. Two contestants are selected from among the villagers. One man is given the empty basket. The other, with hands tied behind his back, is led to the tub and told to eat the apple. The first man has to run, picking up all the eggs and placing them in the basket, before the second has finished his apple. The one who accomplishes his task first receives the eggs as reward. After this contest people go to the tavern to eat and to drink to the winner's health. The *eiergaren* is as exciting a game to adults as the *eiertikken* is to children.

VERJAARDAG VAN PRINSES JULIANA, Birthday of Her Royal Highness Princess Juliana.   *April* 30

This national holiday is celebrated with great rejoicing by all classes of people. Little girls are dressed in white frocks and orange scarfs. All the official buildings are illumined with electric lights which flash out the initial *J*. Bands play in the city squares and a general air of festivity marks all gatherings in public places.

*LUILAKFEEST, Sluggards' Feast.
                              The Saturday before Whitsunday*

On the Saturday before Whitsunday in some of the Eastern Provinces, children still welcome spring with ceremonies inherited from pagan times. The boys and girls rise early and gather green boughs in the woods. Then they dip the branches in water and stealthily fasten them over the doors of "sluggards," or folk who have overslept. When the late risers finally open their doors the cunningly arranged wet branches tumble on their heads and give them a drenching. The children, who are lurking near, often chase the lazy ones, beating them with green branches and singing old folk ditties about the sluggard. Probably this custom originally was intended as an early spring purification rite.

*PINKSTEREN, Whitsuntide. *The fiftieth day after Easter and the days immediately following*

The Whitsuntide holidays generally are celebrated with picnics, excursions to the country or attendance at a *Kermis,* or fair which, with its barkers, side shows and stalls of tempting food, resembles a glorified circus. On Whit-Monday children have a school holiday and everyone dresses in new spring clothes. In olden times it was customary in some places for poor women to beg through the village streets at Whitsuntide. The women always were accompanied by a little flower-decked girl, who sat in a cart. People called the child *Pinksterbloem* or "Whitsuntide Flower." Inhabitants of the Hudson Valley in New York State still call Whitsunday *Pinkster* Sunday, in memory of their early Dutch ancestors.

VERJAARDAG VAN HARE MAJESTEIT KONINGIN WILHELMINA, Birthday of Her Majesty Queen Wilhelmina.

August 31

This is a national holiday observed similarly to the birthday of Her Royal Highness Princess Juliana.

LEIDEN ONTZET, Leyden Day.   *October* 3

This is the anniversary of the lifting of the Siege of Leyden by the Spaniards, in 1574. History records that the first person to venture out from the besieged city was an orphan boy. In the deserted Spanish camp the lad discovered an iron pot filled with *klapstuk,* a mixture of mashed potatoes, carrots and onions boiled together with a piece of meat. *Klapstuk* became a traditional dish with patriotic Netherlanders, who serve it for dinner on every third of October.

Festivals of the Netherlanders

SINT MAARTEN, Saint Martin.   *November* 11

Boys and girls build great bonfires in honor of Saint Martin. After singing and dancing about the fires they light Chinese lanterns and go, two or three abreast, to the neighborhood houses. The children serenade the villagers, singing school songs and rhymes about Saint Martin and how he was cold and needed wood for a fire. The various households reward the children with pennies, which are spent later for many kinds of cookies and sweets.

SINT NICOLAAS AVOND, Saint Nicholas' Eve.   *December* 5

Saint Nicholas, fourth century Bishop of Spain, is the gift-bringer of Dutch children. His feast is the occasion for family reunions, untold surprises for both adults and children, and great rejoicing for boys and girls. According to old folk tradition, on every fifth of December Saint Nicholas rides through the air on his white horse. He jumps from roof to roof and finally slips down the chimney and fills the children's wooden shoes—or baskets, in some parts of the country—which stand in a row, awaiting his coming. The boys and girls leave hay and carrots for the saint's white horse. If the children have been good, Saint Nicholas leaves toys and sweets; if naughty, they get nothing. After the saint has finished his work he climbs up the chimney and is off to another house. On Saint Nicholas' Eve the good saint, accompanied by *Zwarte Piet,* or Black Peter the Moor, who carries a stout rod and a yawning bag, make their appearance at every door in the village. In anticipation of the visit a large white sheet is spread on the floor. As the children sing little songs of welcome to Saint Nicholas the door suddenly bursts open and a shower of goodies falls upon the sheet. While the youngsters are picking up the sweets, the saint, dressed in ecclesiastical vestments, enters the room and questions the little ones on their past behavior. *Zwarte Piet* threatens bad children with his rod, and opens his sack to show how he will carry them away. Finally Saint Nicholas says farewell and the children are packed off to bed. Then the elders have their "surprises"— parcels and bundles that are mysteriously wrapped and appear from mysterious quarters. Hot punch, chocolate, boiled chestnuts served hot with butter and sugar, and many other delicacies are eaten on this occasion. Early in the morning the children patter to the chimney corner to discover what Saint Nicholas has left. Their wooden shoes are overflowing with gifts— toys; sweets; *taai-taai,* crisp ginger cakes baked in traditional patterns; sweet chocolate letters; pink and white candy hearts; hard spiced cakes; and the initials of the child's given name baked in pastry, *letterbanket,* filled with rich almond paste. Roast goose is the traditional food served for the Saint Nicholas feast. There are also marvelous cakes, baked to represent Saint Nicholas, birds, fish and fantastic animals.

SINT THOMAS, Saint Thomas. *December* 21

Possibly because December 21 is the shortest day in the year, children shout "Lazybones, lazybones!" at the person caught lying in bed the longest on Saint Thomas' Day.

BETWEEN DECEMBER 24 AND JANUARY 6.

During this period young boys go through the village streets making a noise on homemade drumlike contrivances called *rommelpot,* and begging for pennies ". . . to buy bread." Although the meaning of the custom is obscure, it possibly originated in a desire to drive evil spirits from the homes by creating a terrific din.

246

Festivals of the Netherlanders

EERSTE KERSTDAG, Christmas. *December* 25

Christmas and the day following generally are spent quietly at home in family gatherings and reunions. Church is attended in the morning. In humble homes bread pudding often is served as dessert at the hearty noonday dinner. Long fat loaves of bread, which are sweet and stuffed with raisins, are a favorite accompaniment to tea, coffee or hot chocolate. Children revel in their gay Christmas trees, which are hung with red apples and all kinds of goodies and sweets.

TWEEDE KERSTDAG, Second Day of Christmas. *December* 26

Holiday festivities continue on this day.

OUDEJAARS AVOND, New Year's Eve. *December* 31

People attend an early evening church service at which the minister gives a résumé of the year's events and a brief memorial for the parishioners who have died during the past twelve months. He never mentions the dead by name unless they are members of the Royal Family. A special Psalm always is sung at this service.

FESTIVALS OF THE NORWEGIANS

NYTTÅRSDAG, New Year's Day. *January* 1

After attending the morning church services the rest of the day generally is spent quietly in the homes. The New Year's dinner consists of all kinds of cold meats, sausages and appetizers as well as roast pork, roast goose and numerous fancy cakes and sweets. Strong holiday beer and hearty good wishes are passed from host to guest as each bids the other luck and cheer throughout the next twelve months. In the afternoon people make formal New Year calls. The second day of the New Year is characterized by family parties, dinners and dances. Many organizations hold their annual festivities at this time.

TYVENDEDAGEN, Twentieth Day (after Christmas). *January* 13

On this day, which marks the end of Yuletide, the Christmas trees are dismantled and the decorations carefully packed away until the following year. Generally the tree is chopped up and burned in the fireplace. The last Christmas festivities and parties are held on January 13 and the greeting *Glaedelig jul,* Merry Christmas, is used up to and on this day.

Festivals of the Norwegians

*FASTELAVN, Shrovetide.[1]

The Monday preceding Ash Wednesday

The Monday preceding Lent is a gala occasion for boys and girls who, following old tradition, rise at crack of dawn, arm themselves with *fastelavnsris,* birch or evergreen switches, and sally forth to switch all the lazy people they can catch lying in bed. A great deal of competition exists among the children, as custom decrees that they shall receive a toothsome hot cross bun for every victim they spank. The *fastelavnsris* are made with great artistry. Sometimes the switches are tied together and decorated with glittering tinsel and red, blue, orange or yellow paper streamers. A small doll dressed in stiff tarlatan skirts is attached to the topmost branch. Sometimes the switches are hung with bright-colored paper flowers, which drop off on the beds as the children spank their victims. Doubtless the custom of switching with branches originated in an ancient pagan rite of ushering into the village the fruitfulness of spring.

*LANGFREDAG, Long Friday. *The Friday preceding Easter*

Religious services are held in all the churches in memory of Christ's Passion. *Langfredag* is so-called because it was a long day to the suffering Christ.

*PÅSKE, Easter.

The devout attend early morning religious services. Others celebrate the Easter holidays, which begin on Maundy Thursday and continue through Easter Monday, by excursions to the

---

[1] Stars indicate movable feasts that depend on Easter. See table of Easter dates and movable feasts on pages 357-358.

mountains. Towns and cities are deserted and every small mountain hotel or inn is packed to overflowing with people of every class, who come for skiing, tobogganing, skating and other winter sports. In many of these mountain resorts special out-of-door Easter services are held for the benefit of the skiers. Ice carnivals, sports competitions, dances and concerts are important features of the Easter festivities. In the homes Easter is a gala day for the children. For weeks in advance boys and girls begin saving eggshells. They either blow out the contents or else carefully cut the shells in half. The empty shells often are filled with small candies before they are pasted together with strips of paper. Then the children ornament the shells with gay-colored paper cut-outs or painted designs. On Easter morning the egg hunt begins. The eggs are hidden in flower pots, doll beds and odd corners. The boys and girls have a merry time finding eggs their parents have hidden and hiding the eggs they have prepared for the other members of the family.

*PINSE, Whitsunday. *The fiftieth day after Easter*

Services are held in all the churches. At this time of year city glee clubs make trips to the country, and country glee clubs hold conventions in the cities. Singing contests are held from village to village and town to town.

SYTTENDE MAI, Independence Day. *May 17*

The anniversary of the drawing up of the Constitution at Eidsvold in 1814 and Norway's independence are observed throughout the country with the flying of flags, military salutes, band music, parades, processions of children carrying flags, patriotic speeches and public demonstrations of many kinds.

Festivals of the Norwegians

SANKT HANS AFTEN, Saint John's Eve.   *June* 23

In many parts of Norway a little girl is chosen as mid-summer queen. Crowned either with flowers or with a traditional bridal crown, she is led through the village by a gay procession of boys and girls. The village fiddler, playing a native wedding march, precedes the children, who wear flowers and peasant costumes. *Sankthansbål,* or Saint John's bonfires, are built on the heights. These fires, made from logs and tar-soaked barrels, may be seen for several miles. Young people, singing the old folk songs of their native valleys, go out on the water in gaily decked boats and watch the burning bonfires, which are reflected a hundred times in the clear waters of fjords and lakes. Although *Sankt Hans Aften* is celebrated throughout the country with bonfires, folk dances and other festivities, the historical significance of the festival is preserved in all its beauty in the open-air museums at Maihaugen, near Lillehammer, and at the Norwegian Folk Museum at Bygdöy, near Oslo.

SANKT HANS DAG, Saint John's Day.   *June* 24

The frolics, dances and sports of the previous night are continued throughout this day.

OLSOK, Saint Olav's Day.   *July* 29

The anniversary of the death of Saint Olav in 1030 at the battle of Stiklestad, near Trondheim, is celebrated throughout Norway. Saint Olav, Norway's patron saint, introduced Christianity and consolidated the kingdom. He ruled the country from 1015 to 1028. Annual vesper services are held in Trondheim Cathedral. Special celebrations take place at Maihaugen, near Lillehammer, and at the Trondheim Folk Museum.

MIKKELSMESSE, Michaelmas. *September 29*

At about this time it is usual for herdsmen to drive the cattle back from mountain pastures and put them in winter quarters on the farms.

FLYTTEDAG, Moving Day. *Sometime during the Autumn*

It is customary in Bergen and other large towns for servants in search of employment to go about from place to place looking for new positions. Peasant girls and men from all parts of Norway come into town on this day. Dressed in the colorful costumes of their respective valleys, they often ride in little carts or wagons which are piled high with gaily painted hope chests or bundles bulging with clothing and other worldly possessions. Market places and streets are thronged with city folk and peasants, who meet to buy and sell animals, chickens, eggs, goat's milk and cheeses, as well as weavings, carvings and other types of handicraft. City men and housewives hold interviews and select their help for the year from among the scores of rosy-cheeked country servants who crowd into the towns in the hope of finding city employment.

JULAFTEN, Christmas Eve. *December 24*

Christmas preparations are begun weeks in advance. The family pig and calf are slaughtered and the meat made into all kinds of delicacies, such as the pork and veal sausages that when sliced reveal various decorative patterns of stars, spirals or geometric designs. The *lutefisk,* or Christmas cod, is slowly dried, then soaked in lye until it swells to a trembling jellylike mass. Among the baked delicacies of the season are fancy gingerbreads and animal cookies for the Christmas tree, as well as delicious coffee breads and small cakes to serve with coffee or punch. The semi-annual family washing is done, houses are scrubbed, brasses and coppers polished, curtains hung and enough wood chopped to suffice for a fortnight of Christmas fires. To the Norwegian peasant *Jul* is the season of peace on earth and good will toward all God's creatures. Consequently, sheaves of wheat placed in the yards or on top of houses or outbuildings furnish plentiful holiday cheer for the birds of the air. Generally the poles are made from spruce trees, with little tufts of branches left at the top, so that while eating, the birds may have a firm foothold as well as protection against snow and wind. Farm animals are provided with extra feedings and nobody thinks of hunting or harming wild animals or birds during the Christmas season. Christmas Eve begins officially with the ringing of the five o'clock church chimes. Stores and shops are closed and "the Christmas peace" descends over every Norwegian town and hamlet. In the homes everything is in readiness for the holiday. Sometimes cold snacks are served before five o'clock. The entire family, including the master and mistress, children, guests and servants, gathers to partake of the traditional *mölje,* or rich liquid in which the Christmas meats are cooked. *Mölje* is served hot with *fladbröd,* flat, hard Norwegian bread, which each one dips into the soup. In rural districts everyone dons national costume, while in cities formal dress is worn. At five o'clock the father of the family usually reads the Christmas story from the Bible. The doors are thrown open and the glittering Christmas tree revealed to the eager children. The tree is lighted with white candles and decorated with all kinds of tempting cooky animals, gilded nuts, eggshell toys, red apples and gingerbread figures. The presents are piled beneath its branches. After the presents have been opened and admired, young and old join hands and walk about the tree, singing well-loved Christmas carols. Then supper is served. After the usual holiday hot and cold appetizers the *lutefisk* appears, which, after its lye bath, has been boiled and is served with drawn butter and boiled potatoes. Then there are *ribbens-stek,* pork ribs, accompanied by boiled potatoes and sauerkraut. Cakes and sweets and *risengrynsgröt,* or rice porridge, end the meal. The porridge is made with a single almond in it, and whoever finds the nut will, it is said, be the first one to marry in the coming year. The *Julenisse,* a small gnome with a red pointed cap and long flowing beard who dwells in the barn and looks out for the welfare of the family, must have his share of Christmas cheer. Even today children remember the little man with a bowl of *risengrynsgröt*—which surely is appreciated, because by morning it always is gone!

JULEDAG, Christmas. *December 25*

Everybody attends Christmas morning church services. As a rule, the day is spent quietly at home. In the afternoon boys and girls sometimes try out their new skis, skates or sleds, but few parties are held on *Juledag.* The day following, however (the second day of Christmas), friends and relatives visit, eat, drink and give parties. These festivities continue until January 13. Throughout this season breakfast is a gay and tremendous meal. Long tables, decorated in the holiday spirit, groan under thirty or forty different kinds of delicious hot and cold dishes. *Aquavit* and other strong drinks accompany the food and make the holiday breakfasts really gala occasions. Between Christmas and the New Year, feasting and parties are held throughout the country.

ANDEN JULEDAG, Second Christmas Day. *December 26*

In olden times Saint Stephen's Day, the day following Christmas, was devoted to mad horse-racing over the icy roads. According to an old rhyme:

Festivals of the Norwegians

"Saint Stephen was a stable boy,
He watered his five foals."

Today *Anden Juledag* is celebrated with a continuation of the Christmas festivities.

NYTTÅRSAFTEN, New Year's Eve.   *December* 31

Young people dressed in fantastic costumes and masks go visiting in groups of ten, fifteen or more. At every house the visitors stop for refreshments and dancing. Often the night's festivities are ended with morning breakfast at the house of a friend or neighbor.

FESTIVALS OF THE POLES

THE Polish peasant's holiday calendar begins on December 24, Christmas Eve, with the appearance of the first star, rather than on January first, New Year's Day. The entire period from December 24, Christmas Eve, to January 6, Three Kings' Day, is regarded as *Boże Narodzenie,* or "Christmas Time" in Poland. Customs vary from village to village and from town to town. Certain ceremonies are performed on one date in one locality and on another in other parts of the country. All the holiday customs mentioned are likely to occur sometime during the two-week "Christmas" period. Each province and hamlet has its own distinctive traditions that often are unknown in other communities. Certain outstanding Yuletide customs are observed throughout the length and breadth of Poland, however, and these are the customs described under the general heading of "Christmas Time."

Boże Narodzenie, Christmas Time (from *Wilia,* on Christmas Eve, to Three Kings' Day, or Epiphany).
December 24–January 6

With the appearance of the first star, the Christmas fast is broken and everyone partakes of the traditional *Wilia,* or supper. The head of the household breaks an *oplatek* with each guest and exchanges wishes for health and happiness. *Oplatki* are semi-transparent wheat-flour wafers, which are made in cast-iron molds and stamped with pictures of the Nativity. *Oplatki* are sent in letters to absent relatives and friends. In many rural communities *oplatki* later are divided among cattle and farm animals, as they too must share in the blessings of the Christmas season. Straw is spread under the linen feast cloth in memory of the manger birth. In some parts of Poland an empty place is set for the poor stranger who may come to the door. The *Wilia* includes many traditional foods, such as *barszcz,* or beetroot soup, which often is served with mushroom patties, almond soup, all kinds of fish, *kluski z makiem,* or a sort of poppy-seed paste, wheat or rice with honey sauce, many kinds of small honey or seed cakes and other dainties too numerous to mention. The Christmas tree usually occupies the place of honor in a room by itself. It is lighted with colored candles and decorated with nuts and apples and numberless homemade ornaments fashioned from eggshells, bits of colored paper, straw and daubs of paint. In some parts of Poland "The Little Star" is said to bring Christmas gifts to the children, but no presents are opened until after singing the traditional Christmas carols. At midnight all pious folk attend the Shepherds' Mass, and as the notes of the shepherds' flutes are heard above the joyous pealing of the organ, people say that the ox and the ass—the animals present at Christ's birth—kneel in adoration and speak the language of men. In Polish villages, between Christmas Eve and Three Kings' Day boys sometimes go from house to house singing *kolendy,* or Christmas carols. Sometimes they give *szopka,* or Punch and Judy Christmas plays, with crude little box-theatres and marionettes manipulated from sticks inserted in the stage floors. The marionettes have flexible legs and hands and are moved rhythmically by the sticks. The rôles they represent are both traditional and local in character. For instance, King Herod, his Knights, Death and the Devil (who kill the wicked Herod) appear in every

257

play. Then there are numerous humorous characters typifying
the town drunkard, the village Jew and his wife, the gypsy man
with his bear, a Krakovian couple or other persons familiar to
the district in which the show is given. The size and shape of
the theatres and the local characters vary according to town
and village. The *szopka*, however, with its quaint figures and
traditional singing dialogues, is an ancient Polish institution
that originated centuries ago. Sometimes, instead of carrying a
star or *szopka*, the leader of the band, who is called *Turon* or
Klapak, represents a fantastic beast, with cloth-covered body
and grotesque head. By a clever manipulation of the strings
Turon opens and closes his enormous jaws. This trick affords
endless delight to the spectators, especially the small boys, who
toss apples into the creature's mouth. *Turon* expresses thanks
with elaborate bows, high jumps and other amusing antics. In
many parts of Poland boys carry through the village an illumined paper star, which is fastened to a long pole and revolves
like a pinwheel. The boys go from house to house, singing traditional carols and are rewarded with little gifts of coins and
sweets. On Three Kings' Day villagers mark over their doors
the initials of the Kings and the date, believing that thus their
homes will be protected from harm.

Święto Matki Boskiej Gromnicznej, Mother of God Who
      Saves Us from Thunder, Feast of Purification, Can-
      dlemas.   *February 2*

On this day people take candles to church to have them
blessed. The sanctified taper is carried home and used throughout the year as a protection against thunder, lightning, disease
and other disaster. Should death occur, the candle is lighted
and placed in the hand of the dying.

Festivals of the Poles

*Zapusty, Fat Thursday.[1]
The Thursday before the beginning of Lent

The Lenten fast always begins on Friday. On the Thursday before Lent everyone holds high festival. Typical of the day's feasting are *paczki,* a special kind of fried doughnut, and other rich foods. Carnival balls and dances continue until midnight, when Lent begins.

*Wielki Piątek, Great Friday. *The Friday preceding Easter*

The church bells are silent on this day, so people say they "have all gone to Rome." People eat no hot food from Good Friday until Easter Sunday, but fast on dry bread and roasted potatoes. Holy Friday, however, is a busy occasion for Polish housewives, who knead and roll out dough for the many elaborate Easter cakes for which they are famous. Houses are cleaned and preparations continued for the Easter feast. Village girls vie with one another in the decoration of Easter eggs for the *swiecone,* or Easter hallow-fare. The eggs, which are ornamented in three ways, may be classified as (1) *malowanki,* eggs painted in solid colors with natural substances, such as vegetable skins, roots or grains; (2) *pisanki,* eggs batiked in marvelous traditional designs, chiefly animal or geometrical figures, that have been handed down for generations from mother to daughter; (3) *skrobanki,* eggs dyed in solid colors upon which the outlines of birds, flowers and animals are delicately scratched with a sharp instrument. The girls often bestow these beautifully ornamented eggs upon their sweethearts as tokens of special favor. In the churches the replica of Christ's body is laid in the sepulchre and covered with flowers. Groups of people go from church to church to worship at the tomb.

[1] Stars indicate movable feasts that depend on Easter. See table of Easter dates and movable feasts on pages 357–358.

259

This custom is regarded almost as a social event in Krakow and many other large towns.

*WIELKA SOBOTA, Great Saturday. *The Saturday before Easter*

Housewives cover a large table with their finest linen and best dishes and lay out the cold *swiecone,* or hallow-fare, which the priest comes and blesses. Sometimes a little lamb, symbolizing the Lamb of God, is cunningly fashioned from butter or sugar and given the place of honor in the center of the table. Red paper cut-outs and festoons of green give added color to the tempting array of eggs, chickens, suckling pigs, Easter loaves and wheaten cakes, hams, headcheese and coils of sausage, which encircle great piles of shelled hard-boiled eggs. The priest makes the village rounds, sprinkles the tables with holy water and blesses the hallow-fare, which remains untouched until the following day. Many people, too poor to have a large feast table, carry to church baskets of cheese, cakes, eggs and other Easter foods to be blessed there. The "blessing of fire and water" is an important ceremony in some homes. The old fire is extinguished and a new one kindled from a lighted taper brought from church. A bottle of water, blessed at church, is carried home and kept as a preventive against disease in cattle or fruit trees. On Easter Eve the famous Resurrection Service is held. The figure of the risen Christ dominates the altar, which blazes with scores of lighted tapers.

*WIELKANOC, Easter.

As the bells peal forth on Easter morning people say that they "have flown back from Rome." Old and young don festive attire and attend the joyous Easter Mass. In the homes the holiday feast consists of the cold hallow-fare, for no fire is lighted on this sacred day. It is customary for the head of the family to cut a colored egg and share a piece with everyone present. As the egg is eaten good wishes are exchanged, such as "Best luck throughout the year" or "We wish you a happy alleluia." In Eastern Poland there is an old peasant belief in a subterranean world inhabited by folk who never see the sun. Boys and girls often throw gaily painted eggshells into the streams, so their message of spring may reach the race dwelling in darkness.

*DRUGIE ŚWIĘTO WIELKANOCNE, Easter Monday.
The day after Easter

Smigus or *dyngus* is the name applied to an ancient festival that permits the boys to duck all the village girls on Easter Monday. In towns and cities the lads squirt their victims with perfume. In some village communities bands of boys often chase after the girls and drench them with buckets of water as they cry out, *"Smigus."* In other places the boys capture the strongest, most energetic girl in the village, drag her to the water's edge and give her a complete wetting. The *smigus* festival is said to date back to the tenth century, when the Poles accepted Christianity and were baptized *en masse*.

ŚWIĘTO PIERWSZEGO MAJA, May Day.   *May* 1

In some parts of Poland boys and girls decorate green branches with ribbons and colored eggshells. Then they go from house to house, singing and begging for gifts of money, eggs or cakes. The households that give presents are rewarded with twigs of green, which are said to bring blessings to animals and crops.

ŚWIĘTO TRZECIEGO MAJA, Constitution Day.   *May* 3

This patriotic holiday is in honor of the ratification of the progressive Polish constitution of 1794. Among other liberal measures, the constitution established a Ministry of Education.

*ŻIELONE ŚWIATKI, Pentecost.
The Thursday following the fiftieth day after Easter

Throughout Poland green branches, purple flag and birch garlands, symbolic of reawakened spring, are used as decorations in the houses and over doors and windows. In rural districts servants gather outside the manor houses and rhythmically crack their long whips. This ceremony symbolizes a wish for joy to the master and mistress of the house. This festival begins on Thursday and continues until the following Thursday.

*BOŻE CIALO, Corpus Christi.
The Thursday following Trinity Sunday

Small chapel-like altars constructed of green boughs are erected in many different parts of the village. Pictures of the Virgin, lighted tapers and garlands of larkspur, cornflowers and other spring blossoms make every altar a shrine of beauty. After Mass the church bells ring joyously. Processions led by the priest, who holds the Monstrance aloft under a scarlet canopy, make the rounds of the village altars. White-clad girls throw flowers before the slowly advancing procession, which is composed of singing choir boys, women carrying the holy pictures, and dignified elders bearing colorful church banners. Religious ceremonies and blessing of altars continue for a week. Processions also are held in towns and cities as well as in villages.

*LEJKONIK, Horse Festival.
The second Thursday after Corpus Christi

This is a local festival, occurring only in Kraków, where a

man dressed like a Tartar prances through the market on a gaily trapped hobby horse, in commemoration of olden times when a breathless horseman carried news of the Tartar defeat to Kraków.

Noc Świętojańska, Saint John's Eve.   *June 23*

Boys and girls dance about *sobotki,* or lighted bonfires, singing ancient songs. The boys jump through the flames as a fertility charm. On this night girls perform a secret rite, which has descended from pagan times. Each girl weaves a garland of wild flowers, decorates it with gay ribbons and fastens a lighted candle across the center. Then she throws the wreath far out into the stream. Should the wreath drift to shore, it is a sign that the girl never will marry; if it sinks, she will die before the year ends; if it floats downstream, she will surely wed. Since superstition says that the boy who catches a wreath will marry the girl to whom it belongs, the boys hide in boats along the river banks and try to capture their sweetheart's garlands. The festival ends with laughter and singing as the boys finally take the girls upstream in their boats. In towns and cities *bengalskie ognie,* or skyrockets, and other fireworks are used as modern additions to the ancient festival.

Dożynki, Harvest Festival.
                    End of August or middle of September

The end of the harvest is marked by the *dożynki,* or harvest festival, which still is observed on large estates in many parts of Poland. Each year President Moscicki has a *dożynki* to which peasants from all over the country bring gifts of harvest fruits. When the harvest is gathered, the reapers fashion wreaths of grain, flowers, nuts and corn. These wreaths are decorated with ribbons and carried in procession to the master and mistress of the estate. The reapers are welcomed and invited to enter the house, where they feast, dance and sing as the guests of the mansion. The first dance usually is opened by the master and mistress, who choose as their respective partners the girl who presented the wreath and the best farm worker. Traditional songs and dances accompany each part of the *dożynki* festival. The harvest wreaths are hung on the walls, where they remain until the following year.

ZADUSZKI, All Souls' Day.   *November 2*

The church bells toll continuously on this day of memorial for the souls of the dead. Vespers are sung in the churchyard or in the mortuary chapel. People give small money gifts to wandering holy men, who offer prayers and petitions for the deceased. Lighted candles and flowers are placed on the graves. According to ancient legend, these offerings drive away the Bad Angel and help the Lord, who comes on this night to count the number of souls belonging to Him.

DZIEŃ ŚWIĘTEGO MARCINA, Saint Martin's Day.   *November 11*

When snowflakes begin to fly, Polish children say "Saint Martin is coming on his white horse." In some places little horseshoe-shaped cakes are eaten as reminders of the good saint's horse.

ŚWIĘTO NIEPODLEGŁOŚCI, Independence Day.   *November 11*

This national holiday celebrates the gaining of Polish independence in 1918, under President Pilsudski. The day is observed with special church services.

Festivals of the Poles

Noc ŚwiĘtego Andreja, Saint Andrew's Eve.   *November* 29

On this night boys and girls have many unique ways of looking into the future and determining whom they will wed. *Andrzejki* is the term applied to fortune-telling on this night. Cherry branches afford one favorite method. Young girls break off dry branches, place them in wet sand and tend them carefully. If the branch blossoms by Christmas it is said the girls will marry within the year, so cherry blossoms frequently are found at Yuletide in Polish homes. Future events are also foretold by pouring liquid wax into cold water. Various shapes are formed when the wax hardens, such as hearts, ships, hammers and so on, and from these symbols the boys and girls read their fate.

Dzień ŚwiĘtej Barbary, Saint Barbara's Day.   *December* 4

This is a day regarded as important in weather prophecy. If Saint Barbara's Day comes with rain, say the peasants, Christmas will come with ice; if Saint Barbara's Day comes with ice, Christmas will come with rain.

FESTIVALS OF THE PORTUGUESE

Anno Novo, New Year's Day.   *January* 1

The New Year is begun with special services in the churches. Friends and relatives visit from house to house, greeting one another with *"Boas Festas"* and exchanging good wishes and congratulations. In some places the village band goes through the streets playing stirring airs. Whenever the musicians happen to pass the house of one of their members they stop and play a special selection. Peasants declare that a person will act during the twelve months as he behaves on the first day of the year. For this reason youngsters look well to their manners, and older people conduct themselves circumspectly!

Dia Dos Reis, Day of the Kings.   *January* 6

In all parts of the country peasants perform Epiphany plays in honor of the Magi. Bands of carolers go about, singing greetings and begging gifts, for they, like the kings of old, are weary and come from afar. In some places, family groups visit one another from house to house. The guests stand at the door and beg admittance, to sing to the Christ Child. After receiving a hearty welcome and singing special carols in honor of the Infant Jesus, the guests are entertained with wines and sweets. Gifts are exchanged on this day. This is a great festival for children, whose mothers often give them a party and a

266

Festivals of the Portuguese

bolo-Rei, or special Epiphany cake. Within the ring-shaped
pastry are hidden all kinds of amulets or little fortune-telling
trinkets, and a single dried lima bean. The child who finds the
bean is crowned king of the party and promises to "make the
cake" for his playmates the following year.

*CARNAVAL, Carnival.[1] *The Sunday, Monday and Tuesday
preceding Ash Wednesday*

The last three days before Ash Wednesday culminate the
pre-Lenten festivities, which begin several weeks earlier. Even
as recently as a hundred years ago the Lisbon carnival was
characterized as a time of license, with obscene jokes, coarse
horseplay and battles with eggs, oranges, flour and water pre-
dominating. Nowadays the public festivities in Lisbon are restricted, for the most part, to processions of gay flower-decked
cars, music and parades of merrymakers in fancy costumes.
Balls, parties and dances are held at this season. In the provinces, Carnival continues to be celebrated with much of its old-
time gaiety and abandon. Mummers and musicians, the burial
in effigy of King Carnival, old folk plays and dramas are features of the festivities.

DOMINGO DE RAMOS, Palm Sunday.
The Sunday preceding Easter

In North Portugal people take to church *ramos,* or half-
hoops decorated with spring flowers. The priest blesses the
ramos, which later are carried in procession. These hoops are
carefully preserved in the homes and burned, if necessary, as a
protection against thunder and lightning. In the district of
Alentejo peasants put in the fields small crosses that are
adorned at the points with rosemary sprays.

[1] Stars indicate movable feasts that depend on Easter. See table of Easter
dates and movable feasts on pages 357–358.

267

The Book of Festivals

*PASCHOA, Easter.

Many of the churches are decorated with white flowers. Special Easter music is sung during the Masses, which are attended by old and young, rich and poor. After the services families eat a holiday meal and visit among friends and neighbors. In some places people exchange presents of colored paper cornucopias which are filled with sugared almonds. *Folar* is a popular Easter cake. It is flat and round and decorated on top with colored eggs.

*QUINTA-FEIRA DA ESPIGA, Ear of Wheat Thursday, Ascension
    Day.   *The fortieth day after Easter*

On this day peasants make bouquets of olive and wheat, poppies and daisies. The olive and wheat symbolize wishes for a plentiful harvest, the poppy stands for peace, and the daisy for money. A bit of wheat is kept in the house as a sign of prosperity throughout the coming year. Medicinal plants and herbs are gathered and prepared for home remedies and magic spells.

*PENTECOSTE, Pentecost, Whitsunday.
                                        The fiftieth day after Easter

The anniversary of the descent of the Holy Ghost on the disciples is celebrated with special Masses in the churches. In some of the Azores the local Holy Ghost societies issue free food tickets to the poor. Long elaborately decorated tables which groan under all kinds of bread, meat and other tempting foods are set up in the main streets of the town. Food and drink are distributed to the poor of the community while the band plays and villagers who have contributed to the feast act as hosts and hostesses to their less fortunate neighbors. The distribution of food usually continues until Corpus Christi Day.

268

Festivals of the Portuguese

SANTO ANTONIO, Saint Anthony.   *June* 13

One of the country's most popular saints is Saint Anthony, patron of Lisbon. The Eve is celebrated by building bonfires, around which the young people dance. Children prepare little street altars in the saint's honor. Boxes and tables are covered with white cloth and decorated with flowers, tapers, images and gaudy pictures depicting the life and works of the saint. The boys and girls go through the streets begging coppers for *Santo Antonio*. Anthony is the matchmaker saint. On the Eve of his day young maidens try various methods of finding out whom they will wed. One favorite way is for a girl to fill her mouth with water and hold it until she hears a man's name mentioned. The name she hears is sure to be that of her future husband! Epistles, asking Saint Anthony to furnish sweethearts, often are written by young people and posted in the letter-box of Saint Anthony's Church in Lisbon. When love affairs prosper and suitable mates are found, the box receives thank-offerings from the grateful lovers.

VESPERA DE SÃO JOÃO, Saint John's Eve, Midsummer Eve.
June 23

On the night dedicated to Saint John the Baptist, peasant folk still observe many traditional rites connected with fire and water. In some places boys and girls strip a pine tree, decorate it with flowers and greens, and ceremoniously bring it into the village. There the *facho,* as the tree is called, is set up in a prominent place and surrounded with brush and pine logs. Young people dance about the fire and leap through the flames. Mothers often hold sick children over the embers, as the Saint John's fires are thought to possess curative virtue. Cattle and flocks are driven through the ashes so the animals may prosper throughout the coming year. Even the dead embers are thought to be efficacious against storm and evil influences. People say

Saint John's night water possesses great healing power. Before dawn both cattle and children are bathed in rivers or dew, so they may become strong and healthy. Young girls and women wash their faces in spring water or early dew, to make themselves lovely throughout the year. Often the springs are decked with flowers, and water from seven springs is drunk or carried home in garlanded jugs. On Saint John's Eve young people exercise powers of divination, for this is the night of love. Three beans slipped under the pillow at night, cakes in which a grain of maize is hidden, fig leaves passed through the Saint John's fires and touched with midnight dew—all these are instruments for learning whom one will wed. Little pots of *mangerico,* a pungent plant, are decorated with large paper pinks, to which love verses are attached. Often these plants are bought and sold in the markets and exchanged as good luck tokens between friends or lovers.

Sāo Pedro, Saint Peter.   *June* 29

In some parts of the country children erect little shrines on the doorsteps. The altars are charmingly decorated with flowers, holy pictures and lighted tapers. Whenever the children see someone coming they run out and beg coppers "for the poor saint." On this night young girls sometimes play divination games. One favorite method of finding out whom one will marry is to knock at nine different house doors without uttering a word. If absolute silence is maintained throughout the ceremony, the first man seen from the window in the morning will be the girl's lover!

Dia da Nussa Senhora da Assumpção, Day of Our Lady of the Angels, Assumption Day.   *August* 15

Special services are held in the churches in memory of Our Lady, who was crowned Queen of the Angels.

Festivals of the Portuguese

PROCLAMAÇÃO DA REPUBLICA PORTUGUEZA, Founding of the
Portuguese Republic. *October* 5

The anniversary of the founding of the Portuguese Republic in 1910, when Manoel II was deposed and a provisional
presidency established under Theophilo Braga, is observed with
military reviews, parades, patriotic speeches and national music.

DIA DE TODOS OS SANTOS, All Saints' Day. *November* 1

Special Masses are said for the souls of all the saints who
are not remembered by a special day in the calendar.

DIA DOS FINADOS, All Souls' Day. *November* 2

Masses are said for the repose of the souls of all the deceased. Processions of the faithful go to the cemeteries and
visit the graves of the dead. In olden times food offerings for
the departed probably were eaten at the graves. Today, however, *magusto,* or open-air feasts of wine and chestnuts, are prepared for the living. In some places bands of children go about
singing for "bread for God," and are rewarded with food and
drink. Sometimes the singers receive *bolos de festa,* special All
Souls sugar cakes which are flavored with cinnamon and pungent herbs.

FESTA DA IMACULADA CONCEIÇÃO, Feast of the Immaculate Conception. *December* 8

The Virgin Mary is patroness of Portugal. The feast in
her honor is celebrated throughout the country with special
Masses and processions.

Vespera de Natal, Christmas Eve.   *December* 24

Everybody attends Midnight Mass at the churches, where nativity folk plays often are enacted.   Throughout the night groups of carolers go through the streets singing ancient hymns about Jesus and his birth in Bethlehem's humble manger.

Dia da Familia, Day of the Family; Dia de Natal, Christmas.
December 25

Christmas to the Portuguese is a family festival, characterized by reunions of as many relatives as can be gathered together.   The *cepo de Natal,* or Christmas log (which is traditionally of oak), usually is burned on the hospitable hearth, while the family feasts and drinks late into the day.   The charred remains of the log are carefully preserved, to be burned later on should the house be endangered by thunder.   In many places the *consoada,* or Christmas repast, is shared with the spirits of the dead, who are thought at this season to visit their former homes.   Sometimes crumbs from the feast are sprinkled over the hearth, or food is left on the table, that hungry ghosts may have a part in the family's cheer.

Vespera de Anno Novo, New Year's Eve.   *December* 31

Religious services held in the churches are attended by the devout.   Bands of children go about from house to house singing *janeiras,* or ancient New Year songs.   The masked singers, *janeireiros,* often address their words to the master or mistress of the house, whom they praise if generous, and insult if stingy with the traditional presents of wine, apples, nuts, sausages or coins.   In some places people go to the housetops at midnight and "blow away the old year" with trumpets and appropriate verses.

FESTIVALS OF THE RUMANIANS

SFÂNTUL VASILE, Saint Basil's Day; ANUL NOU, New Year's Day. *January* 1

Children welcome the New Year with an ancient fertility rite called *sămănatul,* or sowing. Early in the morning boys stuff pockets and blouses with corn and visit from house to house in the village. Everywhere they throw corn at people and greet them with wishes for a long life, fruitfulness like the trees in early spring, abundance like "the wealthy autumn." In some parts of Rumania the greeting custom is varied by using the *sorcova* instead of corn. The *sorcova* is a stick to which flowers, either real or artificial, are tied. To be quite right, these flowers must be from twigs plucked on Saint Andrew's Eve and coaxed into blossom by Christmas. The boys greet people by singing and lightly brushing their faces with the *sorcova.* Probably this custom survives from Roman times, when people saluted one another with branches of laurel. It is customary for young persons to address the aged, servants their masters, the poor the rich. In return for the greetings money gifts are bestowed. On this occasion presents are exchanged among all classes.

SFINȚŪ 40 MARTIRI, 40 DE SFINȚI, Forty Saints' Day. *March* 9

The weather at this season is particularly important to peasants, who believe it prophesies the weather of forty days

273

following. Forty genuflexions made on the Eve of this holiday and total abstinence from food are said to win the good saints' favor and protection. The farmer inspects his spades and ploughs and puts them in order; his wife sprinkles ashes about the house to keep out the serpent; she carries to church *colaci,* small loaves of bread baked in figures-of-eight and sprinkled with crushed walnuts and honey (which often are called *sfinți-șori,* or "little saints") and presents them as alms to the poor. The *colaci* are a delicacy typical of the day.

*FLORIILE, DUMINECA FLORIILOR, Palm Sunday.[1] .

The Sunday preceding Easter

Since *Floriile* is the harbinger of Easter, the peasant some-times celebrates by donning the new clothes laid aside for the holy Easter feast. He would not consider doing this on any other holiday.

*SĂPTĂMÎNAPATIMILOR, Week of Sufferings.

The week preceding Easter

Since Easter is the greatest festival in the Rumanian calendar, it is anticipated weeks in advance. *Săptămînapatimilor* is the housewife's busiest time. Everybody tries to prepare new or at least clean clothes for the holiday. The houses are scrubbed clean both within and without. Walls are white-washed, window frames and doorways painted red and every-thing put in perfect order. The various holiday cakes and breads are baked, the Easter eggs painted in elaborate tradi-tional designs, and cheese and butter prepared for the Easter feast.

[1] Stars indicate movable feasts that depend on Easter. See table of Eastern Orthodox Easter dates and movable feasts on pages 370–371.

Festivals of the Rumanians

*JOIA MARE, Great Thursday. *The Thursday preceding Easter*

At early dawn, before the cock crows for the third time, peasants burn piles of accumulated rubbish in the yard. These bonfires are said to symbolize the fire beside which Peter stood and denied his Lord, before the third cock-crow. While the men are busy with the fires women folk are sprinkling water around the wells and over the ancestral graves, and fetching back pailfuls for use in the homes.

*VINEREA MARE, Good Friday. *The Friday preceding Easter*

On this day the holy *aier*, or shroud, which is painted with a picture of Christ's entombment, is placed over a table in the center of the church. At the afternoon service the worshipers kneel before the *aier*, kiss it and crawl under the table, which symbolizes the tomb. Later the *aier* is taken around the church by a procession of the faithful, who carry lighted wax tapers. Then the sacred cloth is symbolically buried.

*SÂMBĂTA MARE, Holy Saturday.
The Saturday preceding Easter

At Midnight Mass the bells peal out joyously and the priest, holding up a lighted taper, announces the joyous tidings, "Christ is risen." "He is risen indeed," respond the worshipers in unison, as they kindle their candles from the priest's. The congregation surges out of church with greetings and well-wishes, for Lenten gloom is past and all may partake of the elaborate Easter feast. Young people are particularly cautious to carry home their tapers lighted, for whoever does so thinks he or she will be able to read future events by gazing into the mirror.

The Book of Festivals

*Duminica Paştilor, Easter Sunday.

Easter is celebrated for three days with feasting, merry-making and rejoicing. People exchange the season's greetings before sitting down to the holiday meal. Each person holds a red egg which he knocks against his neighbor's, as he makes the traditional greeting, "Christ is risen." "Verily he is risen," is the reply. It is said that the person holding the uncracked egg will outlive the other. The holiday feast is especially enjoyed because the Rumanian peasant, whether adult or child, observes rigorous fasting throughout the Lenten period. Tender young roast lamb and *pasca,* a delicious cake made from· quantities of cheese, eggs, flour and butter, are prominent among the Easter foods.

*Lunia Paştilor, Easter Monday. *The Monday after Easter*

The Easter festivities continue as everyone visits relatives and friends, exchanges presents and dances on the village green. Young people swing high in the *scrânciob,* a traditional swing, which is set up on the village green where everyone congregates to dance and sing.

*Marţia Paştilor, Easter Tuesday.
The Tuesday after Easter

The third day of Easter continues the holiday sports and festivities.

Ajunul Zilei de Sfântul Gheorghe, Saint George's Eve.
April 22

On this mystic Eve, when evil spirits are thought to stalk through stables and steal the milk of cows and sheep, to enter the homes and frighten babies and cause doubts and fears to trouble the slumber of innocent maidens, wise folk safeguard their homes and farm buildings by decorating windows and doors with trailing vines and fragrant boughs. Shepherds watch over the stalls, to prevent witches from harming the young lambs. And just to save the flocks from disaster, they rise at dawn and play sweet tunes on their horns, for spirits can do no harm within hearing of such music!

ZIUA DE SFÂNTUL GHEORGHE, Saint George's Day.   *April 23*

Early in the morning girls go to the village fountains to fetch pails of water. On the way home they are met by the boys, who splash water in their sweethearts' faces. Later in the day the young folk dance the *Hora,* sing and play games on the village green. One favorite sport is for everybody to provide himself with nettles and try to prick his unsuspecting neighbor in some vulnerable spot. The person doing the most adept pricking is considered the best player. Saint George's Day, the great festival of spring, foretells the weather for the coming summer months.

*SĂRBĂTOAREA BLAJINILOR, Feast of the Blajini.
                          The second Monday after Easter*

In some parts of Rumania peasants believe in the existence of the *Blajini,* the Kindly Ones, the lost race which lives to the south on the banks of the river fed by all the streams of the world. The *Blajini,* dwelling apart as they do, know nothing of the world of men. Therefore, on the Monday following Easter Monday women throw red Easter-egg shells on running streams, so the *Blajini* on finding them may celebrate the Easter feast.

ARMINDINI, First of May; SĂRBĂTOAREA MUNCII, Labor Day.
May 1

This festival, although no longer universally celebrated, is regarded as a day to be spent out of doors, in fields and meadows. Roast lamb and red wine are features of the picnic meal. Young and old dance and sing and rejoice in the coming of spring. May first is also Rumania's labor holiday. As such it is celebrated with parades, speeches and public demonstration.

*SÂMBĂTA MORȚILOR, Saturday of the Dead.
The Eve of the eighth Sunday after Easter

On this anniversary, which falls on the Eve of the eighth Sunday after Easter (Trinity Eve), all sorts of alms are given, either for the repose of souls of the dead or to insure peace in the next world to souls of the living. Everybody contributes according to his means. A favorite way of giving is to fill jars with water, wine or food, decorate the vessels with flowers or greens and send them to relatives, friends or needy acquaintances. The gifts are joyously accepted, the food eaten and the wine consumed in remembrance of the person named with the present. Women, more than men, visit the graves of their dead on this day.

*SFÂNTA TREIME, DUMINICA RUSALIILOR, Holy Trinity.
The eighth Sunday after Easter

No peasant works on Trinity for fear of the *Russalii,* said by tradition to be three ill-natured women—the daughters of an Emperor—who, never having received much attention while on earth, now revenge themselves toward mankind in general. The *Russalii* bring death and destruction. They cause storms and great winds. They harm babies and work evil unless one uses proper spells. Sprigs of wormwood hidden under the pillow on Trinity Eve are thought to prevent the *Russalii's* night ravages, while wormwood tucked into the belt affords protection on Trinity Day.

Sfântul Ilie Profetul, Saint Elie. *July* 20

Dreaded by the peasants is Saint Elie, or Elijah, who, they say, on this day drives his chariot through the heavens and chases after devils. When it lightens, the chariot is sending forth tongues of fire; when it thunders, the wheels are rumbling across the clouds. Saint Elie's Day is strictly observed, both as a church feast and as an occasion when peasants take special precautions against the devils whom the saint chases into out-of-the-way corners. In case of thunder, lighting the Easter taper or placing an ax in the yard and sprinkling it with salt is said to avert harm from the house.

Ajunul Zilei de Sfântul Andrei, Saint Andrew's Eve.
November 29

On this night *strigoii,* or vampires, are thought to rise from their tombs, carrying their coffins on their heads. They walk about the homes where once they lived. Before dark, women anoint locks and casements with garlic to keep out the vampires, who try to harm mortals. On Saint Andrew's Eve the vampires fight among themselves at the crossroads, but with the first cock-crow they again betake themselves to the graveyard.

Sfântul Andrei Primul Apostol, Saint Andrew's Day.
November 30

Mothers take the children to the garden, where they pluck

twigs from the fruit trees—cherry, pear, apricot or plum—or sprays from rose or other flowering vines. Then they put the twigs together into small clusters. Each member of the family, from the old grandmother to the babe-in-arms, is assigned a bunch, which is placed in water and tended with the greatest care. The twigs of "lucky" members of the family will flower in time for the winter holidays.

Sfântul Ignat, Saint Ignacius.   *December* 19

On this day the family pig, which since the beginning of Advent has been pampered and fed with delicacies, is slaughtered for the Christmas holidays. Every household that can afford a pig prepares enough meat for its own use and to share with the poor and unfortunate.

Noaptea de Crăciun, Ajunul Crăciunului, Christmas Eve.
December 24

On the *Ajun*, or Eve of the twenty-fourth, the last of Advent, every household has a *turtă*, the symbolic cake made from countless layers of dry paper-thin dough, prepared with crushed walnuts, honey, melted sugar or sometimes with the juice of pounded hemp seed. According to tradition, the leaves of the *turtă* represent the Christ Child's swaddling clothes. In some places the making of the *turtă*—which always is prepared on December 23—is accompanied by a curious rite for causing fruit trees to bear. The housewife plunges her hands into the dough pan, then, with fingers covered with paste, she follows her husband to the orchard and stands before first one, then another of the fruit trees. The peasant carries an ax and threatens to cut down the trees because "they are useless and bear no fruit." The wife intervenes and pleads for each tree in turn. Surely, she declares, during the next summer the trees will bear as much fruit as the dough that sticks to her fingers! From dawn until night boys run about from house to house in the neighborhood shouting, "Good morning to Uncle Eve (*Moş Ajun*)," and singing *colinde,* or long recitations about Christmas, the sun, the moon and the stars, the master and mistress of the house and their various interests and foibles. The lads receive apples, dried fruits, cakes and coins in return for the greetings. On the morning of the twenty-fourth the village priest, accompanied by the sacristan and a lad carrying a kettle of holy water, makes the rounds of his parishioners' homes. The priest dips into the water with his *sfeştoc,* or bunch of sweet basil, sprinkles the house and blesses it. Then the housewife drops a coin into the kettle, gives the priest a present of hemp and invites him to sit down and partake of wine and Christmas fare.

CRĂCIUN, Christmas; NAŞTEREA DOMNULUI, Birth of the Lord.
December 25

From Christmas until New Year's Eve boys go about singing of the holy birth and carrying the *steaua,* a great wooden star, which is covered with decorated paper and hung with little tinkling bells. The star, illuminated from within by a candle, is decorated with a transparency of the Baby Jesus and the Magi Kings. The lads stop at each door, tinkle the bells on the star and chant carols of the Nativity. Throughout the Christmas season, dramatic performances of the story of Christ's birth are enacted in many towns and villages. In Valachia these presentations are known as *Vicleim;* in Moldavia and Transylvania, they are called *Irozi.* Usually the actors number ten or more persons, and include Herod, the Magi, a clown, a comical old man and other traditional characters. Popular plays, satirical in character, and various types of puppet shows also are shown from village to village at this time of year. The principal food at the Christmas dinner is roast pig. *Colaci,* or wheat loaves of varying sizes, are important in the holiday menu.

AJUNUL ANULUI NOU, New Year's Eve.   *December* 31

Boys and men make village rounds after dark and announce the New Year with ringing bells, cracking whips and the recital of innumei. ble verses about *Bădica Traian,* the Emperor Trajan, and the bull which pulls the plough across a meadow. This ancient custom, which is called *Pluguşcrul,* or "little plough," probably originated in the Roman *Opalia,* the festival for Ops, goddess of fertility. Formerly it waɔ customary for the singers to carry about a toy plough; nowadays the *buhai,* or "bull," takes the place of the plough. The bull is a crude sort of musical contrivance fashioned from a small wooden barrel, a piece of dried skin and a stout horsehair cord. By twanging the cord in a certain way the device emits a deep roaring noise which closely resembles the bellowing of an angry bull. As the *buhai* bellows, the boys recite traditional verses that tell how many oxen ploughed a field and got stuck in the furrow. On this Eve many miracles are thought to occur. The gates of Paradise are said to open, and a wish made at this lucky moment is certain to be fulfilled. Folk say that at midnight horses and cows have human speech, but since it is unlucky to eavesdrop, nobody ever hears what they have to say.

FESTIVALS OF THE RUSSIANS

I

NEPRERYVKA is the workers' holiday. *Nepreryvka,* meaning the discontinuation of the week days, is the name the Soviet government has bestowed on every sixth day in the week. It takes the place of the Sunday observed in Tzarist Russia. It is a protest against the holidays formerly observed by the Christian Church.

Things change overnight in the Soviet Union. After twenty years of anti-religious propaganda among adults and school children, the government is beginning to adopt a somewhat more neutral attitude toward religious belief and individual observance of church holidays. Many of the churches, formerly called anti-religious museums, now are known as Museums of the History of Religion. The churches that are kept open for worship are attended principally by the older generation.

Officially, the observance of all holy days has been abolished. Instead of the stately religious festivals of Christmas and Easter, which probably assumed greater dignity and magnificence in the Orthodox Church of pre-revolutionary Russia than of almost any other country, the outstanding days of the Communist calendar are the International Labor Days and the anniversary of the Bolshevik Revolution. Modern Communist

283

processions have supplanted the Orthodox processions of the Cross. Pictures of revolutionary heroes have been substituted for the jewel-encrusted ikons of former days. Red banners bearing such slogans as "Religion is opium for the people," and "Religion is incompatible with Socialism," now float aloft instead of richly embroidered religious standards of the Church. The singing of the *International* is substituted for the intoning of priests, and the shouts of workers for penitential prayers.

January 21, the anniversary of Lenin's death; May 1 and 2, International Labor Days; and November 7 and 8, the anniversary of the Bolshevik Revolution, are the only official holidays of the Soviet year. All other anniversaries are non-official in character and consequently are subject to change. The manner of celebrating the days, as described in the following list, is according to the year 1936.

GODOVSHCHINA SMERTI LENINA, Anniversary of Lenin's Death.[1]

January 21

In Moscow the day is observed by a great demonstration. A concert, beginning with a funeral march, is held in the theatre, which is decorated with red banners and appropriate mottoes. The *International* is sung and speeches made by prominent Party leaders. A film presents scenes from Lenin's life and works.

The same day also commemorates the Bloody Sunday of January 9, 1905.

MEZHDUNARODNYI ZHENSKI DEN', International Woman's Day.

On this anniversary, which was inaugurated in 1910, women of the Soviet Union receive honors for distinguished service in

[1] The holidays listed with dates are the only *official* holidays of the Soviet year. All other anniversaries are non-official and subject to change.

various fields of endeavor, for example, in industry, aviation, animal husbandry, agriculture or military service.

DEN' PARIZHSKOI KOMMUNY, Anniversary of the Paris Commune of 1871.

The anniversary of the first proletarian revolution is observed with speeches, parades and demonstrations among Communist groups the world over.

DEN' INTERNATZIONALA, International Labor Days.   *May 1, 2*

Portraits of the revolutionary heroes are carried in enormous parades. Masses of red streamers and banners are waved aloft. Each flag bears some popular Soviet slogan or announces a noteworthy achievement of a factory or institution. The forces of the international proletariat are inspected. Speeches, dancing, free food and drink mark these days as the great carnival season of the Communist year.

DEN' KONSTITUTZII, Constitution Day. *As a rule between the last week of June and the second week of July*

This day is celebrated by an annual physical culture parade. In 1936, for instance, athletes marched through Moscow's Red Square, carrying aloft models of light airplanes, swimming pools, boxing rings, ships, yachts and the like. In this way the young Soviet athletes demonstrated before the country's leaders their progress and achievements in the field of sports.

VSESOYUZNYI DEN' AVIATZII, Aviation Day.

The achievements of Soviet air pilots are honored on this day.

INTERNATZIONAL'NYI DEN' KOMSOMOLA, International Youth Day.

According to Krupskaya, Madam Lenin, the first Sunday of September was set aside to encourage the youth movement of the Soviet Union. Originally the day was one of protest against war. After 1921 it represented the struggle of youth for a united front. Now the day stands for the betterment of young people in education and work. The occasion is celebrated by speeches, parades and demonstrations.

GODOVSHCHINA SOYUZA KOMSOMOLA, Anniversary of the Establishment of the Union of Communist Youth.

Speeches and lectures remind the country's youth of the ideals and principles of the Communist Party.

DEN' OKTYABRSKOI PROLETARSKOI REVOLYUTZII, Anniversary of the Bolshevik Revolution.   *November 7, 8*

Amid the booming of cannon and the drone of circling airplanes, the new troops of the Red Army are drawn up in Moscow's Red Square to recite the oath of service. Huge parades, speeches and concerts celebrate the great anniversary of the Soviet government.

II

DAYS OBSERVED BY THE EASTERN ORTHODOX CHURCH

THE official holy days of the Eastern Orthodox Church are observed by members in all parts of the world. The festivals always are celebrated by special services in the churches and, in many instances, by religious rites and fasts on the part of the individual.

Festivals of the Russians

In the Russian Church, Easter is the holiday of holidays, the day above all other days. In addition to Easter, other great holidays are Epiphany, the Presentation of Christ in the Temple, Annunciation, Ascension, Holy Ghost Day, Transfiguration, Assumption of the Virgin, Birth of the Virgin, Elevation of the Cross, Presentation of the Virgin and Christmas. These twelve great days, which are marked red in the calendar, were school as well as church holidays in Tzarist Russia. The name-days of the Tzar and of the Empress also were celebrated as great festival occasions.

Many of the traditional folk customs surrounding Christmas, Epiphany and Easter—the three most sacred holidays of the Eastern Church—still are observed by Russians living in the United States and other countries. Oftentimes the original character of the practice has been forgotten or changed to meet the demands of a new environment. Whether this is the case or not, these festival survivals are a precious heritage from the Old Russia that has passed away.

In some parts of rural America, Russian and Ukrainian lads still carry abroad an illumined star on Christmas Eve. They sing tidings of peace and good will from door to door in the community, and receive in return small offerings of goodies or coins. In other places the priest leads his parishioners to the river on Epiphany Day to bless the ice-bound waters in strict accordance with ancient rites.

In many Russian homes in the United States the traditional Christmas and Easter foods are eaten. On Christmas Eve a meal of *koutia,* a dish of rice or wheat in honey, *ouzvaar,* a compote of dried fruits and nuts, candy, and *pryanik,* or gingerbread, are partaken of when the first star appears in the sky. During Butter Week, as the week preceding Lent is called, *bliny,* or raised rye-flour pancakes, are eaten with butter and

287

sour cream, and sometimes, also, with herring, caviar and other delicacies. At Eastertime a special cake called *koulich* is prepared, together with *paskha,* a potcheese dish, and the inevitable colored eggs, which recall the resurrection of Christ.

Wherever two or three Russians are gathered together one still finds the old festivals, old foods and old folk customs which, since time immemorial, have added charm and romance to the solemn festivals of the Eastern Orthodox Church.

DEN' SVYATOVO VASIL'YA, Saint Basil's Day; OBREZANIYE GOS-
PODNE, Day of the Circumcision; NOVYI GOD, New
Year's Day.   *January* 1 *O.S. (January* 14 *N.S.)*

This church holiday commemorates the death of Saint Vasily (Basil). In olden times people used to say that "Ilya comes on Vasily's Day," meaning that on the first of the year comes the sun god, the *Perun* of pagan times, later known as Elijah or Ilya. With the arrival of Ilya the peasants thought the corn began to grow.

SOCHEL'NIK, Epiphany Eve. *January* 5 *O.S. (January* 18 *N.S.)*

The Eve of Christ's baptism in the Jordan is observed by special services in the churches. Epiphany Eve is a time when Russian girls play all kinds of fortune-telling games. A shoe thrown outside the gate is thought to prophesy the direction from which a handsome husband will appear. A girl wishing to know the name of the man she will marry goes out at midnight and asks the first youth she meets, "What is your name?" Other means of looking into the future are by mirrors, wedding rings, egg yolks dropped into water, and many other devices familiar to young people of every land.

Festivals of the Russians

†Bogoyavleniye, Epiphany.[2]

January 6 O.S. (January 19 N.S.)

In pre-revolutionary Russia the Blessing of Waters was a ceremony of great pomp and splendor. A solemn procession led by church officials and priests went to the banks of streams or rivers. There the ice was broken, the crucifix lowered, and the waters blessed by the clergy. Men jumping into the icy waters to recover the cross were thought to receive special blessing. The Blessing of Waters continues among Russians in many parts of the United States. On January 6, water sanctified in the churches is carried home and placed near the ikons.

†Sreteniye Gospodne, Presentation of Christ in the Temple.

February 2 O.S. (February 15 N.S.)

The presentation of Christ in the Temple, forty days after his birth, is observed by special church services.

*Maslyanitza, Butter Week, Carnival.[3]

The week preceding Lent

The carnival season is termed "Butter Week" because of the many good things that are eaten before the seven-week Lenten fast begins. *Bliny,* the famous coarse flour pancakes that are served with butter and sour cream, fish, and all kinds of rich foods are enjoyed during this period. Fancy balls, parties, dances and weddings characterize the gayest season in the year. Peasants of pre-revolutionary Russia used to hold country fairs and indulge in all kinds of merrymaking during Butter Week.

---

[2] Days marked by a dagger (†) are the twelve great days of the Russian Church.

[3] Stars indicate movable feasts that depend on Easter. See table of Eastern Orthodox Easter dates and movable feasts on pages 370–371.

*NACHALO VELIKOVO POSTA, Beginning of Lent.

The first Sunday in Lent

At the Sunday morning church service priest and parishioners ask forgiveness for sins they may have committed during the past year. Sunday afternoon at four o'clock all festivities cease and Lenten services are held in the churches. The first, fourth and last weeks of Lent are most strictly observed. The first week marks the beginning of Lent. The fourth, which is called the Adoration of the Cross, commemorates Christ's crucifixion. During the last week, which is considered the holiest of all, operas, theatres and other places of amusement were closed in Tzarist Russia.

†BLAGOVESHCHENIYE PRESVYATOI BOGORODITZY, Annunciation of the Virgin. *March 25 O.S. (April 7 N.S.)*

This is such a great festival in the church calendar that peasants declare: "Even the birds do not nest on Annunciation." According to old Russian lore, the weather of this day foretells whether Easter will be rainy or fair.

*LAZAREVO VOSKRESENIYE, Lazarus Saturday.

The Saturday before Willow Sunday

The Saturday morning church service is devoted to the memory of Lazarus, whom Christ raised from the dead. At the evening service pussywillows are blessed. The blessed branches are distributed among the worshipers, who carry them home and place them above the ikons. These willows never are thrown out, but eventually are burned as sacred objects. According to ancient folk practice, people used to beat children with willow branches wishing them to be ". . . tall like the willow, healthy like water, and rich like the soil."

Festivals of the Russians

*VKHOD GOSPODEN' V YERUSALIM, Willow Sunday, Entrance of the Lord into Jerusalem.

The Sunday preceding Easter

Christ's triumphal entry into Jerusalem is observed with special services in the churches. The day is popularly called Willow Sunday because willows instead of palms are blessed in the churches.

*VELIKII CHETVERG, Great Thursday.

The Thursday preceding Easter

At the morning service the highest dignitary of the church performs the traditional ceremony of washing the feet of the priests. At the evening service, the twelve Gospel accounts of the crucifixion are read, as devout worshipers stand with burning candles. According to ancient custom, the tapers should be taken home lighted. Young girls make a wish as they carry their candles, for wishes with blessed candles surely come true! On the house door a cross is made with the candle, which later is placed near the ikon. In case of storm the blessed taper used to be lighted and carried around the house.

*VELIKAYA PYATNITZA, Great Friday.

The Friday preceding Easter

A representation of Christ's sepulchre is carried to the center of the church, where it is covered with flowers and kissed by the congregation. The church is draped in black, and priests wear black vestments for the burial service of Good Friday night.

*VELIKAYA SUBBOTA, Great Saturday.

The Saturday preceding Easter

At the impressive midnight service the resurrection is celebrated by clergy and congregation. Friends and relatives kiss
one another three times with the customary exchange of saluta-
tions, "Christ is risen" and "Indeed he is risen." Red eggs,
symbolic of the resurrection, are distributed among the worshipers. Food for the Easter table is blessed at the Great Saturday service. After the midnight service worshipers return to
their homes and feast, starting with the food previously blessed
in church. The meal lasts until early morning.

*†PASKHA, Easter.

Easter is the most joyous and impressive holiday of the
Russian year. On the holiday table are many traditional foods,
such as roast pig, turkey, sausages, sweet tarts and cakes and
paskha, a potcheese which is made in a wooden mold, garnished
with sweets and imprinted with a cross on the sides. Among the
most typical holiday cakes are *baba,* a large round cake, and
flat sweet cakes, not to mention *koulich,* the most sacred of all
Russian Easter sweets. *Koulich* is made according to traditional
formula. Pillows often are placed around the dough pan in
which the sponge is left to rise, for any jarring may cause the
koulich to fall. Men declare that they are forced to leave the
house on this day, because good housewives object to the coming
and going of heavy feet. *Koulich* is a tall cake, usually marked
with the initials X B, which stand for the Russian words,
"Christ is risen." On Easter Sunday and Monday the men
visit, but Easter Tuesday is reserved for the women to call on
their friends. In rural districts of pre-revolutionary Russia it
was customary for boys and girls to swing, dance, play games
and all kinds of musical instruments on these days. The church
bells did not cease ringing throughout this period.

Festivals of the Russians

DEN' GEORGIYA POBEDONOSTZA, Saint George's Day.
April 23 O.S. (May 6 N.S.)

This festival honors the patron of the Military Order of Saint George's Cross. The day is observed with special services in the churches and reunions of military officers and *Kavalier,* or recipients of the Saint George's decoration. Dinners and celebrations are held for military men of all ranks.

PERENESENIYE MOSHCHEI NIKOLAYA CHUDOTVORTZA, Saint Nicholas. *May 9 O.S. (May 22 N.S.)*

Saint Nicholas is the patron of Russia, of travelers and of young married couples. The day commemorates the moving of the saint's relics from Mir-Lickyi to Bargrad.

DEN' SVYATOVO KONSTANTINA I SVYATOI YELENY, Saints Constantine and Elena. *May 21 O.S. (June 3 N.S.)*

This day, in honor of Constantine the Great and his mother Elena, is observed by special church services.

*†VOZNESENIYE, Ascension. *The fortieth day after Easter*

The day that marks Christ's ascension to heaven is observed by special services in the churches.

*KANOON SVYATOYI TROITZY, Trinity Eve.
The Saturday preceding Trinity

In the United States the churches are decorated with flowers, greens and birch branches, just as they used to be in Old Russia. The floors are strewn with fragrant grasses.

*DEN' SVYATOI TROITZY, Trinity.

The fiftieth day after Easter

This was formerly the great spring festival of Russia. Homes and ikons are decorated with fresh birch branches, to symbolize the revival of nature. According to an old superstition, the person who brings no flowers to church on this day must shed as many tears for his sins as there are dewdrops on his birch twig.

*†SOSHESTVIYE SVYATOVO DUKHA, Holy Ghost Day.

The day after Trinity

This purely church holiday is observed with special services.

DEN' PETRA E PAVLA, Saints Peter and Paul.

June 29 O.S. (July 12 N.S.)

This church holiday which commemorates the martyrdom of the two great evangelists is also an important Russian name-day.

†PREOBRAZHENIYE GOSPODNE, Transfiguration.

August 6 O.S. (August 19 N.S.)

On this church day, honey, as well as pears, apples, plums and other fruits, is brought to the churches for divine blessing.

†USPENIYE PRESVYATOI BOGORODITZY, Assumption of the Virgin Mary. *August 15 O.S. (August 28 N.S.)*

This church holiday commemorates the taking of the Virgin to heaven.

Festivals of the Russians

USEKNOVENIYE GLAVY IOANNA ZLATOUSTA, Beheading of Saint John the Baptist.

August 29 *O.S.* (*September* 11 *N.S.*)

This anniversary of the martyrdom of Saint John is observed with special church services.

†ROZHDENIYE PRESVYATOI BOGORODITZY, Birth of the Virgin.

September 8 *O.S.* (*September* 27 *N.S.*)

This church holiday is observed with special services.

†VOZDVIZHENIYE, Elevation of the Cross.

September 14 *O.S.* (*September* 27 *N.S.*)

This feast honors the miraculous apparition of the cross which Constantine was said to have seen when preparing to fight Maxentius, in 312 A.D. The famous litany, "Lord have mercy," is chanted in the churches, as the priest lowers and raises the cross to symbolize the repeated elevation of the holy object after its discovery by Saint Elena.

POKROV PRESVYAOI BOGORODITZY, Intercession of the Holy Virgin. *October* 1 *O.S.* (*October* 14 *N.S.*)

This church holiday commemorates Saint Andrew's vision of the Holy Virgin in the tenth century. Saint Andrew beheld the Virgin with her veil spread protectingly over the Christians whom she prayed God to save. Early in the twelfth century the Russian Church established this anniversary as a festival.

NACHALO ROZHDESTVENSKOVO POSTA, Beginning of Christmas Lent. *November* 14 *O.S.* (*November* 27 *N.S.*)

The beginning of Advent, or the four-week period of preparation for Christmas.

†Vvedeniye vo Khram, Presentation of the Virgin.
November 21 O.S. (December 4 N.S.)

A church holiday honors the presentation of Mary in the Temple at three years of age.

Den' Svyatovo Nikolaya Chudotvortza, Saint Nicholas.
December 6 O.S. (December 19 N.S.)

This church anniversary celebrates the death-day of Saint Nicholas of Bari, patron of young couples.

Sochelnik, Christmas Eve.
December 24 O.S. (January 6 N.S.)

In some parts of rural Russia it was customary for peasants masquerading as cows, pigs, goats and other manger animals to go from house to house in the village singing *kolyady,* or songs of the shepherds and of Christ's miraculous birth. In return for their carols the mummers were given gifts of coins, eggs, chickens, sausages, nuts and sweets. Survivals of this custom are found in different parts of the United States. In some communities Russians still sing the first *kolyada* on Christmas Eve, receiving in return money for charitable purposes. After the evening church service, supper is served, the Christmas tree lighted and gifts exchanged.

†Rozhdestvo Khristovo, Christmas.
December 25 O.S. (January 7 N.S.)

The day usually is observed with family reunions and a holiday dinner at which roast goose is the *pièce de résistance.* Children's parties, masquerades and balls formerly made the Russian Christmas a brilliant social occasion.

FESTIVALS OF THE SPANIARDS

Año Nuevo, New Year. *January* 1

According to an old superstition, the luck of the entire year depends upon the first day. A gold coin in the pocket means plenty of gold during the next twelve months, while empty pockets foretell a lean year ahead. Eating a good meal and drinking good wine symbolize abundance of food and drink the whole year round. Meeting a beggar is considered bad luck, while coming face to face with a rich man is a propitious sign. After attending the New Year church services people go home to enjoy family reunions, feasting and holiday cheer.

Día de los Reyes Magos, The Day of the Kings, Epiphany.
January 6

Little children eagerly await the arrival of Epiphany Eve, when, they are told, the Three Kings—Gaspar, Melchor and Baltazar—travel through Spain with gifts of sweets and baubles for all good boys and girls. At night children stuff their shoes with straw and place them on the balconies. By morning the Magi's horses have eaten the straw. In its place the Kings leave toys, cookies and all kinds of sweetmeats. On Epiphany Eve parents often blacken sleeping children's cheeks with charcoal. The next day the boys and girls rush to the mirror to see if Baltazar, the black King, has kissed them in the night! In

Madrid groups of men and lads used to go out on Epiphany Eve "to meet the Kings." They carried a tall ladder and made a terrific din on horns, trumpets and drums. The men went about looking for some credulous person whom they could induce to join in the search for the Kings. When a victim was found he was given a bell-decked mule collar and ordered to take the ladder. From time to time his tormentors bade him mount the ladder and look about for the Magi. Often the rude jesters let the ladder fall at the risk of the poor simpleton's neck. This type of practical joking went so far that city authorities finally prohibited the practice of "meeting the Kings."

DÍA DE SAN ANTÓN, Day of Saint Anthony.   *January 17*

On the day of Saint Anthony, patron of horses, asses, mules and other four-footed beasts, people of Madrid deck their animals with flowers and ribbons and drive them to the church of San Antonio. The priest administers a barley wafer to the strange communicants, sprinkles them with consecrated water and blesses them against accident and disease throughout the coming year. All day the procession of animals goes through the city streets, and throngs of admiring bystanders watch the antics of mules, horses and oxen as they unwillingly march toward the sanctuary.

*CARNAVAL, Carnival.[1]
                    The three days preceding Ash Wednesday

The last three days of Carnival, which culminate the pre-Lenten period of merrymaking and amusement, are given over to feasting and mirth. Gambling, bull fights, weddings, masquerade parties and dances are celebrated in every town and vil-

[1] Stars indicate movable feasts that depend on Easter. See table of Easter dates and movable feasts on pages 357–358.

lage. In Madrid the *Prado* is a scene of picturesque revelry. Gay masqueraders, battles of flowers, showers of confetti and throngs of vendors crowd the driveway, which seems suddenly transformed into a gigantic fair.

*Miercoles de Cenizas, Entierro de la Sardina, Burial of the Sardine. *Ash Wednesday, the first day of Lent*

Ash Wednesday, the first day of Lent, is celebrated throughout Spain with the *Entierro de la Sardina,* the Burial of the Sardine, an ancient ceremonial symbolizing the burial of worldly joys during the Lenten fast. Gay Sevillians fashion a strip of pork in the semblance of a sardine. The sardine is interred with pomp and ceremony, as a reminder that abstinence from meat has begun and the eating of fish will continue for the next six weeks. In Madrid a sausage-link sometimes is substituted for the sardine. A great throng annually goes to the banks of the river Manzanares, where the sausage is buried. After this final pre-Lenten ceremony people go to Ash Wednesday church services, where their foreheads are marked with ashes to symbolize the beginning of the penitential fast.

San José, Saint Joseph. *March* 19

The feast of Saint Joseph is observed with great splendor in Valencia, where *fallas,* or picturesque bonfires, are the unique feature of the celebration. The festival, which is given under municipal auspices, is planned long in advance. *Fallas* artists, working in studios or lofts, fashion grotesque or satiric images of animals, houses, gods or human beings. These figures, set up throughout the city, are admired and enjoyed by vast crowds of merrymakers. A week or more of bull fights, parades, fireworks, music, dancing and eating makes Saint Joseph's feast a memorable occasion. Just at midnight torches are set to the sixty or more *fallas,* and all Valencia rejoices as the city bursts into a blaze of light.

*DOMINGO DE RAMOS, Palm Sunday.

The Sunday preceding Easter

Early in the morning people go to church to have palms and olive branches blessed by the archbishop. The consecrated branches are reverently carried home and fastened to the balconies as a protection against storm and lightning during the next twelve months. Palm Sunday is the occasion of many confirmations. Processions of little white-veiled maidens and small shy lads in fresh new suits fill all the streets, as children go to or from their first communion.

*JUEVES SANTO, Holy Thursday.

The Thursday preceding Easter

From Holy Thursday until Saturday church bells stop ringing and no vehicles are allowed to move through the principal streets of towns and cities. The gloom of Passion Week and the sufferings of Christ seem uppermost in the minds of the black-clad women and solemn-faced men who throng cathedrals and churches.

*VIERNES SANTO, Good Friday. *The Friday preceding Easter*

Spain is noted for its Good Friday religious processions, which are among the most impressive and elaborate in the world. Life-sized *pasos,* or sculptured images, represent different characters in the Passion story. These *pasos,* dressed in costly garments, are mounted on platforms that are carried in processions of various organizations or trade guilds. Many of the *pasos* are masterpieces, originating at the hands of famous fifteenth or sixteenth century wood carvers. The Last Supper, the agony in the garden, the crucifixion and other Passion scenes are represented with exquisite workmanship and realistic detail. On Good Friday the effigies, accompanied by cross-bearers, black-robed penitents with tall lighted tapers, civic authorities in uniform, clergy in magnificent robes and officials of every rank, are borne in solemn procession through the streets of Seville, Toledo and other important Spanish cities.

*SABADO DE GLORIA, Holy Saturday.

The Saturday preceding Easter

At the Holy Saturday church services the bells, which have not been rung since Holy Thursday, peal forth their resurrection message. The black veil shrouding the high altar suddenly is torn aside, revealing the altar in a blaze of light. In Seville the great Paschal Candle, which burns until Ascension Day, is blessed and lighted during the cathedral service.

*DOMINGO DE RESURECCION, PASCUA FLORIDA, DOMINGO DE GLORIA, Easter.

Easter, with its music and flowers, its gay sunshine and bright new clothes, is looked upon as the most joyful day in the Spanish calendar. After morning Mass and the exchange of Easter greetings people throng cafés and restaurants, to break the Lenten fast with rich food and native wine. In the afternoon, everybody in Madrid, Seville and other cities attends bull fights, where famous matadors exhibit their skill before thousands of frantically waving, excited spectators.

DOS DE MAYO, Second of May. *May 2*

The Second of May commemorates the anniversary of the

battle, in 1808, of Madrid (the *Prado*), where the Madrid citizens started the war of independence by revolting against the French general, Murat. Several hundred patriots were killed on this occasion. In the capital the anniversary is observed with great ceremony. Church bells toll. Houses and public buildings are hung with crape and garlands of cypress. In all the churches Mass is celebrated for the heroes of the revolution, while great military parades do honor to the memory of the dead.

SAN ISIDRO LABRADOR, Saint Isidore the Ploughman. *May* 15

The anniversary of *San Isidro,* the twelfth century patron of farmers and of Madrid, is celebrated with great ceremony in the Spanish capital. Flags, banners and rich tapestries adorn walls and balconies. Church bells peal forth joyously. A colorful procession of pilgrims moves toward San Isidro's Hermitage, which is built on the barren hill overlooking the Manzanares. The day is a great *fiesta* for all classes and ages. Streets and plazas are filled with vendors selling sweets and fruits, pictures of the saint and small pottery or glass pig-bells which when rung are thought to frighten off the evil effects of thunder and lightning. Typical of the Ploughman's *fête* are the little whistle-stemmed glass roses sold by every vendor. Throughout the day the tooting of the whistles furnishes a cheery accompaniment to the merriment that flourishes on all sides. Music, dancing, eating, *pelota* games and side-shows are enjoyed by the worshipers, who first pay homage to San Isidro's shrine. San Isidro is beloved by the peasantry, who invoke his aid in seasons of drought. According to legend, Isidro was a peasant like themselves. He labored for Don Juan de Vargas on a farm outside Madrid. Although the servant was devout and hardworking, jealous tongues made Don Juan suspect him of laxity in his work. One day the master spied upon his servant. To his astonishment, Vargas beheld an angel and a yoke of white oxen ploughing the field at Isidro's side. The vision finally convinced the master of his servant's faithfulness—for he knew Isidro was beloved of God.

*PENTECOSTES, DOMINGO DE PENTECOSTES, Pentecost.
The fiftieth day after Easter

At Roncevalles, in Navarre, an annual procession of black-clad penitents with crosses tied to their backs toils up the steep hillside to attend Mass at the Monastery of Roncevalles. According to tradition, this procession originated as an act of penance among twenty-three families that desired to atone for sins they had committed during the year. The penitents are garbed in black robes and hoods, with only slits for the eyes. Their arms are outstretched to support the heavy crosses. The penitents chant a solemn *Miserere* and make the weary ascent from the village to the monastery, which is situated about two miles up the hillside.

*CORPUS CRISTI, Corpus Christi.
The Thursday after Trinity Sunday

Throughout Spain, Corpus Christi is celebrated with magnificent pageantry and processions of the Host. In many towns and cities the streets are hidden with fragrant flowers and aromatic herbs. The priest, arrayed in costly red and gold robes, carries aloft the sacrament as he walks beneath a crimson silk canopy borne by four choristers. A procession of officials and clergy follows the priest, who often is preceded by the village band. Lighted tapers, incense, flowers and banners combine to make the Corpus Christi procession among the most beautiful religious festivals of the year.

LA NOCHE DE SAN JUAN, Saint John's Eve.   *June 23*

Throughout Spain, *hogueras,* or bonfires, are lighted in honor of *San Juan,* the saint of the summer solstice. On this night people walk through the dew or bathe in the sea, to make the skin lovely and the body healthy and strong. Young maidens resort to charms and omens, for Saint John is the friend of lovers. A favorite method of looking into the future is to place a bowl of water outside the window. An egg broken into the water just at the hour of midnight is thought to assume shapes significant in the young girl's destiny. On Saint John's Eve shops do a brisk business in heart-shaped cakes, to say nothing of the fruits and sweets which each gallant *caballero* purchases for his dark-eyed *dama.*

DÍA DE TODOS LOS SANTOS, All Saints' Day.   *November 1*

On this day Masses are said for the souls of the faithful departed, particularly those of the family dead. Cemeteries are visited and graves decorated with flowers and wreaths.

DÍA DE LOS DIFUNTOS, Day of the Dead, All Souls' Day.

November 2

This day, which is dedicated to the memory of souls in Purgatory, is celebrated with special prayers and Masses for the dead. Throughout Spain, all the theatres give performances of the famous drama *Don Juan Tenorio.*

NOCHE BUENA, Christmas Eve.   *December 24*

In almost every Spanish town and village the Christmas markets are special features of the holiday season. Throughout this day streets and plazas are lined with stalls heaped high with oranges, melons and lemons, flowers of all colors, children's toys, piles of *turron, mazapan* and other favorite Christmas sweets. The streets are flooded with laughter and music, with jostling good-natured men and gaily dressed peasant women; and everywhere dark-eyed, eager children run from booth to booth admiring, touching, exclaiming over the little nativity scenes which on *Noche Buena* hold place of honor in every Spanish home. Some of these scenes are made of cardboard, some of plaster. Sometimes the figures of Jesus and the Holy Family are so crude as to be well within the means of even the humblest purse. Often, however, they are elaborate in workmanship and costly in price. Toward evening crowds begin to thin out and housewives, with baskets overflowing with foodstuffs and toys, start homeward to prepare the evening meal. Usually the gatherings of *Noche Buena* are family affairs to which outsiders are not expected to come. As twelve o'clock strikes, the church bells peal forth and everybody goes to Midnight Mass.

"Esta noche es Noche-Buena,
Y no es noche de dormir,"

says an old Spanish verse, which means that this is the Good Night and therefore it is not meant for sleep.

NAVIDAD, Christmas Day.   *December* 25

Everybody attends church services, which are characterized by joyous Christmas music. On this day patrons receive calls or holiday reminders from washerwoman, postman, bootblack, baker's boy, garbage man and many others who have rendered services during the past year. All these public servants as well as family domestics are remembered with money presents. In some districts the priest and the doctor are given gifts at this season, while the well-to-do people always make a practice of sending food and luxuries to their less fortunate neighbors. After the Christmas luncheon the day is spent in merrymaking, strolling through streets and plazas, greeting friends. In Cadiz children observe the old rite of swinging at Christmastide. Swings are set up in the courtyards. Throughout the holidays and until Carnival, young people gather in the evenings and swing to the accompaniment of song and laughter. The custom of Christmas swinging probably originated in a very old magical rite, once intended to help the sun in its gradual upward course to the highest point in the summer sky.

Noche Vieja, New Year's Eve.   *December* 31

The *tertulia,* or New Year's Eve party, is a gay affair for young people, who have a unique way of "matching partners" for the coming year. The names of the men and women guests are written separately on slips of paper, which are numbered in pairs and then drawn by lot. The man and woman who draw the same number become partners, not only for the evening but for the entire year. Custom demands that the young man send his *novia* flowers or sweets on the day following the party and that he be her escort at the social functions of the next twelve months. On this night it is also customary for the *madrileños,* the people of Madrid, to go to the *Puerta del Sol* in front of the Department of the Interior building. When the clock on top of the building strikes twelve, they swallow twelve grapes, one with each stroke of the hour.

FESTIVALS OF THE SWEDES

NYÅRSDAGEN, New Year's Day.   *January* 1

Everyone attends morning church services, after which the
day is spent quietly at home. The New Year's dinner is a dupli-
cate of the Christmas feast, which always includes *smörgåsbord,* or a magnificent array of appetizers; *lutfisk,* an especially
prepared stockfish, usually served with a light cream sauce and
boiled potatoes; the holiday ham; *risgrynsgröt,* or rice pudding
dessert, which contains a "lucky" almond; various kinds of
wine, and claret sweetened with sugar and flavored with almonds, raisins, dried orange peel, cinnamon, cloves and carda-
mon. The *glögg,* as this drink is called, is set aflame before
serving.

TRETTONDEDAG JUL, Holy Kings' Day, Epiphany.   *January* 6

This church holiday which commemorates the Magi's finding of Jesus in the manger was celebrated during the Middle
Ages with ecclesiastical folk plays. Today it is customary for
Stjärngossar, or Star Boys, to present an annual pageant which
dramatizes the march of the Holy Kings from the East. The
lads wear white garments and white cone-shaped caps that are
adorned with pompons and symbols of the moon and stars. They
carry white paper stars attached to long poles. The stars are
illumined from within by lighted candles. Judas is a tradi-

307

tional character who often accompanies the *Stjärngossar*. He wears a huge false nose and carries a money-bag jingling with the thirty pieces of silver.

TJUGONDAG KNUT, Saint Knut's Day.   *January* 13

On Saint Knut's Day, the twentieth day after Christmas, Yuletide comes to an official close. The day is celebrated with a dance and the dismantling of the Christmas tree, which is lighted for the last time. In some parts of the country the young people dance around the Yule table while the old folk sing:

> *"Twentieth day Knut*
> *Driveth Yule out."*

According to some authorities the name of Saint Knut's Day is derived from Canute the Great's laws, written between 1017 and 1036, which commanded that there should be no fasting between Christmas and the Epiphany Octave.

*FASTLAGEN, Lenten Period.[1]   *The forty-day fast (excluding*
                                 Sundays) that precedes Easter

During this period every Swedish home is decorated with bunches of fine birch switches trimmed with colored chicken or rooster feathers—red, pink, blue, green—and little printed verses. The birch twigs are picked in bud at the beginning of Lent and placed in water. As the weeks advance, the leaves gradually come out. Originally people used these branches for beating one another, as a sort of spring purification rite, but today they serve purely decorative purposes. *Fastlagsbullar* or *Fettisdagsbullar* (Fat Tuesday buns), special buns made with wheat flour and served with hot milk, cream and little chunks of

[1] Stars indicate movable feasts that depend on Easter. See table of Easter dates and movable feasts on pages 357–358.

marzipan, are one of the few luxuries eaten during the abstemious Lenten period.

MARIE BEBÅDELSEDAG, Annunciation.   *March* 25

This is a church holiday observed with religious services. In olden times Värmland peasants used to practice many quaint customs on Annunciation Eve, which was significant in popular weather lore. People honored the sun by eating supper before sunset and retiring without aid of artificial light. As the cranes arrive in Sweden at about this time, parents always told the children that the birds would come into the houses with lights, to make sure that everyone was in bed.

*LANGFREDAGEN, Good Friday. *The Friday preceding Easter*

The day is observed with special church services in commemoration of Christ's Passion and crucifixion. In Stockholm the theatres are closed and great oratorios are sung in the Royal Opera House.

*PÅSKDAGEN, Easter.

Throughout the country, people color eggs for Easter and decorate them with flowers or amusing rhymes. Since skiing and other winter sports are at their height in Dalarne and many of the northern provinces at this season, people from Stockholm and other cities of the south often spend the Easter holidays in the country.

*ANNANDAG PÅSK, Second Day of Easter.
The Monday after Easter

This day sees the continuation of the Easter sports and festivities.

VALBORGSMÄSSOAFTON, Walpurgis Night. *April* 30

This festival has survived from Viking days, when warriors of old celebrated an annual feast in honor of returning spring. Bonfires lighted on the mountain tops were thought to frighten away demons of darkness and gloom. Today the festival is observed throughout the land by lighting fires on hills and mountain tops, as symbols of welcome to the lengthening days. On this night students of Upsala University don their white velvet caps for the first time, pin sprays of spring flowers in their lapels and march from their fraternities and club houses, singing traditional Swedish spring songs. The bonfires that blaze from every height flare dramatically against the dusky horizon. Many Stockholm folk celebrate the festival at Skansen, the city's open-air museum and animal park, where a tremendous bonfire of logs and tar-barrels blazes from the heights of the Reindeer Mountain.

FÖRSTA MAJ, First of May. *May* 1

The festivities of *Valborgsmässoafton* continue. The day is also observed, as in all parts of Europe, with parades of labor organizations, political speeches and public demonstrations.

*KRISTI HIMMELFÄRDSDAG, Ascension Day.
The fortieth day after Easter

This religious holiday is celebrated by special services in the churches. Many old peasant superstitions exist in regard to this day. One saying is that if a person fishes from dawn until night on Ascension Day he will learn the hour when fish bite best, and be lucky in his angling the whole year through. Another saying is that "the dragon who guards hidden treasures throughout the night, exposes them to view on Ascension, when he sets them out to air."

Festivals of the Swedes

*Pingst, Pentecost, Whitsunday.

The fiftieth day after Easter

This two-day religious holiday is widely observed with excursions to the country, picnics and visits to rural estates. City as well as country folk decorate their houses with branches of green, in welcome to the returning spring. Even Stockholm's old brewer horses share in the holiday, as their collars and wagon shafts are adorned with greens.

Flaggans Dag, Flag Day.   *June 6*

Flag Day, the nameday of His Majesty King Gustaf V, is celebrated throughout Sweden with patriotic meets, parades and the raising of flags over castles and huts. In Stockholm the celebration centers at the Stadium. The Swedish national anthem is sung by a chorus of several thousand voices. Then King Gustaf awards the national flags to various schools, sport clubs and organizations. In the evening the festival continues at Skansen.

Midsommar, Midsummer.   *June 23*

Every town and village throughout the country erects on the village green a *majstång*, or Maypole, which is decorated with garlands, green leaves and fluttering flags. Old and young dance about the Maypole the whole night through, to the witching music of fiddle and fife. Since pagan times *Midsommar* has been the night of rejoicing and merrymaking over the return of summer. Nobody thinks of going to bed. Sometimes dancing is held in the village barns, rather than out of doors. In some places, as in Rättvik, on Lake Siljan, the dancers hold their festivities on the pier of the bridge. Often somebody tumbles into the water when merrymaking and excitement reach a boisterous climax.

The Book of Festivals

GUSTAF ADOLFSDAGEN, Gustavus Adolphus Day. *November 6*

This day is the anniversary of the Battle of Lützen, in 1632, when Wallenstein was defeated and Gustavus Adolphus killed. Throughout the country the holiday is marked by patriotic demonstrations. In Skansen the occasion is observed with special ceremony. Enormous bonfires are built on Reindeer Mountain. Processions of students carrying lighted torches march through the museum grounds. An honor guard, garbed in the uniforms of the Thirty Years' War, surrounds the bust of Gustavus Adolphus and renders tribute to Sweden's great leader.

MÅRTEN GÅS, Martin's Goose Day. *November 11*

From Skåne, the province famous for geese, comes the old-time custom of feasting on goose. The typical foods which are eaten at the great family *Mårten Gås* parties are roast goose, luscious with stuffings of apples and prunes, sauerkraut and green cabbage. Blood soup also is highly esteemed. This concoction is made from the wings and blood as well as the neck, heart and liver of the goose. Additional ingredients are dried apples and prunes and flavoring of ginger, pepper, vinegar, sugar and wine.

LUCIADAGEN, Saint Lucia's Day. *December 13*

The Swedish Yuletide is opened officially by the "Lucia Bride," who usually is represented by some young feminine member of the household. According to ancient Catholic tradition, Lucia was a medieval saint who went about carrying food and drink to the hungry folk of her district. Saint Lucia is the embodiment of the Christmas spirit, in her white dress, crimson sash and traditional *lingon*-leaf crown, adorned with lighted candles. She wakens each member of the household

312

early and leaves steaming coffee, newly baked bread and buns at the bedside. Sometimes Lucia is accompanied by baker lads. These boys carry *Lussikattor,* or Lucia cats—cat-shaped saffron buns with raisin eyes. Many folk beliefs exist in connection with Saint Lucia's day, which is the harbinger of Yule. The year's threshing, spinning and weaving must be finished and everything put in order for the Christmas holidays. According to an old proverb, if one celebrates with due lavishness prosperity will continue throughout the next twelve months.

JULAFTON, Christmas Eve.   *December* 24

On Christmas Eve the ancient rite of *doppa i grytan,* "dipping bread in the pot," is celebrated in the kitchen of many Swedish homes. The room is festive with paper garlands and lighted candles. The freshly scrubbed floor is strewn either with straw—in memory of the manger birth—or with fragrant juniper twigs. As family, guests and household servants assemble, each person sticks a piece of *wort* bread on a fork and dips it into the kettle of pork and sausage drippings. According to old tradition, this bread is eaten "for luck," before the feast begins, by master and mistress and each member of the household. Then toasts are drunk from *glögg,* the concoction of wine, rum, spices and herbs, which is lighted and poured over lumps of sugar. After laughter and jests and the exchange of wishes for a *God Jul,* the company sits down in the dining room to a dinner consisting of an elaborate array of *smörgåsbord; lutfisk* served with boiled potatoes or with green peas and drawn butter; and *potatiskorf,* a kind of sausage made with potato, pork, beef and herbs and packed into casings. The Christmas ham, roast goose and prunes, *lingon* berries stewed in sugar, and last but not least the *gröt,* or rich rice porridge, all are important features of the holiday feast. The *gröt* is cooked with milk and sugar and decorated on top with intricate designs in cinnamon.

An almond hidden within foretells who will marry first during the coming year. Each guest makes a jingle before he can take his portion of *gröt*. After the holiday meal the doors are opened and the Christmas tree, lighted with many candles, is revealed in its full glory. The head of the family reads the nativity story. Then everyone joins in singing the well-loved Christmas carols. The *Julbock,* or Yule goat, Sweden's gift-bearer, throws presents through the door. Much merriment prevails over opening the gifts, which always are wrapped in white paper, sealed with red wax, and accompanied with amusing rhymes.

JULDAGEN, Christmas.   *December* 25

No matter how late the Christmas Eve revels continue, everyone is up betimes to attend *Julotta,* the early holiday Mass. In country districts lighted candles placed in farmhouse windows shine across the path of the prancing horses as they carry sleigh loads of worshipers across the frosted earth. Each sleigh is lighted by a torch. When people arrive at the churchyard they throw their torches into a great bonfire. The church is lighted with hundreds of candles and many voices sing the nativity hymns. Christmas, which is regarded as a holy day, is spent quietly in the homes.

ANNANDAG JUL, Second Day after Christmas.   *December* 26

The second, like the first day after Christmas, is spent rather quietly. Church services are attended. From *Annandag Jul* to *Tjugondag Knut* dancing and all kinds of festivities are held from house to house in the neighborhood. Quantities of rich holiday foods are consumed and all kinds of merrymaking indulged in by young and old.

FESTIVALS OF THE SWISS

SWITZERLAND is a country of fête days and festivals. Yet with the exception of August first, the Anniversary of the Founding of the Swiss Confederation, which is the country's one nationally celebrated day, all other holidays are purely local in character. Just as each canton has its own beautiful traditional costumes that have descended from father to son and from mother to daughter for many generations, so each canton possesses its own local feast days and festivals.

When one realizes that the Confederation of Switzerland consists of twenty cantons and three half-cantons—namely, Appenzell (including Inner Rhoden and Ausser Rhoden), Basle (including Basle Stadt and Basle Land) and Unterwalden (including Obwalden and Nidwalden)—and that each canton is really a small sovereign state, one does not wonder that two cantons rarely celebrate the same festival in the same manner or on the same date.

Religion plays an added part in creating festival differences. Central Switzerland, consisting of the cantons of Zug, Schwyz and Unterwalden, is strictly Roman Catholic. Eastern Switzerland follows the teachings of Zwingli, and Western Switzerland those of Calvin. Consequently, even such a widely recognized church holiday as Good Friday is likely to be observed in one part of the country but not in another.

In the holiday list that follows, an effort has been made to indicate, whenever possible, the particular locality to which festivi-

ties belong, and to show that other celebrations may be known
only to given communities.

Neujahrstag, New Year's Day. *January* 1

Amateur dramatic performances, visiting among friends
and general merrymaking characterize the first day of the New
Year, which generally is observed as a quiet holiday. Housewives vie with one another in making a special New Year's
bread rich with milk, butter, eggs and raisins. January first is
significant in peasant weather lore, as a red sky predicts storms,
fire and war. In some parts of the country peasants declare that
meeting a woman the first thing on New Year's Day is certain
to bring ill luck, although encounters with men or children are
looked upon as good omens.

Berchtolds Tag, Berchtold's Day. *January* 2

In many parts of Switzerland the second day of January
is devoted to gay neighborhood parties. Early in the fall the
children begin to hoard supplies of nuts for Berchtold's Day,
when they indulge in "nut feasts." Singing, yodeling and
other kinds of wholesome entertainment are features of the
Berchtold parties.

*Fastnacht, Carnival.[1] *Sometime before Lent*

This day, which varies from canton to canton, brings to a
close the pre-Lenten festivities. Parties, balls, dances and
parades and all kinds of merrymaking are featured during the
weeks preceding *Fastnacht*. Parades of adults and children are
features of the day's celebration, especially in Basle. In some

---

[1] Stars indicate movable feasts that depend on Easter. See table of Easter
dates and movable feasts on pages 357–358.

parts of Switzerland processions of fantastically-garbed children, singing and carrying the national flag, go through the streets of towns and villages. Boys often masquerade in costumes suggesting their fathers' professions, while girls dress as fairies. A fine *Fastnacht* cake abundantly flavored with caraway seeds is the crowning delight of the children's party. Bonfires, dancing and general gaiety end the carnival season.

*Ostern, Easter.

After attending the morning church service, which features magnificent Easter music, the day is spent in merrymaking and festivity. Games with gaily decorated Easter eggs are important to the young people, especially those living in towns and smaller villages. Parents often hide colored eggs under the trees and then call the children to "see what the Easter bunny has left for them." Boys love to match eggs with their friends, as the one who smashes the most eggs reaps the largest reward. In some parts of the country there is a lively egg competition in which one group throws a certain number of eggs into a flat basket while another covers a given distance on foot or horseback. Children get presents of chocolate bunnies and confection eggs on this day. In many sections of Switzerland the holidays continue through Easter Monday.

Sechseläuten, Six o'Clock Ringing Feast. *Sometime in April*

This is a picturesque festival celebrated annually in Zurich in honor of the passing of winter and the arrival of spring. Winter, represented by *Bögg,* a huge wooden effigy covered with white cotton wool and stuffed with firecrackers and gunpowder, is formally "executed" at six o'clock, when the ringing of bells announces the close of the working day. In the early forenoon a procession of school children escorts through the streets a triumphal float representing Spring and her attendant maidens. Following Spring comes *Bögg* accompanied by jeering clowns. The procession winds along the banks of the river Limmat to the head of the lake, where *Bögg* is left in the square to await his fate. Meanwhile members of various town guilds parade through the streets in historic costume, while the boys and girls who accompany Spring are given a colorful ball in *Tonhalle*. At six o'clock everybody gathers in the square to witness the burning of *Bögg*. Bonfires are lighted on the surrounding mountain as the people rejoice in winter's annual defeat.

NAEFELSERFAHRT, Pilgrimage to Näfels.

The first Thursday in April

An annual pilgrimage is made to Näfels, in the canton of Glarus, in memory of the victory of 600 Glarus men, April 9, 1388, over 6,000 Austrian soldiers. A procession visits each of the eleven memorial stones marking the eleven unsuccessful attacks of the Austrians. After reading the historical account of the battle, a hymn is sung and special High Mass celebrated.

MAITAG VORABEND, May Day Eve.   *April* 30

The ancient custom of planting the *Maitannli,* the May pine tree, on May Day Eve still is celebrated in certain villages of the Seeland and Burgdorf regions, in the canton of Berne. Village lads steal into the forest on this night and cut down small pine trees which they deck with flowers and ribbons and plant before the homes of the girls they love. Usually the pine tree is set before the sweetheart's bedchamber window. Sometimes it is placed in front of the gate, and occasionally on the roof. The bearer of the symbolic tree usually is welcomed and entertained by the girl and her family. If a girl is haughty and unpopular among the village boys she is likely to receive a grotesque straw puppet in place of the traditional *Maitannli.*

*Ausflug Nach Tellskapelle, Pilgrimage to William Tell's Chapel. *The Friday after Ascension*

Every year the people of Uri make pilgrimage to William Tell's rustic shrine at Tellsplatte, on the southern shore of Lake Lucerne. Mass is celebrated and a sermon delivered in honor of the archer of Altdorf, who, according to tradition, killed Gessler, the mythical Austrian bailiff, and incited the Forest cantons to independence.

Mitsommer Fest, Midsummer. *June* 24

On this festival the peasants of some parts of Switzerland visit the high mountain pastures where their goats and cows have grazed since the opening of the season. Family parties ascend steep mountain paths and gather at the shepherds' chalets, where they enjoy such pastoral foods as cheese, butter, cream and milk. A special kind of bread which consists of sweetened dough mixed with butter and aniseed and baked in fancy shapes, is the only food the peasants bring with them. The day is spent in dancing, singing, playing games and gathering mountain flowers. Finally the animals are herded and driven down the mountain paths, to the accompaniment of tinkling cowbells and the songs and cries of shepherds.

Sempachfeier, Anniversary of the Battle of Sempach (observed in the canton of Lucerne). *July* 9

A procession composed of government officials, students, clergy and citizens of Sempach makes annual pilgrimage to the battlefield that marks the defeat of the Austrians on July 9,

1386. The ancient battlefield chapel is visited, documents relative to the victory are read and religious services celebrated. At the conclusion of the exercises the people return to Sempach, where the holiday is observed further with banquets, speeches and special music.

SANKT PLACIDUSFEST, Saint Placidus Festival.   *July* 11

Since the eighth century this annual religious fête has been observed at the Abbey of Disentis, in the Grisons Oberland, in commemoration of the abbey's founding in 614 A.D. by Saints Sigisbert and Placidus. The anniversary marks the beheading of Saint Placidus near the abbey. Each year the relics of the two saints are carried in solemn procession from the abbey to the village church, and back through the village to the abbey.

UNABHÄNGIGKEITSTAG, Independence Day.   *August* 1

The anniversary of the founding of the perpetual league of the communities of Uri, Schwyz and Unterwalden on August 1, 1291—the beginning of the Swiss confederation—is celebrated each year throughout Switzerland by the pealing of bells, displays of fireworks and the lighting of bonfires on hills and mountains. Flags and banners fly from every house, gay processions march through the streets, and choral societies meet to sing folk songs and ancient ballads. The lighting of bonfires on important holidays is an old Swiss custom, passed down from medieval days when fires built on the mountains were used to flash from village to village the news of some great victory.

SCHÄFER SONNTAG, Shepherd Sunday.
The second Sunday in September

In the Valais this festival celebrates the return of the sheep from summer pasture in the Alpine region above Brigue. As the sun rises on the Alpine plateau of Belalp, sheep owners and peasants gather to attend open-air Mass and pray for the safe return of flocks. The shepherds, meanwhile, have assembled their animals on the mountain and started them down toward the plateau. The villagers anxiously watch for the appearance of the beasts. As they descend the mountain everyone lends a hand in penning the sheep in a great overnight enclosure. A hearty "Sheep Dinner" brings the day to a fitting close. The day following, owners sort their sheep, wash them in the lake and prepare for the task of shearing.

AUSSCHIESSET, Shooting Festival.   *Sometime in October*

This festival is celebrated annually at Thun, in the Bernese Oberland. A picturesque shooting contest is participated in by men and youths in medieval dress, who shoot at a target representing Gessler, the hated Austrian oppressor. According to legend, William Tell shot Gessler in the narrow pass near Küssnacht. Today Swiss archers vie with one another in trying to pierce Gessler's heart. A man dressed as William Tell removes the arrows as they are shot into the effigy. Drummers announce each successful shot. The victor is rewarded with loud drumming, a handsome prize and the privilege of carrying Gessler's riddled picture through the streets of the town. An amusing feature of the day's celebration is the jester, called *Fulu Hund,* who wears the grotesque masque that men of Thun brought back from the battle of Morat, June 22, 1476. The *Fulu Hund* delights in chasing small boys and girls and in performing wild antics in the streets. When the festival is over, the masque of *Fulu Hund* is returned to its place of honor in the local museum.

SAMICHLAUS, Saint Nicholas.   *December 6*

In some sections of Switzerland Christmas begins on December 6, when Saint Nicholas, armed with a pack of cookies, prunes and red-cheeked apples, parades through the streets and rewards obedient children with his coveted gifts. At this season many towns and villages hold peasant fairs where gifts and sweets and cunningly constructed toys are exhibited before the eyes of eager youngsters and indulgent parents. Saint Nicholas Day often is regarded as the time when rents, mortgages and other obligations must be met.

Heiliger Abend, Christmas Eve.   *December* 24

In some parts of Switzerland, *Christkindli,* or the Christ Child, the gift-bearer of Swiss children, is said to make village rounds on Christmas Eve, in a sleigh drawn by six fine reindeer. *Christkindli* carries a load of toys and gifts, to say nothing of glittering trees that are well laden with oranges and apples, nuts and cookies baked in many fantastic shapes. The family gathers about the Christmas tree to sing carols and listen to the reading of the nativity story. Then the presents are distributed and everyone makes merry until it is time for Midnight Mass. In some parts of the country superstitions exist regarding the miracles of Christmas Eve. It is said that young people wishing to foretell future events should drink from nine different fountains while the midnight church bells are ringing. Then they hasten to church, where they will behold their future mates standing on the steps! Dumb animals are thought to be blessed with human speech at the midnight hours; housewives clip their chickens' wings between eleven and twelve at night, so their fowls may be saved from beasts of prey; and old folk predict the weather for the coming year by means of onion peelings filled with salt. In some villages it is customary for boys and girls to go after dark from house to house. The children tinkle cowbells, yodel and sing. The householders reward them with gifts of apples, nuts and other goodies.

Festivals of the Swiss

WEIHNACHTEN, Christmas. *December 25*

Christmas marks the beginning of the winter sports, such as skiing, sledding and tobogganing. Between Christmas and New Year's Day people visit friends and relatives. Outdoor sports, *Jass* or other card parties, and afternoon coffee gatherings make the last week of the year a gala occasion for both young and old.

SYLVESTER, Saint Sylvester's Day. *December 31*

People say that whoever gets up last in the morning will be Sylvester in the home, and whoever reaches school last will be Sylvester at school. These sluggards are greeted, both at home and school, with deafening shouts of "Sylvester!" Bonfires burn on the mountains and church bells ring out joyous harmonies in honor of the passing of the old year and the beginning of the new. In some villages youths thresh grain on especially constructed platforms, as this rite is supposed to insure a plentiful harvest in the coming year. Carolers often go from house to house in the village, singing and offering New Year wishes.

FESTIVALS OF THE SYRIANS

SYRIA is a country in which many races and divergent faiths are represented. The majority of the population is Mohammedan. To this group belong various races and religious sects, such as the Kurds, Bedouins, the Ismailites (including the Druses, the Ansariah and many other divisions). The Jews are found extensively in larger towns and cities. The Christians represent probably a fifth or more of the country's population. The greatest number of Christians belong to the Greek Orthodox Church, which has patriarchal seats both in Jerusalem and in Antioch. Catholics, mostly Melkites or Uniate Greeks, United Syrians and Maronites, are numerous in Syria. Various Protestant sects also are represented.

These marked divergencies in religious belief mean that Syria is blessed with more than the usual number of holidays and saints' days. Since for centuries the Greek Orthodox Church has been recognized more or less as the country's national Christian Church, the holidays of this body have been mainly selected as representing the real folk festivities of the Syrian people. This choice has been further strengthened by the fact that the Greek Catholics observe practically the same folk traditions and festivals as those of their Greek Orthodox neighbors. The Maronites, on the other hand, are concentrated chiefly in the Lebanon district, and consequently their holiday customs are not typical of the country at large.

The festivals of the Jews and the Mohammedans are given

elsewhere.[1] It is interesting to note, however, that in many instances both Christians and Mohammedans observe the same holidays and venerate the same saints, under different names, each group in its own way and according to its own religious traditions. Probably the Mohammedans took these early festivals with them from Christian times before they were converted to the faith of Islam. One of the most striking examples of this overlapping of religious festivals is observable in the veneration of Saint George. Saint George, the most famous of Christian saints, whose day falls on April 23 in the Old Style calendar and May 6 in the New, is known as *al-Khidr* among the various sects of Islam. Saint George has numerous shrines throughout Syria. One of the most important is in the monastery at Humeira, between Homs and Tripoli, where both Christians and Moslems make annual pilgrimages and perform sacred vows before the same saint. In olden days *al-Khidr* was identified in Moslem belief with the prophet Elijah. Now the worship of Elijah has been transferred to Saint George, with perhaps the one exception of his veneration at the Haifa shrine at the foot of Mount Carmel.

The celebration of Epiphany Eve, known as *Lailat-al-Qadr* to Islam, furnishes another example of a festival that holds special significance for both Christians and Moslems. According to the Greek Orthodox Church this day marks the anniversary of Christ's baptism, or the "appearance" of the Holy Spirit and its descent upon Christ. To the Mohammedans it signifies the night when the Koran descended to Mohammed from heaven. A series of folk practices and beliefs has grown up about this night, when people think the gates of heaven are open and three wishes made at the proper moment are sure to be fulfilled! In the same way the Christians have their folk beliefs connected with Epiphany. Thus both groups observe the same occasion

[1] See pages 202–209 and 236–239.

but in a totally different manner. And this is the way in which folk festivals have grown since the beginning of time.

‘Īd al-Khitān, Day of the Circumcision; ‘Īd Ras al-Sanah, New Year's Day. *January 1 O.S. (January 14 N.S.)*

Presents and good wishes are exchanged among relatives and friends. Bands of children go from door to door offering New Year greetings. In return they receive gifts of coins and money. On this day men call in groups from house to house and are served with sweets and coffee. The day following, the women visit their friends and neighbors.

Lailat-al-Qadr, Epiphany Eve.
January 5 O.S. (January 18 N.S.)

This Eve is considered by the Latin Church as the time when the Magi presented gifts to the Infant Christ; by the Greek as the anniversary of his baptism. Bottles of water are brought to the church for consecration. After this sanctification of the water the priest visits his parishioners' homes and blesses them, sprinkling holy water in each room and on the house inmates. In the interior of Syria, children visit the banks of streams and rivers. There they fashion little syringes, made from reeds and manipulated with a stick, to which a bit of cloth is tied. The children chase one another, squirting water as they run. According to ancient folk belief, this is the wonder night of the year. The trees are said to bow at midnight in honor of Jesus. Housewives prepare dough, hide a silver coin within it, wrap it in a cloth and hang it from a branch. At midnight the dough is believed to become leaven. This lump of risen dough is kept as yeast throughout the year. To the very holy, special blessings are thought to occur, such as the traditional "miracle of increase," when, so people say, a housewife finds that her dough has doubled in quantity, or her half-empty jars again are full of wine. *Lailat-al-Qadr* is honored no less by Mohammedans than Christians, for according to Moslem belief this was the night when the Angel Gabriel brought down the Koran to Mohammed from heaven. An old tradition says that the gates of Paradise open on this night and three wishes, made at just the right moment, are sure to be fulfilled. For this reason Mohammedans always visit the housetops during the month of *Ramadan* to make petitions and offer prayers. It is said also in Moslem tradition that the exact "Night of Fate" is not known to mortals, but that it falls on one of the nights of *Ramadan*. On that night praises of the Prophet are chanted antiphonally from one minaret to another. This beautiful old custom is called *Tarawih Ramadan,* or "bidding farewell to *Ramadan*."

'ĪD AL-GHITĀS, Epiphany. *January 6 O.S. (January 19 N.S.)*

Special church services commemorate Christ's baptism in the Jordan.

DUKHUL AL-SAYYID ILA-L-HAYKAL, Entrance of the Lord into the Temple. *February 2 O.S. (February 15 N.S.)*

The fortieth day after Christ's birth, when he was presented in the Temple and the Virgin was purified, is observed by special church services.

'ĪD MAR YOUHANNA MARŪN, Saint John Maron. *February 9*

The birthday of the fourth century saint who founded the Maronite Order is a legal holiday in Mount Lebanon. In the United States, if the day falls within the week it is generally celebrated on the Sunday following. The anniversary is observed with Masses in the churches, with banquets and with meetings of religious societies.

*AL-MARFA', Carnival.[2]   *The week preceding Lent*

Carnival represents the Syrian Thanksgiving, as well as the season of merrymaking and rejoicing that precedes the strict self-denial of Lent. Beginning with Sunday, when friends and relatives exchange calls, the people feast, drink wine and enjoy the fruits of their labors in field and orchard.

*KHAMIS AL-MARFA', Carnival Thursday.
The Thursday of the week preceding Lent

This day is known popularly as "Drunkard's Thursday," because the festivities of eating and drinking reach their height at this time. The family sheep is slaughtered. After the work is finished a great fire is built and a plentiful feast prepared. The chief delicacies of the meal are rice with lamb, stuffed grape leaves, squash, figs stewed with molasses and pine seeds, dried raisins and other fruits. After the feast all dance and sing to the accompaniment of reed pipe and tambourine.

*AWWAL AL-SAUM AL-KABĪR, Beginning of Lent.
The first Sunday in Lent

Sunday night at midnight festivities cease and the Lenten fast begins.

'ID AL-ARBA'IN SHAHID, Forty Martyrs.   *March 9*

According to legend, forty believers, condemned to be

[2] Stars indicate movable feasts that depend on Easter. See table of Eastern Orthodox Easter dates and movable feasts on pages 370–371. Jewish and Mohammedan groups observe the festivals described on pages 202–209 and 236–239.

drowned for their faith, were led by heathen soldiers to the river. There the Christians miraculously received crowns. of glory as they cast themselves into the stream. One man drew back, however, and his guard, suddenly converted, threw himself into the river and was crowned as the fortieth martyr. The anniversary is observed with special church services.

*SABT AL-'AZAR, Lazarus Saturday.

The Saturday before Palm Sunday

This day is observed by Syrians of the Greek churches. The school teacher, accompanied by his pupils, goes from house to house chanting about Lazarus' resurrection. In return for the songs the little band is given gifts of eggs and coins.

*AḤAD AL-SHA'ANĪN, Palm Sunday.

The Sunday preceding Easter

Among Syrians of the Greek faith, children attired in gala robes enter the church with palms, olive branches and candles, in commemoration of Christ's triumphal entry into Jerusalem. Crosses made of palm leaves are presented at the gates of the church.

*KHAMIS AL-JASAD, Holy Thursday.

The Thursday preceding Easter

At the Holy Thursday service the priest performs the traditional foot-washing ceremony upon the feet of twelve good men of the parish. In Jerusalem this is an impressive public ceremony in which the patriarchs and twelve bishops take part.

The Book of Festivals

*AL-JUM'AH AL-HAZINAH, Sorrowful Friday.

The Friday preceding Easter

Among Syrians of the Greek faith the cross of Christ is buried symbolically in the flower-covered tomb. Perfumed water is sprinkled over sepulchre and congregation.

*AL-'ĪD AL-KABIR, The Great Festival, Easter.

This is a day of feasting and visiting among friends and relatives. Guests are served with Easter eggs and special cakes. In the Greek churches the priest gives each worshiper a red egg in token of Christ's blood and resurrection. Easter is the greatest and most joyous feast day in the Eastern Christian churches.

'ĪD MAR JURJUS, Saint George's Day.

April 23 O.S. (May 6 N.S.)

According to tradition, Saint George, or *Mar Jurjus* as he is called by Christian Syrians, killed the dragon at Lydd—or, according to another tradition, at Beirut. Today several monasteries mark the site where the saint is said to have revealed himself. According to the Moslems, Saint George, known as *al-Khidr*, once was identified with the prophet Elijah. Both Christians and Moslems worship Saint George in their own way and under their own name. The monastery at Humeira is the scene of a great annual folk festival attended by hundreds of devout worshipers from many different parts of Syria.

*'ĪD AL-ṢU'ŪD, Ascension.   *The fortieth day after Easter*

The ascension of Christ, the fortieth day after his resurrection, is observed with special church services.

330

Festivals of the Syrians

'ĪD AL 'ANṢARAH, Pentecost.   *The fiftieth day after Easter*

The descent of the Holy Ghost is observed with special church services.

'ĪD HAMATAY AL-RŬSŬL BUTRUS WA BULUS, Saints Peter and
Paul.   *June 29 O.S. (July 12 N.S.)*

Special church services honor the martyrdom of the two great evangelists.

'ĪD AL-TAJALLI, Transfiguration.
August 6 O.S. (August 19 N.S.)

Special church services commemorate Christ's transfiguration on Mount Tabor, in the presence of Saints Peter, James and John.

'ĪD RAḲAD-AI-SAYYIDAH, Assumption of the Virgin.
August 15 O.S. (August 28 N.S.)

This church festival is characterized by offerings of new wheat and small three-cornered cakes to the Blessed Virgin. According to a sixth century Syrian text, "The Apostles ordered that there should be a commemoration of the Blessèd One on account of the vine-bearing branches and the trees bearing fruit, that the clouds of hail might not come and destroy them." Near Damascus the Assumption Feast is celebrated at the Monastery of the Virgin at Saidnaya, whither people flock from all parts of the country. Both Christians and Moslems celebrate the feast, the folk of each town keeping themselves aloof from the others. Down in the monastery orchard, where tradition says the Virgin appeared to Justinian, the various groups eat, dance and hold horse races and other types of entertainment.

MAHRAJAN, Festival of the Soul.   *September* 1

On September 1, 1920, Lebanon, which is under the French mandate, received her independence in internal affairs and was granted her former boundaries.   In the United States the anniversary assumes the character of a national festival of the people from Lebanon and is attended by thousands of Syrians from all over the country.   For the past seven years *Mahrajan* has been held in Bridgeport, Connecticut.   Features of the celebration are folk dancing, folk music and demonstrations that recall the native culture of Syrians from the Lebanon district.   The *Mahrajan,* which is of ancient Persian origin, is a native folk festival that has been transplanted to new world soil.

'ĪD RAF'AL-SALĪB, Elevation of the Cross.
September 14 *O.S.* (*September* 27 *N.S.*)

This church festival commemorates Constantine's vision of the cross in the year 312.

'ĪD AL-BARBARAH, Saint Barbara.
December 4 *O.S.* (*December* 17 *N.S.*)

In Syrian homes a feast table, laden with sweets and decorated with colored candles, is prepared in the center of the room.   The boys and girls march in, singing a chant to Saint Barbara.   The children take sweetmeats to the homes of the poor.   Sometimes the boys masquerade from house to house, demanding blessings and gifts wherever they go.

'ĪD MAR NIKULA AL-'AJAIBI, Saint Nicholas Thaumaturgus.
December 6 *O.S.* (*December* 19 *N.S.*)

Special Masses are said in the churches for the fourth century Wonder Worker. An account of the saint's labors and persecutions is read.

BEIRAMUN 'ĪD AL MILAD, Christmas Eve.
December 24 O.S. (*January 6 N.S.*)

The Midnight Mass is significant of the Christmas season. The church bells, which are played skilfully by village lads, ring out glad tidings of Christ's birth. After communion the priest passes on the *salaam,* or peace token, to members of his congregation.

'ĪD AL MILAD, Christmas. *December 25 O.S.* (*January 7 N.S.*)

Christmas Day is a family festival enjoyed by young and old. After a special dinner friends and relatives begin calling on one another. Among Syrians of the United States guests are served with Oriental coffee and goodies typical of the season. *Baklawa, burma, mulabas* and other holiday cakes as well as nuts, oranges, candies and fine native wine are among the good things offered at every home.

FESTIVALS OF THE YUGOSLAVS

THE festivals of the Yugoslavs represent a mixture of many different folk cultures and religious faiths. The Kingdom of Yugoslavia, established after the World War, is composed of the pre-war kingdoms of Serbia and Montenegro, as well as the provinces of Bosnia, Carinthia, Carniola, Croatia, Dalmatia, Hertzegovina, Slavonia, Slovenia, South Serbia, Voyvodina (Banat, Bachka, Srem). The inhabitants of each of these provinces jealously guard their own old folk customs, superstitions, modes of dress and religious belief.

The Independent Serbian Orthodox Church, which was founded by Saint Sava, Serbia's twelfth century royal monk and national patron saint, represents Yugoslavia's predominant religious group. Roman Catholicism finds especially fertile ground in Croatia and Slovenia. Bosnia, on the other hand, boasts a large Moslem population. A small minority of Greek Catholics exists in some of the provinces, while Jews are scattered throughout the Kingdom.

In spite of the many differences in background, custom and religion, it must be remembered that the Yugoslavs are all South Slavs. In this fact lies their common tradition and their bond of unity.

In describing the festivals of the Yugoslavs, it will be noted that most of the dates are given according to the Julian, or Old Style calendar, which is observed by the majority of the country's inhabitants. Where customs are characteristic of some particular locality, mention is made of that fact. All Roman Catholic holidays are celebrated according to the Gregorian, or New Style calendar. The principal Mohammedan and Jewish festivals are described elsewhere, under the headings of those particular groups.[1]

Nova Godina, New Year; Obrezanje Gospodnje, Circumcision of the Lord. *January* 1 *O.S.* (*January* 14 *N.S.*)

Croatians attach great significance to the drawing of water on New Year's Day. Often sacrifices are offered to fountains and wells, to make the waters pure and the crops fruitful during the coming year. Serbians generally spend New Year's Eve visiting among friends and relatives and wishing one another a Happy New Year.

Bogoyavlyeniye, Epiphany.
January 6 *O.S.* (*January* 19 *N.S.*)

According to old Serbian folk belief, the heavens open at midnight on Epiphany Eve and God fulfils any wish made at this moment. Throughout Yugoslavia the ceremony of Blessing the Waters is performed in Serbian orthodox communities. In Belgrade the rite is particularly impressive. Priests and high church dignitaries go in procession to the junction of the Sava and the Danube, where, in the presence of military and state officials, the waters are blessed and the crucifix cast into the river. Young men compete to recover the cross. The lad who retrieves it is blessed by the priest and rewarded with a substantial gold piece. After the ceremony people carry home bottles of the blessed water, which has been placed in large receptacles

[1] Festivals of the Mohammedans, pages 236–239; Mohammedan calendar, pages 372–374; Festivals of the Jews, pages 202–209; Jewish calendar, pages 362–367.

beside the river bank. The priest visits his parishioners' houses and sprinkles them with *vodica,* the sanctified water.

RODYEN DAN KRALYICE MAYKE, Birthday of the Queen Mother Mariya. *January* 9

Special services honoring the Queen Mother Mariya are held in Belgrade Cathedral and other churches throughout the land. On this day, the Queen Mother, who is patroness of many women's welfare organizations, gives large sums of money to the various charities in which she is interested. The anniversary is observed with special exhibitions and demonstrations of work for women and girls. Campaigns for raising funds are held at this time.

SVETI SAVA, Saint Sava. *January* 14 *O.S.* (*January* 27 *N.S.*)

On this day Serbians celebrate the anniversary of *Sveti Sava,* their national patron, as well as the patron of schools and education. *Sveti Sava* was born in 1174, a crown prince of the Nemanich dynasty. He renounced his right to the throne and took the vows of a monk. Later he became both the cultural and spiritual leader of his people. He founded the Independent Serbian Orthodox Church, and liberated it from Greek influence. On the day dedicated to the great saint, boys and girls recite poems, sing and dance in his honor. One typical Sava song is:

"Let us acclaim Sveti Sava with love,
 Let us dedicate our schools and churches to that holy head,
 Yonder wreaths and yonder glory, where our Holy Sava rests.
 Sing to him, O Serbians. Sing to him songs of praise."

Throughout Serbian Yugoslavia, *Sveti Sava* is celebrated with special church services, speeches and choral singing.

Festivals of the Yugoslavs

*BELA NEDELYA, White Week.[2]   *The week preceding Lent*

Only white meat, such as chicken, is eaten during the week preceding Lent. At dinner the father often says, "What shall we give the children?" The mother replies, "The neck or the wing." "And what shall the older people eat?" "The white meat!" says the mother teasingly, this being considered the best part of the chicken.

*LAZAREVA SUBOTA, Lazarus Saturday.
                    The Saturday preceding Palm Sunday

Groups of children carrying willow branches and ringing little bells go from house to house singing about Lazarus and how Christ raised him from the dead. In return for their songs the children receive gifts of fruit and candy which they save for a Palm Sunday feast. The resurrection of Lazarus symbolizes the renewal of spring after the long dreary winter.

*CVETI, Day of Flowers, Palm Sunday.
                    The Sunday preceding Easter

Cveti derives its name from the many beautiful flower customs Yugoslavs practice at this season. On Palm Sunday Eve girls throw handfuls of fragrant blossoms into basins of water. The following day they bathe in this water, believing that it will make them lovely throughout the year. On *Cveti* maidens sow flower and flax seeds, while shepherds decorate their beasts

---

[2] Stars indicate movable feasts that depend on Easter. A table of the Easter dates as observed by the Independent Serbian Orthodox Church is given on pages 370–371. For Easter dates observed especially by Roman Catholics of Croatia and Slovenia, see pages 357–358. Mohammedans of Bosnia and elsewhere observe the Mohammedan festivals described on pages 236–239. Jews follow the festivals described on pages 202–209.

with garlands and greens. Branches of willow, blessed in church, later are carried about the fields, for the blessed willows are thought to protect against thunder and storm. Often the branches are placed over house doors, on roofs, above animal stalls and in the gardens. Boys make wreaths of the willows and place them on the heads of the girls they love. People always take the consecrated branches to invalids and shut-ins.

*VELIKI CHETVRTAK, Great Thursday.
The Thursday preceding Easter

On this day girls and women decorate the eggs which feature in all the Easter ceremonies and sports. In many parts of the country, flowers, birds and conventional designs are traced in white on a background of red, yellow or green. In some places the first egg to be colored is thought to possess special virtue. When cut and fed to children it is believed to keep them healthy and cure them of fright. Sometimes black mourning eggs, known as *korotna jaja,* are laid on graves. In bereaved Montenegrin families, eggs are boiled in alum water, to dye them black. Orthodox Serbs, holding lighted candles, go to church to participate in the longest night service of the year. The priest reads the apostolic message from all twelve apostles.

*VELIKI PETAK, Good Friday. *The Friday preceding Easter*

On this day Serbian women burn candles in memory of Christ's death, and take offerings of food and flowers to church. All children who come to services are given portions of boiled wheat in commemoration of the resurrection of the soul, and dried fruit (usually raisins and prunes), to symbolize the blessing of the earth's fruits. Throughout Holy Week, food is provided for the parish poor. On Good Friday the church bells are silent. In their place boards are beaten together. At the burial

338

service in memory of Christ, a sepulchre is covered with flowers. As the picture of the Savior's body is laid within the tomb, the choir chants a famous hymn called *Plach Majke Boziye,* the "Cry of Mother Mary," which describes the Virgin's agony at beholding the death of her Son.

*Velika Subota, Holy Saturday.
> *The Saturday preceding Easter*

In Roman Catholic communities the priest blesses huge Easter bonfires, which are built near the church. Church tapers and parishioners' Easter candles are lighted from the sacred flames. People carry home live embers and kindle new fires on the hearth from the *puzmenak* or sacred Easter fire. In some villages, cattle are driven through the ashes of the bonfires, in order to protect them from witches. On Holy Saturday or the day following, it is customary for people to take bread, meat, eggs, cheese and salt to church to be blessed by the priest.

*Uskrs, Easter, Resurrection from the Dead.

In Serbian Orthodox communities the Easter service commences shortly before midnight, the traditional hour of Christ's resurrection from the dead. A procession formed by priests, choir and worshipers goes around the church three times. The church bells peal forth joyously after their silence of the penitential days. The most dramatic moment of the ceremony is when the choir sings the great Easter hymn, *Hristos Voskrese!* "Christ is risen from the dead." Friends and neighbors greet one another with the traditional words, *Hristos voskrese!* "Christ is risen," and receive the response, *Vo istinu voskrese!* "Truly, he has risen!" Young people celebrate Easter with dancing, singing and playing games with artistically dyed and decorated eggs. One favorite sport is to crack one's egg against that of a neighbor. The possessor of the stronger egg "collects" the damaged ones of his opponent. This custom of egg cracking is known as *tutsanye*. The Easter dinner is a sumptuous repast, including meat, sweets, *pereca,* a special kind of biscuit which is eaten with Easter eggs, and many other unaccustomed delicacies. In the lowlands of Yugoslavia roast pig is the favorite Easter meat, whereas roast lamb is usual in mountainous regions.

DYURDYEV DAN, Saint George's Day.
April 23 *O.S.* (*May* 6 *N.S.*)

For fear of being ridiculed and called sleepy heads, Serbian men and boys rise early on *Dyurdyev Dan,* if on no other day in the year. "If he cannot even get up on *Dyurdyev Dan,* he is an incurable lazybones," is an old folk saying, which illustrates one reason why no man wants to be caught napping after daybreak. According to the old custom called *uranak,* male members of a community rise while it is dark and go to the woods in carts or other conveyances. They load their wagons with greens and carry them back to the village, where they decorate houses, schools, halls and public buildings with the fragrant boughs. *Dyurdyev Dan* marks the beginning of out-of-door sports and bathing. In some places girls celebrate the Eve of the festival by scattering flowers and herbs in water brought from ponds and streams, for bathing in this water is said to make them strong and lovely! If the weather is sufficiently warm, men and boys go swimming in the rivers, while girls splash and frolic in garden pools. Young people often rock in branches of the dogwood trees, as a charm for virility and strength. In some places animals are decorated with flowers and garlands in honor of Saint George.

Festivals of the Yugoslavs

ZRINSKI FRANKOPAN DAN, Memorial Day for Counts Zrinski
and Frankopan. *April* 30

Croatians celebrate this anniversary in commemoration of
the execution, in 1671, of Count Peter Zrinski and Marquis
Francis Kristo Frankopan, two great patriots who attempted to
separate the Yugoslav provinces from the Austrian Empire, and
unite them in a separate national state. The day is observed
with memorial services, national music and public demonstrations.

CHIRILO I METODIYE, Saints Cyril and Methodius.
May 11 *O.S.* (*May* 24 *N.S.*)

This church holiday commemorates the life and works of
the brothers who converted the Slavs to Christianity in the
ninth century. The two missionaries were highly esteemed for
their great piety and learning. The brothers invented the Slav
alphabet called *Chirilica,* and translated both liturgy and Bible
into the old Slav language which could be read and understood
by the masses. The anniversary is celebrated with special
church services and movements for promoting Slav culture and
adult education.

*DUHOVI, Holy Trinity. *The fiftieth day after Easter*

The floor of the church is covered with grass and flowers.
During morning services wreaths are woven which later are
taken home and hung, symbols of blessing, beneath the ikons
or above the doors.

VIDOV-DAN, Saint Vitus' Day. *June* 15 *O.S.* (*June* 28 *N.S.*)

This great memorial day, which commemorates the fall of
the Serbian medieval empire on the field of Kosovo in 1389, is

341

celebrated throughout Serbia with *Vidov-danski pomen,* or special church services, and with parades and athletic carnivals. *Vidov-dan,* originally significant in Yugoslav history as the anniversary of the battle of Kosovo, likewise commemorates a series of historic events. Chief among these events are the victory of the Serbs over the Turks in 1912 (which resulted in liberating the historic field of Kosovo), and the signing of the Treaty of Versailles, in 1918, at the request of the Serbian delegation at the Peace Conference.

IVAN-DAN, Saint John's Day.   *June 24 O.S. (July 7 N.S.)*

Herbs plucked on Saint John's Eve are thought to possess healing and supernatural virtue. In some parts of Yugoslavia girls gather herbs before sundown. As they pick the plants, they sing special songs known as *Ivanjsko Cveche,* and weave the herbs into fragrant garlands. Wherever these wreaths are hung—in the houses, on hedges, sheep pens, in fields or gardens —they are thought to bring blessings and health to men and beasts. On Saint John's Eve also, young people build huge bonfires on the hillsides and in the fields. Crowned with garlands of flowers and greens, they jump through the embers at midnight, and then dance about the fires to the plaintive accompaniment of bagpipe and flute. Old people say that the heavens open thrice on Saint John's Night and that God will fulfil wishes made at the moment the miracle occurs. Both human beings and animals should bathe on Saint John's Day, because the waters of streams and rivers are thought to impart special strength at this season.

RODYEN DAN KRALYA, Birthday of King Peter II.

September 6

At the morning church service in honor of Yugoslavia's

boy monarch, a special prayer called *mnogolestvije,* or "many summers," is offered for the King. In this ancient ritual, health, happiness, long life and inspiration are asked for the young ruler. Each year on the King's birthday, three boys of the same age, selected from each of the provinces of Slovenia, Croatia and Serbia, are invited to come to Belgrade as King Peter's birthday guests. The boys, who come from the mountainous, inland and coast districts of the country, spend two or three happy days with their young host. They indulge in all kinds of boyish sports and amusements, including gymnastic demonstrations, fishing, boating, tree climbing and radio tinkering. In Yugoslav communities in the United States King Peter's thirteenth birthday, in 1936, was observed by inviting thirteen boys thirteen years old to a party, where they ate a large birthday cake decorated with thirteen candles. The lads made speeches about the qualities they admired in the King and told of their own dreams and ambitions. The boys are making plans and saving money to attend King Peter's coronation in 1941.

SVETI MARTIN, Saint Martin. *November* 11

This festival is the occasion for drinking the first new wine, eating roast goose and rejoicing in the autumn harvest. In some parts of Croatia it is customary to send food and wine to the pastures, so the shepherds can make merry and hold a feast in honor of the herd.

DAN UJEDINYENYA, Unity Day. *December* 1

The anniversary of the proclamation of the Kingdom of the Serbs, Croats and Slovenes, in 1918, is celebrated with prayers for national unity and memorial services for the fallen heroes of all wars. The exercises in Belgrade are attended by the King and officials from all parts of the Kingdom. Lectures, national music, parades and public meetings are features of the celebration.

DECHIYI DAN, Children's Day; MATERITSE, Mother's Day; OCHICHI, Father's Day.   *Sometime in December*

Shortly before Christmas, on a Sunday known as *Dechiyi Dan,* parents tie up the children and refuse to let them go until they promise to be good, and offer some childish token in return for their freedom. On the following Sunday, known as *Materitse,* or Mother's Day, boys and girls watch the chance of tying up their mother, whom they let go only upon payment of sweets and goodies. On the third Sunday, *Ochichi,* or Father's Day, the children plot to secure their father firmly to a chair or to bind him fast to his bed. The father has difficulty in "buying himself out of bondage," as the boys and girls refuse to release him until he promises substantial gifts such as coats, shoes, dresses or other coveted presents. Usually the father pays his forfeit at Christmas.

BADNYI DAN, Christmas Eve.
December 24 O.S. (January 6 N.S.)

The day before Christmas the men of the family rise before dawn and go to the forest with the ox team, to find a young oak for the *badnyak,* or Yule log. The tree is selected with care and its cutting is performed with ceremonial precision. The sign of the cross is made before the ax touches the trunk. The oak must fall toward the east, at the moment of sunrise. Should the branches of the *badnyak* touch those of any other tree, bad luck is sure to disturb the family during the coming year. When father and sons bring home the *badnyak,* their arrival is hailed

344

with song and pistol shots. In the evening the tree is placed in the fireplace with one end extending toward the room. The small upper branches are reserved for sweeping out the chimney. Following ancient custom, the head of the house empties a cup of wine and throws grain over the *badnyak,* with a wish for plenty of wine and grain during the coming season. The mother scatters straw over the floor in memory of Jesus' humble manger birth. As the mother drops the straw over the floor she clucks like a hen, and the children, following after in a row, peep like small chickens. Then the father stands before the fire and throws walnuts into the four corners of the room—for Christmas goes to the east, west, north and south. Should boys and girls eat the nuts on any other night during the holidays, they are warned they will have toothache! Before eating the Christmas Eve supper the father places a lighted wax candle in the wheat bin and prays for prosperity, health, good harvest and plentiful flocks during the next twelve months. Then a toast is made to the *badnyak* and a light supper is eaten. On this holy night some Serbians observe the old custom of laying sacking over the straw-strewn floor, allowing the children to eat the Christmas repast from the floor instead of the table. No meat is eaten for the Christmas Eve supper. Fish, beans, onions and other vegetables, as well as white wheat bread are among the special Christmas Eve foods. Since it is considered unlucky to let the *badnyak* log burn out, certain members of the family keep vigil with it throughout the night.

Božic, Christmas.   *December 25 O.S. (January 7 N.S.)*

Early on Christmas morning, weather permitting, a fire is built in the courtyard and a whole suckling pig, called *peche-nitsa,* is roasted on a spit. Relatives and neighbors greet one another with the traditional words: *Mir božiyi! Hristos se rodi!* "God's peace! Christ is born!" Then everybody kisses everybody else three times and forgives all the differences and quarrels of the past year. According to an old Croatian superstition, angels pass over springs on Christmas Eve, touching them with their wings and making them pure. For this reason special ceremony is attached to drawing water on Christmas Day. At dawn girls carry their pitchers to the village fountains. Before filling them, however, they throw basil and grain into the water, with a wish for cleanliness and plentiful harvest. The first water drawn is used to make the *tchessnitza,* or Christmas cake, in which the housewife bakes a gold or silver coin. The cake is divided and eaten at the midday dinner. The person finding the coin in his or her piece is thought to be lucky throughout the year. The family gathers around the blazing *badnyak* log early, to await the coming of *polaznik,* a village lad, who must be the first to enter the house with Christmas blessings. *Polaznik* knocks at the door. He runs into the room and throws a handful of grain at each member of the family, crying, *Hristos se rodi!* "Christ is born." *Vo istinu se rodi!* "Truly he is born," respond the others as they in turn throw grain on *polaznik.* *Polaznik* strikes the log so that the sparks fly, wishing, meanwhile, for as many sheep, cows, oxen and pigs as there are sparks in the fire. Then he pours a little wine on the log and leaves a coin on the protruding end, so the family may have plenty during the next twelve months. *Polaznik* is not permitted to leave the house for the entire day. In return for his good wishes he is treated with food and drink and hearty good cheer. Serbians call the twelve days between Christmas and Epiphany *nekršteni dani,* or unbaptized days, because Jesus was unbaptized during this period. All kinds of demons, and especially the souls of unbaptized children, are thought to roam abroad trying to harm human beings who spin, weave, wash or perform any other forbidden tasks during the holy season. For this reason people lay aside their usual work and devote themselves to feasting, merrymaking and visiting friends.

Festivals of the Yugoslavs

MLADENCI, Holy Innocents' Day.   *December 28*

On this day Croatian mothers switch the boys and girls "to make them healthy and strong." Then the children, in their turn, go from house to house, vigorously switching all the neighbors and receiving little gifts of goodies and coins. In Herzegovina the day is known as *Ženski Dan,* "Women's Day," because it is customary for the women to go about visiting one another. In the evening young people gather at some neighbor's house, where they sing and dance far into the night.

SILVESTESTROVO VECHE, Saint Sylvester's Eve.
December 31 *O.S.* (*January* 13 *N.S.*)

On December 31, a hilarious *Silvestestrovo Veche* is celebrated, with singing, dancing and drinking. Promptly at midnight the lights are extinguished. A moment later, the host wishes his guests a Happy New Year and kisses his wife or mother. His guests follow his example. Croats and Slovenes follow the custom of kissing on this night, while Serbians do so on Christmas Day.

347

PART II

THE STORY OF THE CALENDARS

I

THE ARMENIAN CALENDAR

THE Armenian calendar is confusing because of its many seeming contradictions and variations. The reason for conflicting festival dates is easily understood, however, when one considers that the Armenians always adapt their holidays to correspond with those of the countries in which they are living. Armenians dwelling in Greece or in Jerusalem, for example, use the Julian, or Old Style calendar, which still is employed in Eastern Orthodox countries.

On account of business conditions, Armenians in the United States, as well as many other nationalities, generally celebrate on the Sunday following, all holidays that fall within the week. If January 6 (the fixed date of the Armenian Christmas), for example, falls on a week-day, it is observed on the next Sunday. With the exception of Christmas, most Armenian holidays are calculated according to the Gregorian, or New Style calendar, in use in the western world.

In reckoning the movable feasts commemorated by Armenians in the United States, it is helpful to remember that Christ's Presentation comes forty days after Christmas; Christ's Ascension, forty days after Easter; Pentecost, fifty days after Easter; *Etchmiadzin,* on the second Sunday after Pentecost; *Vartavar,* or Transfiguration, ninety-eight days after Easter; Assumption of the Virgin, on the nearest Sunday to August 15, either before

351

or after; the Raising of the Cross, on the Sunday nearest September 15.

For the sake of greater convenience, the principal Armenian holidays may be classified according to:

I. THE LORD'S HOLIDAYS

   The first five days are termed *Daghavar,* or Main Holidays.
   1. Christmas
   2. Easter
   3. Vartavar, Transfiguration of Christ
   4. Assumption of the Virgin
   5. Holy Cross Day
   6. Baptism of Christ
   7. Presentation of Christ in the Temple
   8. Ascension of Christ
   9. Pentecost

II. SAINTS' DAYS

   Days of the Virgin Mary, of the Apostles, Prophets, Church Fathers, Kings, Princes, Generals, Soldiers, Martyrs, Virgins, Hermits.

III. NATIONAL HOLIDAYS

   1. Saints Thaddeus and Bartholomew
   2. Saint Gregory the Illuminator
   3. Saints Sahag and Mesrob
   4. Saints Vartan and Ghevont
   5. Saint Tarkmanchatch
   6. Saint Etchmiadzin

II

THE CHINESE CALENDAR

WHEN the Chinese Republic was established in 1912, the old-style Chinese calendar was discarded in favor of the Gregorian calendar used in the western world. In spite of the official change, however, many of the Chinese people still adhere to the old-style calendar. Native festivals are observed according to the old lunar calendar even in Chinese communities of San Francisco, New York and elsewhere.

According to the calendar reforms of 104 B.C., the first day of the year always begins with the first new moon after the sun enters Aquarius. This fixes the date of the New Year as not earlier than January 21 nor later than February 19.

The old Chinese calendar, which is principally lunar in character, consists of the twelve months, or moons, known as the First, Second, Third, etc. The new moon marks the beginning of each month and the fifteenth day of the month accords with the new moon. Each month is composed of twenty-nine or thirty days, with one intercalary month added in every thirty, in order to make the lunar year correspond to the solar. Whenever an intercalary month is added, any festival the change may affect is celebrated in the regular, instead of in the intercalary month. The First, Eleventh and Twelfth Moons never are duplicated. The additional month comes at variable intervals, sometimes at the beginning of the year and sometimes at other periods. The reason for this irregularity probably is best explained by the fact that China is an agricultural country. The intercalary month, therefore, is added whenever it will cause the least disturbance to the Chinese farmer's traditional periods for plowing, planting and harvesting of crops.

The resulting advantage of this manipulation of the months is that the old Chinese calendar consistently retains its seasonal character. The first three months of the year—February, March, April—are spring. The second three—May, June, July—are summer. The third three—August, September, October—are autumn. The last three—November, December, January—are winter. The vernal equinox, which in the western calendar comes about March 20, in the Chinese is about the first day of the Second Moon; the autumn equinox, which falls about September 23 in western reckoning, takes place on about the ninth day of the Ninth Moon in the Chinese. The summer and winter solstices, which in the western calendar come respectively on about June 21 and December 22, in the Chinese are approximately on the fifth day of the Fifth Moon and on the eleventh day of the Eleventh Moon.

Festival customs and festival dates vary in different parts of China. Even though the legends of the different holidays are essentially the same throughout the country, the practices of rural folk oftentimes are quite unfamiliar to their city neighbors and vice versa. Because of calendar diversities and variations in celebrations, it is almost impossible to give wholly accurate information about the great feast days of the Chinese.

III

THE GREGORIAN CALENDAR

THE Gregorian, or civil calendar, now universally followed by Christian nations, rapidly is becoming the official system of reckoning time, even in China, Japan, India, Turkey and other countries which for hundreds of years have followed their own religious calendars. The Gregorian calendar was introduced by order of Pope Gregory's papal bull of March 1, 1582.

According to the Julian calendar, instituted by Julius Caesar in 46 B.C., the year was too long by eleven minutes and fourteen seconds. In the course of 128 years the error had crept up to a day; after a few centuries the equinox had turned back toward the beginning of the year. The equinox, which began on March 25 in Julius Caesar's day, fell on March 21 at the time of the Council of Nice, in 325 A.D. By 1582 it had retrograded to March 11. To the pious peasant who for centuries had tilled his soil, planted his grain and harvested his crops according to the holy days and feast days of the Church, it now seemed as if all signs had failed. The sun and the moon no longer performed their appointed tasks. The seasons had become "hit or miss." The farmer's whole world went topsy-turvy. Agriculture and religion no longer agreed!

At the peak of this crisis, when the calendar had slowed up by ten days, Pope Gregory, with the help of the most able astronomers and scientists of his time, harmonized the civil and the astronomical calendars by changing the date of October 5, 1582, to October 15. This Gregorian, or New Style calendar, which issued from Rome and was adopted promptly by all Roman Catholic countries, was viewed with suspicion and dislike by Protestant Great Britain and the English colonies in America. So stubbornly did the British oppose the calendar reform that they continued to begin their year on March 25 (in accordance with the Julian, or Old Style calendar) until the reign of George II, in 1752.

By the time Great Britain and the American colonies finally adopted the New Style calendar, an eleven-day variation existed between the two. The rate of variation between the Julian and the Gregorian calendars may be seen by the following table:

Year	*Amount of Variation*
From 1582 to 1700	10 days
From 1700 to 1800	11 days
From 1800 to 1900	12 days
Since 1900	13 days

As is explained under the section dealing with the Julian calendar, any Julian (or Old Style, abbreviated O.S.) date may be converted into the Gregorian (or New Style, abbreviated N.S.) by adding thirteen days to the Julian date.

Although considerable variation exists among the calendars of the Armenian, Greek, Roman, Russian and other national Christian Churches, they all agree fundamentally, inasmuch as they follow in chronological order the events in the life of Jesus, from the time of his birth, through his Passion, resurrection, ascension, and the descent of the Holy Ghost. The seasons of the Christian calendars therefore are dependent upon the holy days of the Church. Easter, the pivotal festival of the Christian year (since it determines the dates of all the movable feasts of the Church), is a lunar date set in the midst of a solar calendar.

Easter always is reckoned as the first Sunday after the paschal full moon[1] of the vernal equinox (March 21). If the full moon occurs on a Sunday, Easter is observed on the Sunday following. Easter never comes before March 22 or after April 25 (N.S.).

Following is a table of the Easter dates according to the Gregorian calendar:

DATES OF EASTER

Year	Date	Year	Date
1938	April 17	1945	April 1
1939	April 9	1946	April 21
1940*	March 24	1947	April 6
1941	April 13	1948*	March 28
1942	April 5	1949	April 17
1943	April 25	1950	April 9
1944*	April 9		

* Leap year.

PRINCIPAL MOVABLE FEASTS THAT DEPEND ON THE DATE OF EASTER

Shrove Tuesday—The last day before Lent.
Ash Wednesday—The first day of Lent.
Lent—The forty week days (beginning with Ash Wednesday) that immediately precede Easter.
Mid-Lent Sunday—The fourth Sunday in Lent.

[1] It must be remembered that the "full moon" that regulates Easter does not refer to the actual moon in the sky, but to an "imaginary" moon, set as the fourteenth day of the calendar moon.

357

The Book of Festivals

Palm Sunday—The Sunday preceding Easter.

Maundy Thursday—The Thursday preceding Easter.

Good Friday—The Friday preceding Easter.

Holy Saturday—The Saturday preceding Easter.

Easter Monday and Tuesday—The two days following Easter.

Low Sunday—The Sunday after Easter.

Ascension Day—The fortieth day after Easter.

Whitsunday or Pentecost—The fiftieth day after Easter.

Whitsuntide—The week beginning with Whitsunday, especially the first three days.

Trinity Sunday—The fifty-seventh day after Easter.

Corpus Christi—The Thursday after Trinity Sunday.

For description of these feasts see Glossary on page 377.

IV

THE HINDU CALENDAR

THE present Hindu calendar dates back to about the fifth century B.C., when Greek astrologers were in India calculating the movements of the heavenly bodies. The Hindu year, which is divided into twelve months, is both lunar and solar in character. Although the solar system is widely followed in Bengal, including Orissa, and in the Malāyalam and Tamil sections of Madras, the lunar system, which obtains in other parts of India, regulates native feast days and religious festivals and therefore is important for present purposes.

To the twelve-month Hindu year, an intercalary month is added to every month having two new moons, or once in about every two and a half or three years. In northern India the New Year begins in the month of *Chaitra,* or between March and April, whereas in other parts of the country it commences in *Baisakha,* or between April and May. Following is a table giving the Sanskrit names of the months, together with their English equivalents:

1. *Baisakha* (April–May)
2. *Jyaishtha* (May–June)
3. *Asarha* (June–July)
4. *Sravana* (July–August)
5. *Bhadra* (August–September)
6. *Asvina* (September–October)

7. *Kartika* (October–November)
8. *Aghrana* (November–December)
9. *Pausha* (December–January)
10. *Magha* (January–February)
11. *Phalguna* (February–March)
12. *Chaitra* (March–April)

Each lunar month has two fortnights—the bright and the dark—or the fortnight of the waxing moon, which ends with the full moon, and the period of the waning moon, which ends with the new moon.

The Hindu year is divided into six seasons,[1] each one covering a two-month period. Originally the seasons were planned to coincide with the course of the sun, but at the present time each season lags behind by about three weeks. The seasons are:

1. *Grīshma* (Hot Weather)
2. *Varshā* (Rainy Season)
3. *Sárat* (Autumn)
4. *Hēmanta* (Dewy)
5. *Seeta* (Winter)
6. *Vasanta* (Spring)

Lunar days of the week are called *tithi;* solar, *bara.* The desired suffix is added to the Sanskrit names for the various planets:

1. *Rābi* (*tithi* or *bara*), Day of the Sun—Sunday
2. *Sōmo,* Day of the Moon—Monday
3. *Mangala,* Day of Mars—Tuesday
4. *Budha,* Day of Mercury—Wednesday
5. *Brihaspati,* Day of Jupiter—Thursday
6. *Sukra,* Day of Venus—Friday
7. *Sani,* Day of Saturn—Saturday

To the Hindus some days are lucky, others are unlucky, but this is determined according to the birth date of the individual

[1] Kalidasa, regarded by the Hindus as the greatest of Sanskrit poets, has described the six seasons in his poem entitled, *The Seasons.* With delicate precision and exquisite imagery he paints the pageant of the changing seasons as they pass before the eyes of two young Hindu lovers. See *Kalidasa: Translations of Shakuntala and Other Works.* Tr. by Arthur W. Ryder. New York, Dutton, 1933. "The Seasons," p. 211–216.

and the position of the sun and the planets. Saturday is generally considered the most unlucky day of the week. Certain days are sacred to some particular god or goddess and therefore are considered propitious for the celebration of specific fasts or religious rites. The events of the year are predicted according to the dominance of different planets. Thus Budha, or Mercury, which was in the ascendancy in 1936, was said to have ruled the heavens as king, while Saturn, the evil counselor, acted as Prime Minister.

According to the Hindus there are four *Yuga,* or eras of time. Mention need be made only of *Kali Yuga,* or the existing "Evil Age," which for purposes of astronomical reckoning was devised by Hindu astronomers in about the fifth century of the Christian era. In Hindu philosophical belief the *Kali Yuga,* or age of materialism, will end in total destruction, out of which the cosmic world will arise.

V

THE JEWISH CALENDAR

THE Jews number their years, not as commonly practiced, but from what old Jewish tradition calculated was the birth of the world. The year 1937–1938 in the civil calendar, for example, is reckoned as 5698 in the Jewish, the year 1938–1939 as 5699, and so on. The beginning of the Jewish year is approximately in September or October.

Since the Jewish calendar is primarily lunar, each month consists of about twenty-nine and one-half days, or the period it takes the moon to travel around the earth. Of course, it would be highly inconvenient to split a day between two months, so it became necessary to alternate the months between twenty-nine and thirty days each. Further modifications were devised in order that *Yom Kippur*, the Day of Atonement (*Tishri* 10), should not fall on Saturday or Sunday, and *Rosh Hashanah*, the New Year (*Tishri* 1), on Sunday. As the lunar year consists of 364 days and the solar of 365, it was necessary to juggle the calendar further by giving an extra month to every three-year cycle, or, more strictly speaking, seven additional months in each nineteen years. The Jewish calendar, consequently, boasts seven leap years (each one consisting of thirteen months) in every nineteen-year period. In this way the various festivals are made to fall within their proper seasons and the scientific basis of the calendar is preserved.

The Story of the Calendars: Jewish

Following the tradition in the Bible, where night precedes the day, the Sabbath, as well as every other Jewish festival, begins the night before.[1]

In the Bible, the days, with the exception of the Sabbath (or Seventh Day), are not distinguished by special names. They are known as First Day, Second Day, etc. In Biblical times the months, too, were known chiefly as First Month, Second Month, etc., though often, also, designated by specific names. After the Babylonian captivity, however, the Jewish months and their corresponding months in the civil calendar acquired the following names:

1. *Tishri*—October (approximate beginning of the Jewish year)
2. *Heshvan*—November
3. *Kislev*—December
4. *Tebet*—January
5. *Shebat*—February
6. *Adar*[2]—March
7. *Nissan*—April
8. *Iyar*—May
9. *Sivan*—June
10. *Tammuz*—July
11. *Ab*—August
12. *Elul*—September

For the sake of convenience, the festivals of the Jewish calendar may be classified according to the following table:

A. THE HIGH HOLY DAYS

These days are neither historical nor agricultural in origin. They are purely religious in character. *Yom Kippur*, the Day

[1] Genesis, ch. I, v. 5—"And God called the light Day, and the darkness he called Night. And the evening and morning were the first day."

[2] *Adar Sheni*, the "second Adar," is the extra month added only in leap years.

of Atonement, the most sacred festival of the year, is the only fast day enjoined in the Torah.

1. *Rosh Hashanah,* New Year (*Tishri* 1).
2. *Yom Kippur,* Day of Atonement (*Tishri* 10).

B. THE GREAT FESTIVALS

These days originally were agricultural festivals of a pastoral people who rejoiced and gave thanks for their crops and harvests. Later the feasts assumed historic significance, thus making them of double importance to the Jewish faith.

1. *Pesach,* Passover (*Nissan* 15–22)—The festival that celebrates the Exodus from Egypt.
2. *Shabuoth,* Feast of Weeks (*Sivan* 6–7)—The festival marking the Later Harvest. Eventually it came to celebrate the Revelation on Mount Sinai.
3. *Succoth,* Feast of Tabernacles (*Tishri* 15–22)—This festival marked the Ingathering of Fruit. Later it came to celebrate the Journey through the Desert.

C. THE MINOR FESTIVALS

In general, these days commemorate some historic event of importance in the life of the Jewish people. These festivals are joyous in character and are anticipated as happy occasions.

1. *Hamishah Assar Bi-Shebat,* New Year of the Trees (*Shebat* 15).
2. *Purim,* Feast of Lots (*Adar* 14).
3. *Lag ba'Omer,* Feast of Scholars (*Iyar* 18).
4. *Simchat Torah,* Rejoicing in the Law (*Tishri* 23).
5. *Chanucah,* Feast of Lights (*Kislev* 25–*Tebet* 2).

D. THE MINOR FASTS

These fast days commemorate some sad event in Jewish history. They serve to strengthen the historic consciousness of the Jewish people.

The Story of the Calendars: Jewish

1. *Ta'anith Esther,* Fast of Esther (*Adar* 13).
2. *Tish'ah b'Ab,* Fast of Ab (*Ab* 9).
3. Fast of *Tammuz* (*Tammuz* 17).
4. Fast of *Gedaliah* (*Tishri* 3).
5. Fast of *Tebet* (*Tebet* 10).

Rosh Hodesh, or the New Moon, the first day of every Jewish month, is observed as a half-holiday. On these days women are given respite from household duties, for, according to tradition, in the time of Moses and Aaron women worshiped the Golden Calf less readily than men. Some pious Jews sanctify the moon by reciting special benedictions in the open air when the moon is visible in full.

Because of the impossibility of furnishing a workable scheme whereby the corresponding dates of the Jewish festivals can be given in the Gregorian calendar, a table of the most important dates in the Jewish calendar (from 1936 to 1951) is offered below. A glance at the table is sufficient to show the variations existing between festival dates from one year to the next.

JEWISH HOLIDAYS AND FASTS

	5697 1936	5698 1937	5699 1938	5700 1939	5701 1940
Rosh Hashanah	Sept. 17–18	Sept. 6–7	Sept. 26–27	Sept. 14–15	Oct. 3–4
Fast of Gedaliah	Sept. 19	Sept. 8	Sept. 28	Sept. 16	Oct. 5
Yom Kippur	Sept. 26	Sept. 15	Oct. 5	Sept. 23	Oct. 12
Succoth	Oct. 1–9	Sept. 20–28	Oct. 10–18	Sept. 28–Oct. 6	Oct. 17–25
Hoshanah Rabah	Oct. 7	Sept. 26	Oct. 16	Oct. 4	Oct. 23
Shemini Atzereth	Oct. 8	Sept. 27	Oct. 17	Oct. 5	Oct. 24
Simchat Torah	Oct. 9	Sept. 28	Oct. 18	Oct. 6	Oct. 25
Chanucah	Dec. 9–16	Nov. 29–Dec. 6	Dec. 18–25	Dec. 7–14	Dec. 25–Jan. 1
			1939		*1941*
Fast of tenth of Tebet	Dec. 24	Dec. 14	Jan. 1	Dec. 22	Jan. 9 Dec. 30

	5697 1937	5698 1938	5699 1939	5700 1940	5701 1941
Ta'anith Esther	Feb. 24	March 16	March 4	March 23	March 12
Purim	Feb. 25	March 17	March 5	March 24	March 13
Pasach (Passover)	March 27–April 3	April 16–23	April 4–11	April 23–30	April 12–19
Shabuoth	May 16–17	June 5–6	May 24–25	June 12–13	June 1–2
Fast of seventeenth of Tammuz	June 26	July 16	July 4	July 23	July 12
Tish'ah b'Ab	July 17	Aug. 6	July 25	Aug. 13	Aug. 2

	5702 1941	5703 1942	5704 1943	5705 1944	5706 1945
Rosh Hashanah	Sept. 22–23	Sept. 12–13	Sept. 30–Oct. 1	Sept. 18–19	Sept. 8–9
Fast of Gedaliah	Sept. 24	Sept. 14	Oct. 2	Sept. 20	Sept. 10
Yom Kippur	Oct. 1	Sept. 21	Oct. 9	Sept. 27	Sept. 17
Succoth	Oct. 6–14	Sept. 26–Oct. 4	Oct. 14–22	Oct. 2–10	Sept. 22–30
Hoshanah Rabah	Oct. 12	Oct. 2	Oct. 20	Oct. 8	Sept. 28
Shemini Atzereth	Oct. 13	Oct. 3	Oct. 21	Oct. 9	Sept. 29
Simchat Torah	Oct. 14	Oct. 4	Oct. 22	Oct. 10	Sept. 30
Chanucah	Dec. 15–22	Dec. 4–11	Dec. 22–29	Dec. 11–18	Nov. 30–Dec. 7

	5702 1942	5703 1943	5704 1944	5705 1945	5706 1946
Fast of tenth of Tebet	Dec. 18		{ Jan. 6 / Dec. 26	Dec. 14	
Ta'anith Esther	March 2	March 20	March 8	Feb. 26	March 16
Purim	March 3	March 21	March 9	Feb. 27	March 17
Pasach (Passover)	April 2–9	April 20–27	April 8–15	April 29–May 6	April 16–23
Shabuoth	May 22–23	June 9–10	March 28–29	May 18–19	June 5–6
Fast of seventeenth of Tammuz	July 2	July 20	July 8	June 28	July 16
Tish'ah b'Ab	July 23	Aug. 10	July 29	July 19	Aug. 6

The Story of the Calendars: Jewish

	5707 1946	5708 1947	5709 1948	5710 1949	5711 1950
Rosh Hashanah	Sept. 26–27	Sept. 15–16	Oct. 4–5	Sept. 24–25	Sept. 12–13
Fast of Gedaliah	Sept. 28	Sept. 17	Oct. 6	Sept. 26	Sept. 14
Yom Kippur	Oct. 5	Sept. 24	Oct. 13	Oct. 3	Sept. 21
Succoth	Oct. 10–18	Sept. 29– Oct. 7	Oct. 18–26	Oct. 8–16	Sept. 26– Oct. 4
Hoshanah Rabah	Oct. 16	Oct. 5	Oct. 24	Oct. 14	Oct. 2
Shemini Atzereth	Oct. 17	Oct. 6	Oct. 25	Oct. 15	Oct. 3
Simchat Torah	Oct. 18	Oct. 7	Oct. 26	Oct. 16	Oct. 4
Chanucah	Dec. 18–25	Dec. 8–15	Dec. 27– Jan. 3	Dec. 16–23	Dec. 4–11

	1947	1948	1949	1950	1951
Fast of tenth of Tebet	{ Jan. 2 { Dec. 23		{ Jan. 11 { Dec. 30	Dec. 19	
Ta'anith Esther	March 5	March 24	March 14	March 2	March 21
Purim	March 6	March 25	March 15	March 3	March 22
Pasach (Passover)	April 5–12	April 24– May 1	April 14–21	April 2–9	April 21–28
Shabuoth	May 25–26	June 13–14	June 3–4	May 22–23	June 10–11
Fast of seventeenth of Tammuz	July 5	July 24	July 14	July 2	July 21
Tish'ah b'Ab	July 26	Aug. 14	Aug. 4	July 23	Aug. 11

VI

THE JULIAN CALENDAR

AT the period of Julius Caesar's accession to power, the ancient civil calendar of the Romans was reckoned by the moon rather than the sun. This system gave 354 days to the year, with intercalary days added now and then, at the discretion of the pontiffs. Unfortunately, the pontiffs saw the opportunity for using the calendar to further their own ends, and began to add or subtract days in conjunction with annual elections or official reappointments, rather than in accordance with movements of the heavenly bodies. As may be readily imagined, the priests' manipulation of the calendar soon led to such confusion that eventually the civil and the astronomical calendars bore but slight resemblance to each other. The seasons fell three months behind time, so that, for example, summer in the civil calendar corresponded to spring in the lunar, and spring in the civil to winter in the lunar.

In the year B.C. 44, Julius Caesar, with the able advice of the Greek astrologer Sosigenēs of Alexandria, ultimately abolished the inaccuracies of the Roman lunar calendar by regulating the civil year in accordance with the movements of the sun. It was calculated that the new solar calendar had approximately 365¼ days. To every fourth or bissextile year one day was added. It took some juggling of the months to straighten out the confusion coincident to the first steps in calendar reform. The new

The Story of the Calendars: Julian

Julian calendar finally took effect in B.C. 46. The names of the months, their order and length were fixed as in present usage.

Although the Julian calendar was slightly altered under Augustus, it remained virtually the same for about sixteen centuries. In the year 1582, Pope Gregory XIII introduced the reforms of the Gregorian, or New Style calendar.

The Julian calendar, although no longer official, continues to be observed as the calendar of the Eastern Church. In 1923, the Church of Greece and the churches under the Œcumenical Patriarchate of Constantinople accepted the Gregorian calendar, except for the celebration of Easter. This explains why both Julian (Old Style) and Gregorian (New Style) dates appear with many of the church festivals listed in this volume under Albanians, Bulgarians, Greeks, Rumanians, Russians (of the Eastern Orthodox Church), Syrians and Yugoslavs.

Since the end of February of 1900, there has been a variation of thirteen days between the Julian, or Old Style calendar (abbreviated O.S.), and the Gregorian, or New Style calendar (abbreviated N.S.). January 6 (O.S.), for example, corresponds to January 19 (N.S.); April 30 (O.S.) is the same as May 13 (N.S.). In other words, dates in the Julian calendar can be converted to those of the Gregorian by adding thirteen days to any given calendar date.

The thirteen-day difference existing between the calendars of the Eastern and the Western Churches resulted in serious variation of the Easter dates. In early times Easter was not celebrated on the same day by all the churches. Some of them observed it on the same date as the Jewish Passover, others after it. It was not until 325 A.D. that the First Œcumenical Council of Nice decreed that Easter (the day upon which numerous other church festivals depend) should be reckoned according to the following rule:

It must fall on the first Sunday after the full moon of the

369

vernal equinox (March 21). Consequently it cannot come earlier than March 22 nor later than April 25.

Some peoples of the Eastern faiths—the Greeks, for example —observe all festivals *with the exception of Easter and days dependent upon it* according to the Gregorian (N.S.) calendar. Russians of the Eastern Orthodox Church, on the contrary, follow the Julian (O.S.) calendar throughout.

DATES OF EASTER

Year	Eastern Orthodox Church		Western Church
1938	April 11 (O.S.)	April 24 (N.S.)	April 17
1939	March 27 (O.S.)	April 9 (N.S.)	April 9
1940	April 15 (O.S.)	April 28 (N.S.)	March 24
1941	April 7 (O.S.)	April 20 (N.S.)	April 13
1942	March 23 (O.S.)	April 5 (N.S.)	April 5
1943	April 12 (O.S.)	April 25 (N.S.)	April 25
1944	April 3 (O.S.)	April 16 (N.S.)	April 9
1945	April 23 (O.S.)	May 6 (N.S.)	April 1
1946	April 8 (O.S.)	April 21 (N.S.)	April 21
1947	March 31 (O.S.)	April 13 (N.S.)	April 6
1948	April 19 (O.S.)	May 2 (N.S.)	March 28
1949	April 11 (O.S.)	April 24 (N.S.)	April 17
1950	March 27 (O.S.)	April 9 (N.S.)	April 9

The following list gives the principal festivals of the Eastern Orthodox Church. The Julian (O.S.) dates are followed in parentheses by the corresponding Gregorian (N.S.) dates. The movable feasts, marked with an asterisk, are dependent upon the Easter date.

1. Circumcision of Our Lord, January 1 O.S. (January 14 N.S.)
2. Epiphany, January 6 O.S. (January 19 N.S.)
3. Presentation of Christ in the Temple, or Purification of the Virgin Mary, February 2 O.S. (February 15 N.S.)

4. Annunciation, March 25 O.S. (April 7 N.S.)

*5. Palm Sunday (Sunday before Easter)

*6. Easter, between March 22–April 25 O.S. (between April 4–May 8 N.S.)

*7. Ascension (40 days after Easter)

*8. Pentecost (50 days after Easter)

9. Nativity of Saint John the Baptist, June 24 O.S. (July 7 N.S.)

10. Saints Peter and Paul, June 29 O.S. (July 12 N.S.)

11. Transfiguration, August 6 O.S. (August 19 N.S.)

12. Assumption of the Blessed Virgin, August 15 O.S. (August 28 N.S.)

13. Beheading of Saint John the Baptist, August 29 O.S. (September 11 N.S.)

14. Nativity of the Blessed Virgin, September 8 O.S. (September 21 N.S.)

15. Exaltation of the Cross, September 14 O.S. (September 27 N.S.)

16. Presentation of the Blessed Virgin, November 21 O.S. (December 4 N.S.)

17. Christmas, December 25 O.S. (January 7 N.S.)

In the Greek calendar there are two Decoration Days and both are dependent upon Easter. The first Decoration Day is celebrated on the Saturday preceding the Saturday before Carnival, or nine days before Carnival. The second Decoration Day falls on the Saturday preceding the Day of Pentecost, or the forty-ninth day after Easter. In other words, these two anniversaries are fifteen weeks apart.

* Movable feasts.

VII

THE MOHAMMEDAN CALENDAR

THE Mohammedan Era, or Era of the *Hijrah* (meaning flight or departure), which is used extensively in Arabia, Egypt and Persia, as well as in many parts of India, China, Syria, Mesopotamia, Albania and certain other countries, dates from July 15 A.D. 622, when Mohammed fled from Mecca to Medina. After the Prophet's death his followers abandoned the ancient Arabian calendar, which had been luni-solar in character for some two hundred years previous to the introduction of Islam. The Mohammedan year became strictly lunar.

Twelve lunar months compose the year of the *Hijrah*. Each month has its approximate beginning with the new moon. Since the Mohammedan year is governed solely by the moon, the seasons "wander" through the year, coming later and later until they retrograde through all the seasons in about thirty-two and a half years,[1] or, according to some Mohammedan authorities, in thirty-six years. The Mohammedan farmer would have a hard time should he attempt to sow or reap according to his calendar! Fortunately, however, he follows the sun rather than the almanac, with the result that his crops flourish quite as abundantly as those of his Christian neighbor.

The years of the *Hijrah* are divided into cycles, each cycle being made up of thirty years. Eleven years in every thirty-year cycle—the second, fifth, seventh, tenth, thirteenth, six-

[1] "The Mohammedan Calendar," *Encyclopaedia Britannica* (11th edition), v. 4, p. 1001.

teenth, eighteenth, twenty-first, twenty-fourth, twenty-sixth and twenty-ninth—are what might be termed "leap" years, consisting of 355 days each. The remaining nineteen years are common, and are composed of 354 days each. The extra day in each of the "leap" years is intercalated at the end of the last month, which consequently always has thirty instead of twenty-nine days. The last month of the nineteen common years has but twenty-nine days. The intercalated day is termed *yaum kabis*. The additional year is known as *sana kabisah*.

According to the Mohammedan calendar, March 14, 1937, marked the 1356th year of the forty-sixth cycle of the *Hijrah*.[2]

The names of the Mohammedan months are given below, together with the number of days belonging to each month:

Name of Month	*Number of Days*[3]
1. *Muharram* (first of *Muharram* commences the Mohammedan year)	30
2. *Safar*	29
3. *Răbī 'Awwal*	30
4. *Răbī 'Thani*	29
5. *Jumadah-l-Oula*	30
6. *Jumadah-l-Akhira*	29
7. *Rajab*	30
8. *Sha'ban*	29
9. *Ramadan*	30
10. *Shawwal*	29
11. *Dhu-l-Ku'dah*	30
12. *Dhu-l-Hijjah*	29
and in intercalary years	30

[2] "Mohammedan Holidays," *Encyclopaedia Britannica* (11th edition), v. 4, p. 1003.

[3] Until recently the number of days in the months varied according to the time the crescent moon was visible to the religious authority who had charge of making the calendar. During the last few years the function of this person has been abolished in practice.

The Book of Festivals

The Mohammedan day, like the Hebrew day, is reckoned from sunset to sunset, and is divided into twice twelve hours, which vary in relation to the season. The hours of the day are from one to twelve, and again from one to twelve. Because the sunset hour varies from day to day, the beginning of the Mohammedan day also changes a few minutes every day. The difference between the beginning of the Mohammedan day and that of the Christian must be kept in mind when computing Moslem dates, otherwise great confusion results. Frequently historians disagree by a day in dating important events, the reason being that one authority uses the Mohammedan and another the Christian reckoning of days.

The chief holidays of Islam are the five festivals relative to the life of Mohammed, its founder. The dates are only approximate, since Mohammedan holidays are computed not according to the calendar but according to the appearance of the moon on the horizon. Thus the same festival, because of the cloudiness or clearness of the sky, may be celebrated in different towns of the same country with a possible variation of twenty-four hours. Similarly, the same festival is likely to be observed in China and in Morocco, for example, on entirely different dates.

The principal Mohammedan holidays and the approximate period of their observation are as follows:

1. *Maulid,* Birthday of Mohammed (approximately the twelfth of the Third Moon, *Răbī 'Thani*).
2. *Al-Isrá,* Vision of the Journey of Mohammed from Mecca to Jerusalem (approximately the fifteenth of the Eighth Moon, *Sha'ban*).
3. *Lailat-al-Qadr,* First Revelation of Mohammed (approximately twenty-fourth of the Tenth Moon, *Ramaḍan*).
4. *'Id-il-Fitr,* End of *Ramaḍan* (approximately first of the Tenth Moon, *Shawwal*).
5. *'Ide Adha,* Feast of Sacrifice (approximately tenth of the Twelfth Moon, *Dhu-l-Ku'dah*).

374

APPENDIX

GLOSSARY OF FAMILIAR RELIGIOUS AND FESTIVAL TERMS

GLOSSARY OF FAMILIAR RELIGIOUS AND FESTIVAL TERMS

ADVENT

The term meaning "the coming of the Savior," which is applied to the four weeks preceding Christ's birth. Advent is recognized by the Christian churches as a period of preparation for Christmas, just as Lent is a preparation for Easter.

ADVENT SUNDAY

The Sunday nearest to the Feast of Saint Andrew (November 30), whether it falls before or after.

ALL FOOLS' DAY

April first, when it is customary to play various good-natured tricks and jokes on one's neighbors. The origin of the day is uncertain.

ALL SAINTS' DAY

November first, the feast commemorating all the saints. As early as the fourth century the Greek Church observed on Trinity Sunday a feast dedicated to all the lesser saints and martyrs who had no special day in their honor. About November 1, 731, when Gregory III consecrated a chapel in Saint Peter's to the memory of all the saints, the date of All Saints was changed to November first. The early English Church called the feast All Hallows, meaning All Holies. (See *Halloween*.) All Saints is the Eve of All Souls' Day.

ALL SOULS' DAY

November 2, a festival dedicated to commemoration of and prayer for the faithful dead who remain in Purgatory.

ANNUNCIATION

March 25, the anniversary of the angel Gabriel's announcement to the Virgin Mary of the mystery of the Incarnation.

ASCENSION

The fortieth day after Easter. This is the anniversary of Christ's ascension into heaven, forty days after his resurrection.

ASH WEDNESDAY

Observed as the first day of Lent in most Christian countries. The name is derived from the old custom of sprinkling ashes on the head in the penitential service of the day.

ASSUMPTION OF THE VIRGIN

August 15. A high festival of the Roman Catholic Church in honor of the Blessed Virgin's ascent to heaven.

BAISAKHI

The Hindu New Year, which falls on the first day of *Baisakha*.

CANDLEMAS

February 2, the fortieth day after the birth of Jesus. The name Candlemas originated from the custom of blessing candles in church on this day and distributing them to worshipers. (See *Groundhog Day, Presentation of Christ, Purification of the Virgin Mary*.)

CARLING SUNDAY

Fifth Sunday in Lent. So called in Great Britain from the custom of eating the traditional carlings, or peas, which have been soaked, fried and seasoned with salt and pepper.

Appendix: Glossary of Familiar Terms

CARNIVAL

The term given to the period of feasting and merrymaking which immediately precedes Lent and is thought to help compensate for the forty days of Lenten abstinence and self-denial. The word "carnival" is derived from the Latin words *carne vale,* meaning "farewell meat."

CHILDERMAS (See *Holy Innocents' Day*)

CHRISTMAS

December 25, the anniversary of the reputed date of the birth of Jesus Christ. This is the greatest of church feast days.

CIRCUMCISION, FEAST OF THE

January first, one week after the Nativity. This feast, commemorating the naming of Jesus and his formal admission into the membership privileges of the Church of Israel, is observed on this date by all Christian Churches except the Armenian. Since Christmas is celebrated on January 6 by the Armenian Church, the Feast of the Circumcision falls on January 13.

COMMENCEMENT

The term applied to the conferring of degrees by colleges and universities, as well as to the graduation exercises of academies and schools.

CORPUS CHRISTI

The Thursday following Trinity Sunday. *Corpus Christi,* meaning "body of Christ," ranks as one of the greatest festivals of the Roman Catholic Church. The day commemorates the institution of the Eucharist and celebrates the doctrine of transubstantiation.

CROSS, DISCOVERY OR INVENTION OF THE

May 3, the feast observed by the Greek and Latin Churches

379

The Book of Festivals

in commemoration of the discovery of the "true cross," in 326 A.D., by Saint Helena, mother of Constantine the Great.

CROSS, ELEVATION OF THE (Known also as *Holy Cross* or *Holy Rood Day*)

A festival observed by the Greek and Latin Churches on September 14. It commemorates the miraculous vision of the cross seen by Constantine in 312 A.D., when he was about to fight Maxentius. According to some authorities Constantine himself instituted the feast in honor of the Holy Cross, which appeared in the heavens with the words, *In hoc signo vinces,* "By this sign you will conquer."

EASTER

The Sunday set aside by the Christian Church to commemorate Christ's resurrection from the dead. According to the Council of Nice, Easter always is reckoned in the Gregorian calendar as the first Sunday after the paschal full moon of the vernal equinox (March 21). Should the full moon occur on a Sunday, Easter falls on the Sunday following. Easter does not come *before* March 22, or *after* April 25.

EASTER MONDAY AND TUESDAY

The first and second days immediately following Easter Sunday. Observed as popular holidays in most European countries.

EASTER SEPULCHRE

A stone or wooden structure that resembles a sepulchre and represents the tomb of Christ. The sepulchre is used extensively in the Holy Week ceremonials of the various Christian Churches.

EPIPHANY (Known also as *Three Kings' Day,* or *Twelfth Night*)

January 6, the twelfth day after Christmas. Epiphany, meaning "manifestation," is the anniversary of three great

380

events in the life of Christ. It commemorates the star's leading of the Three Kings to his manger; the appearance of the Holy Ghost at his baptism in the river Jordan; and the miracle of turning water into wine at the marriage in Cana.

EUCHARIST

The term applied to the sacrament of the Lord's Supper and also to the consecrated wafer and wine used in the communion service.

FEAST OF WEEKS (Also called *Shabuoth*)

A Jewish festival that falls on the fiftieth day after the first day of Passover.

GOOD FRIDAY

The Friday preceding Easter. This day commemorates the Passion of Christ.

GROUNDHOG DAY

February 2. In the United States, Candlemas, which is popularly known by this name, is associated with weather lore. According to tradition, the groundhog comes out of his hole on February 2, looks around, and if he sees his shadow crawls back for another six weeks of cold weather. If, on the contrary, the day is cloudy, the groundhog remains above ground, and mild weather may be expected. (See *Candlemas, Presentation of Christ, Purification of the Virgin Mary*.)

HALLOWEEN

The popular name given to the night of October 31, the Eve of All Souls' Day. (See *All Saints' Day*.)

HOLY INNOCENTS' DAY (Called also *Childermas* in England)

December 28, the anniversary of the slaughter of Bethlehem's innocent children by order of King Herod, who wished to be certain of killing the Infant Jesus.

HOLY SATURDAY

The Saturday immediately preceding Easter. The Easter vigil is observed on this day.

JANAM (Called also *Janma Ashtami*)

A great Hindu festival celebrated during *Bhadra* (August–September) in honor of the birth of the god Krishna.

LENT

The name given to the annual period of fasting and penitence that many churches observe in preparation for the Easter feast. In the Western Church Lent begins on Ash Wednesday and continues for the forty week-days preceding Easter. The six Sundays occurring during the Lenten period are not included, since Sundays always are regarded as feast days.

LOW SUNDAY

The Sunday after Easter. The day is so called because it is of less importance than Easter.

MARTINMAS

November 11, the feast of Saint Martin, which is celebrated in many European countries as the occasion for tasting new wine, eating roast goose and enjoying the fruits of the harvest.

MAULID, BIRTHDAY OF MOHAMMED

The birthday of the Prophet Mohammed, one of the most important festivals of the Moslem calendar.

MAUNDY THURSDAY

The Thursday preceding Easter. The day sometimes is called *dies mandati*, Mandate or Maundy Thursday, from the fact that Jesus washed his disciples' feet on this day and commanded them to do likewise.

MAY DAY

May first, the ancient Druidic feast of Bel, is dedicated in the Christian Church to the memory of the two apostles Saints Philip and James. May Day also is celebrated throughout the world as International Labor Day.

MIDSUMMER DAY (See *Saint John's Day*)

Appendix: Glossary of Familiar Terms

MOTHERING SUNDAY (Called also *Mid-Lent Sunday*)

The fourth Sunday in Lent. According to old British lore children away from home visit their parents on this day. They take gifts to their fathers and mothers. The mother's special present is a simnel, or rich plum cake, which is made according to a traditional formula.

NATIVITY OF THE VIRGIN

A feast celebrated by both the Latin and the Greek Churches on September 8, in memory of the birth of the Virgin Mary.

NEW YEAR'S DAY

The first day of the calendar year.

PALM SUNDAY, PASSION SUNDAY

The Sunday immediately preceding Easter. The name Palm Sunday is derived from the custom of carrying palms, in commemoration of the palms waved before Christ when he made his triumphal entrance into Jerusalem.

PANCAKE DAY (Called also *Shrove Tuesday*)

The Tuesday before Ash Wednesday. In Great Britain, before the Reformation, a bell was rung on Shrove Tuesday, to remind people of confession and shriving by the priest. After the Reformation, when the bell which once summoned people to church became the signal for making pancakes and indulging in all sorts of sports, Shrove Tuesday popularly became known as Pancake Day.

PASCHAL CANDLE

A large candle which is blessed at the church altar on Holy Saturday, lighted and kept burning until Ascension Day.

PASSION OF CHRIST

The term applied to the sufferings of Christ between the time of the Last Supper and his death on the cross.

383

The Book of Festivals

PASSOVER

The annual Jewish festival that begins on the fourteenth day of *Nissan* and continues for eight days following. Passover derives its name from the Biblical story of the Death Angel who "passed over" Jewish homes when he slew the first-born sons of the Egyptians.

PENTECOST

A great feast observed by the Jews on the fiftieth day after the first day of Passover, and by the Christians on the fiftieth day after Easter. (See *Feast of Weeks, Whitsunday*.)

PRESENTATION OF CHRIST

February 2, the anniversary of Mary's presentation of her Son at the Temple forty days after his birth. (See *Candlemas, Groundhog Day, Purification of the Virgin Mary*.)

PRESEPIO

A representation of the manger scene. The *presepio* is found in Italian homes and churches during the Christmas season.

PURIFICATION OF THE VIRGIN MARY (Known also as *Presentation of Christ, Candlemas* and *Groundhog Day*)

February 2, the fortieth day after the birth of Christ. The feast is in honor of the purification of the Virgin and the presentation of her Son at the Temple.

RAMADAN

The ninth lunar month of the Mohammedan year. Ramadan is a period of fasting (from dawn to sunset only) in preparation for *Sheker Baïram,* the great festival with which Ramadan ends. (See *Sheker Baïram*.)

ROGATION DAYS

The Monday, Tuesday and Wednesday preceding Ascension Thursday. The name is derived from the fact that the Litany of the Saints is chanted during the processions of the three days.

Appendix: Glossary of Familiar Terms

SAINT JOHN'S DAY (Known also as *Midsummer Day, Nativity of Saint John the Baptist*)

June 24, the nativity of Saint John the Baptist, presents one of the rare exceptions when a saint is commemorated on the day of his birth, rather than on that of his death. Since June 24 is the time of the summer solstice, the festival is celebrated popularly throughout Europe as Midsummer Day.

SHABUOTH (See *Feast of Weeks*)

SHEKER BAÏRAM

The three-day festival that ends Ramaḍan. People wear new garments, exchange gifts, visit and make merry after the Ramaḍan fast.

SHROVE TUESDAY (Called also *Pancake Day* in England)

The Tuesday before Ash Wednesday, or the last day before Lent. In most Catholic countries Shrove Tuesday is regarded as the culminating day of the carnival festivities.

THANKSGIVING DAY

In the United States, a legal holiday set apart by proclamation of the President as a time of thanksgiving and praise for the mercies of the past year. Thanksgiving usually comes on the last Thursday in November.

THREE KINGS' DAY (See *Twelfth Night*)

TRANSFIGURATION, FEAST OF THE

August 6, a feast held by some branches of the Christian Churches in memory of Christ's transfiguration on Mount Tabor, in the presence of his disciples Peter, James and John.

TRINITY

Fifty-seven days after Easter, or the Sunday following Whitsunday (or Pentecost). The feast commemorates the mystery of the Trinity.

TWELVE DAYS

The name popularly applied to the twelve-day period between Christmas and Epiphany. According to ancient lore the "Twelve Days" are the "image of the year," and anything done during this period reflects on the good or the bad luck of the next twelve months. This belief possibly originated in the Vedic age in India, when the twelve midwinter days were regarded as the time when the genii of the seasons rested in the sun god's home. The twelve days of rest were sacred in character and were looked upon as "a copy of the year." In some Christian countries, witches, ghosts and the souls of unbaptized children are said to roam abroad and do harm to mortals during the twelve-day interval between Jesus' nativity and his baptism.

TWELFTH NIGHT (See *Epiphany, Three Kings' Day*)

VISITATION

July 2, the festival which celebrates the visit of the Virgin Mary to Elizabeth, mother of John the Baptist.

WHITSUNDAY (Called also *Pentecost*)

A festival occurring on the seventh Sunday and the fiftieth day after Easter. Whitsunday commemorates the descent of the Holy Ghost on the Apostles, on the day of Pentecost. The term "whit" is thought by many to mean "white" and to refer to the wearing of white garments by converts who were baptized on this day.

WHITSUNTIDE or PENTECOST

The week commencing with Whitsunday, especially the first three days, known as Whitsunday, Whit-Monday and Whit-Tuesday.

SELECTED BIBLIOGRAPHY ON
FESTIVALS

SELECTED BIBLIOGRAPHY ON FESTIVALS

GENERAL

Breasted, James H.
"The Beginning of Time Measurement and the Origins of Our Calendar." *Scientific Monthly,* v. 41, October, 1935, p. 289–304.

Folk-Lore: a Quarterly Review of Myth, Tradition, Institution and Custom. London, Glaisher, Publication of the Folk-Lore Society (British).
See index to each volume for countries, holidays and customs.

Frazer, James George.
The Golden Bough: A Study in Religion and Magic. 3rd ed. London, Macmillan, 1911–26. 12 vols.
See name of country in v. 12, *Bibliography and General Index,* for material on each country listed below.

Hastings, James, ed.
Encyclopaedia of Religion and Ethics. New York, Scribner's, 1908–1927. v. 1–12 and *Index.*
See name of country in *Index,* for material on each country listed below.

Johnson, W. Branch.
"Whitsuntide in Rustic Europe." *Catholic World,* v. 137, June, 1933, p. 342–346.

Miles, Clement A.
Christmas in Ritual and Tradition, Christian and Pagan. London, Unwin, 1912.
See index for name of country, festival or custom. Good material on the Yuletide cycle.

The Book of Festivals

Walsh, William Shepard.
*Curiosities of Popular Customs and of Rites, Ceremonies, Observ-
ances and Miscellaneous Antiquities.* Philadelphia, Lippincott,
1925.
See index for name of saint, festival or custom.

ALBANIANS

Chater, Melville.
"Europe's Newest Kingdom," *National Geographic Magazine,* v.
59, February, 1931, p. 131–190.
Colored costume plates and descriptions of native customs.

Dozon, Auguste, tr.
Contes Albanais. Paris, Leroux, 1881.
An old collection of folk tales, which furnishes valuable background material
to students of native customs.

Durham, M. E.
High Albania. London, Arnold, 1909.
p. 45 ff., Feast of the Translation of St. Nicholas.

Miller, Elizabeth Cleveland.
Pran of Albania. Garden City, New York, Doubleday, Doran,
1929.
Ch. 4, "Feast Day," p. 51–72. Description of Feast of St. John the Divine.

Peacock, Wadham.
Albania. London, Chapman and Hall, 1914.
Ch. 12, "A Night in Ramazan," p. 142–152; ch. 13, "An Albanian Wed-
ding," p. 153–175.

Pedersen, Holger.
Zur Albanesischen Volkskunde. Copenhagen, Siegfried Michael-
sens Nachfolger, 1898.

AMERICANS

Brown, Abram English.
"The Ups and Downs of Christmas in New England." *New England Magazine,* n.s. v. 29, December, 1903, p. 479–484.

Selected Bibliography

Crawford, Mary Caroline.
Social Life in Old New England. Boston, Little, Brown, 1914.
Chapters 14 and 15 give charming descriptions of early Thanksgiving and Christmas customs.

Dillon, Philip Robert.
American Anniversaries; Every Day in the Year. New York, Philip R. Dillon, 1918.
Well-selected historical material on great American anniversaries.

Earle, Alice Morse.
Customs and Fashions in Old New England. New York, Scribner's, 1902.
Colorful description of the first Thanksgiving, of Christmas and other holidays celebrated in New England.

Hunt, Gaillard.
"A Christmas at Mount Vernon." *Century,* v. 77, December, 1908, p. 188–195.
A description of the celebration in honor of Washington's return to Mount Vernon in 1783.

Jones, Dora M.
"Mount Rubidoux in a Silver Sunrise Service." *Literary Digest,* v. 117, March, 31, 1934, p. 17.

Pickett, LaS. C.
"Old-time Virginia Christmas." *Harper's Bazaar,* v. 41, January, 1907, p. 48–54.

Tittle, Walter, comp.
Colonial Holidays. Garden City, New York, Doubleday, Doran, 1910.
Contemporary accounts of how holidays were celebrated in colonial days.

ARMENIANS

Ananikian, Mardiros H.
"Armenian Mythology." In *Mythology of All Races.* Boston, Marshall Jones, 1925. v. 12, p. 11–100.
An authoritative treatise on Armenian mythology.

391

The Book of Festivals

Boettiger, Louis A.

Armenian Legends and Festivals. Minnesota University, Studies in Social Sciences, no. 14. Minneapolis, University of Minnesota, 1920.

A valuable study of Armenian customs and holidays as related to the Church. A useful handbook for club workers and activities directors.

Ormanian, Malachia.

The Church of Armenia; Her History, Doctrine, Rule, Discipline, Liturgy, Literature and Existing Condition. London, Mowbray, 1912.

Ch. 36, "The System of the Calendar," p. 180–184; ch. 37, "The Dominical Festivals," p. 185–190; ch. 38, "The Commemoration of Saints," p. 191–198.

"The Old Armenia in New America," *Survey,* v. 36, May 6, 1916, p. 167–169.

Werfel, Franz.

The Forty Days of Musa Dagh. New York, Viking Press, 1934.

" 'The Forty Days of Musa Dagh' is a very exciting book; it is at once a story of an astonishing military operation, a study of nationalism, a picture of native Armenian life, and a subtly reactionary bit of special pleading." *New Outlook,* December, 1934.

AUSTRIANS

Adrian, Karl.

Salzburger Volksspiele, Aufzüge und Tänze. Salzburg, A. H. Huber, 1908.

Excellent description of many of the old Austrian folk plays, processions and dances. Words to many of the songs included, and some music.

—— *Von Salzburger Sitt'und Brauch.* Wien, Österreichischer Schulbücherverlag, 1924.

Creed, Virginia.

"Corpus Christi Day in Halstatt." *Foreign Travel,* v. 30, July, 1936, p. 10–11, 29.

Selected Bibliography

Dollar, George.
"Masked Procession of Imst." *Wide World Magazine,* v. 13, April, 1904, p. 23–29.

Dörrer, Anton.
Die Thierseer Passionsspiele, 1799–1935; Ringen um Bestand und Gestalt eines Tiroler Volksbrauches. Innsbruck, Mar. Vereinsbuchhandlung und Buchdruckerei A. G., 1935.

Holme, Charles, ed.
Peasant Art in Austria and Hungary. London, 'The Studio,' Ltd., 1911.
The artistic background of peasant festival customs is well described and illustrated.

Mabie, Hamilton W.
"A Passion Play in the Tyrol." *Outlook,* v. 76, February 6, 1904, p. 341–346.
An account of the Passion Play given in the little town of Brixlegg.

"Merry Maskers of Imst." *National Geographic Magazine,* v. 70, August, 1936, p. 201–208.
Fourteen illustrations with captions.

Saberlandt, Michael.
Österreich, sein Land und Volk und seine Kultur. Wien, Verlag für Volks-und Heimatkunde, 1929.
Ch. 3, "Volkskunde von Österreich."

Vernaleken, Theodor.
Mythen und Bräuche des Volkes in Österreich. Wien, W. Braumüller, 1859.

BELGIANS

Anderson, Isabel.

The Spell of Belgium. Boston, Page, 1915.
Description of the Festival of the Dancing Gilles in Binche at Mardi-Gras, p. 336–338.

Delstanche, Albert.
The Little Towns of Flanders. London, Chatto and Windus, 1906.
Description of the annual Mystery of the Passion at Furnes, p. 23–24.

Omond, George W. T.
Peeps at Many Lands: Belgium. London, Black, 1909.
Contains much excellent material on Belgian processions and children's holidays.

Rooses, Max, ed.
Vlaanderen door de Eeuwen Heen. Amsterdam, "Elsevier," 1912–1913. 2 vols.

Schayes, A. G. B.
Essai Historique sur les Usages, les Croyances, les Traditions, les Cérémonies, et Pratiques Réligieuses et Civiles des Belges Anciens et Modernes. Louvain. Privately printed, 1834.
Contains a wealth of material on Belgian customs and festivals.

Scudamore, Cyril.
Belgium and the Belgians. New York, Dutton, 1903.
"A Chapter of Folk-Lore," p. 341–359.

Wallonia, Liége.
Publication on Belgian folklore. See index to volumes for festivals, music, legends, etc.

BRITISH

Blakeborough, Richard.
Wit, Character, Folklore and Customs of the North Riding of Yorkshire. London, Henry Frowde, 1898.

Brand, John.
Observations on the Popular Antiquities of Great Britain. London, Bohn, 1849. 3 vols.

Chambers, Robert.
The Book of Days: a Miscellany of Popular Antiquities in Connection with the Calendar. London, Chambers, 1863–1864. 2 vols.

Hogg, Major Philip.
A Calendar of Old English Customs Still in Being, 1936. Reading. Privately printed, 1936.

Selected Bibliography

Hone, William.
Every-Day Book and Table Book. London. Printed for Thomas Tegg, 1826. 3 vols.

MacCulloch, John Arnott.
"Celtic." In *Mythology of All Races*. Boston, Marshall Jones, 1918. v. 3, p. 5–213.

Rhŷs, John.
Celtic Folklore, Welsh and Manx. Oxford, Clarendon Press, 1901. 2 vols.

"St. John's Eve." *Catholic World*, v. 139, June, 1934, p. 351–352. St. John's Eve in Ireland.

Sikes, Wirt.
British Goblins, Welsh Folk-Lore, Fairy Mythology, Legends and Traditions. London, Low, Marston, Searle and Rivington, 1880. "Quaint Old Customs," p. 250–337.

Simpson, Eve Blantyre.
Folklore in Lowland Scotland. London, Dent, 1908.

Thiselton-Dyer, T. F.
English Folk-Lore. London, Hardwicke and Bogue, 1878.

Verrall, F. M.
"The Farmer's Year." *Catholic World*, v. 136, October, 1932, p. 87–91.

Williamson, George C.
Curious Survivals; Habits and Customs of the Past That Still Live in the Present. London, Jenkins, Ltd., 1923.

Wood-Martin, W. G.
Traces of the Elder Faiths of Ireland. London, Longmans, Green, 1902. 2 vols.

Wright, A. R.
British Calendar Customs. v. 1. *England. Movable Festivals*. London, Glaisher, 1936.

BULGARIANS

Arnaudov, Mikhail Petrov.
Die Bulgarischen Festbräuche (Bulgarische Bibliothek no. 4). Leipzig, I. Parlapanoff, 1917.
One of the most authentic accounts of native festival customs, observances of Christmas, New Year, Lazarus Day, St. George's Day, Harvest, etc.

"Christmas Customs in South-Eastern Europe." *Bulgarian British Review*, no. 38–39, December, 1931–January, 1932, p. 17. "Bulgaria."

Markham, R. H.
Meet Bulgaria. Sofia, Stopansko Razvitiye Press, 1931.
Ch. 6, "Life in the Village," p. 104–115; ch. 7, "Romance in the Village," p. 116–151.

Muir, Nadejda.
"The Feast of the Epiphany." *Bulgarian British Review*, no. 38–39, December, 1931–January, 1932, p. 18.

"St. Cyril and Methodius Festival." *Bulgarian British Review*, no. 32, May, 1931, p. 7, 14.

"The Easter Festivals in Bulgaria." *Bulgarian British Review*, no. 31, April, 1931, p. 4.

"The Day of the National Awakeners." *Bulgarian British Review*, no. 73–74, November–December, 1934, p. 6–7.

Vessova, A.
"Bulgarian Village Life and Customs." *Bulgarian British Review*, no. 28, January, 1931, p. 9–10.

—— "Village Family Life and Customs in Bulgaria: Marriage Customs." *Bulgarian British Review*, no. 30, March, 1931, p. 10–12.

—— "Village Family Life and Customs in Bulgaria: Births, Deaths and Superstitions." *Bulgarian British Review*, no. 32, May, 1931, p. 9–11.

—— "Village Family Life and Customs in Bulgaria: Village Festivals." *Bulgarian British Review*, no. 35, September, 1931, p. 10–12.

Selected Bibliography

CHINESE

Doré, Henri.
Researches into Chinese Superstitions. Tr. by M. Kennelly.
Shanghai, T'Usewei Printing Press, 1914–1933. 10 vols.
Part I, "Superstitious Practices," v. 1–5; Part II, "Chinese Pantheon,"
v. 6–10.
One of the most authoritative studies on Chinese symbols, folk customs and
festival practices. Profusely illustrated.

Ferguson, John C.
"Chinese." In *Mythology of All Races.* Boston, Marshall Jones,
1928. v. 8, p. 1–203.

Hodous, Lewis.
Folkways in China. London, A. Probsthain, 1929.

Tun Li-ch'en.
Annual Customs and Festivals in Peking (as recorded in the Yen-
Ching Sui-shih-chi). Tr. by Derk Bodde. Peiping, H. Vetch,
1936.
A translation from the Chinese of a work written in 1900. "It is a record,
day by day, and month by month, beginning with Chinese New Year's Day
and taking us throughout the year, of what used to take place in Peking: its
festivals, temple pilgrimages, fairs, customs, and the clothing, foods and
animals of the season."

U. S. Department of Labor, Bureau of Immigration.
Chinese-American Calendar. Comp. by William C. Welch. United
States Government Printing Office, 1928.
A useful guide in computing Chinese dates. Calendar tables from 1849 to
1951.

Werner, E. T. C.
China of the Chinese. London, Pitman, 1919.
Ch. 4, "Ceremonial Institutions," p. 62–107.

Williams, Edward Thomas.
China Yesterday and Today. New York, Crowell, 1932.
Ch. 10, "The Calendar and Its Festivals," p. 205–222.

397

The Book of Festivals

CZECHOSLOVAKS

Máchal, Jan.
"Slavic." In *Mythology of All Races*. Boston, Marshall Jones, 1918. v. 3, p. 217–314.

Němcová, Božena.
Babička; Obrazy Venkovského života. Praha, Aventinum, 1923.
Babička, the old grandmother, gives many charming pictures of rural life, customs and superstitions.

Szalatnay, Rafael D., ed.
Old Bohemian Customs Throughout the Year. New York, Rafael D. Szalatnay [192–?].

Tufnell, Blanche O.
"Czechoslovak Folklore." *Folk-Lore*, v. 35, March, 1924, p. 26–56.
Contains much unusual material on festivals and folk customs.

Zíbrt, Čeněk.
Staročeské Výročni; Obyčeje, Pověry, Slavnosti a Zábavy Prostonárodni. Praha, Jos. R. Vilimka, 1889.
Old Bohemian customs, proverbs, folk songs and dances.

DANES

Bröchner, Jessie.
Danish Life in Town and Country. New York, Putnam's, 1906.
Some information on festivals in ch. 9, "Copenhagen," p. 111–116; ch. 15, "Country Life," p. 188–198.

Mogensen, Brigitte Monrad.
"Almond for Luck." *American-Scandinavian Review*, v. 5, January, 1917, p. 45–50.

Olrik, Axel.
Nordens Trylleviser. Udgivet af Anders Bjerrum og Inger M. Boberg. Copenhagen, J. H. Schultz, 1934.
Authoritative material collected by a great folklorist.

Riis, Jacob A.
The Old Town. New York, Macmillan, 1909.
Old customs and home festivals charmingly described.

Selected Bibliography

ESTONIANS

Eisen, M. J.
Meie Jõulud. Tartu, Eesti Kirjanduse Seltsi Kirjastus, 1931.
—— *Eesti Uuem Mütoloogia.* Tallinn, K. Ü. "Rahvaülikool."

Holmberg, Uno.
"Finno Urgic." In *Mythology of All Races.* Boston, Marshall Jones, 1925. v. 4, p. 1–295.

Kallas, Oskar T.
"Estonian Folklore." *Folk-Lore,* v. 34, June, 1923, p. 101–116.

Kreutzwald, Friedrich R. & H. Neus.
Mythische und Magische Lieder der Ehsten. St. Petersburg, Kaiserliche Akad. der Wissenschaften, 1854.
An authoritative work by the first native scholar to collect data on Estonian folklore and customs.

Kuemme, P. N.
"A Wedding on Kihnu Island." *Estonian Review,* v. 1, September, 1919, p. 108–109.

Loorits, Oskar.
Estnische Volksdichtung und Mythologie. Tartu, Akadeemiline Kooperatiiv, 1932.

Päss, Elmar.
Eesti Liulaul: Runovõrdluse Katse. Tartu, 1933.
Contains folk songs and music.

Sapas, J.
"Heathen Religions of Ancient Estonia." *Estonian Review,* v. 1, October, 1919, p. 144–146.

FINNS

Byrne, Bess S.
"The Northland's Festival of Light; Midsummer Night in Finland." *Travel,* v. 59, August, 1932, p. 26–27, 47.

Holmberg, Uno.
"Finno Urgic." In *Mythology of All Races.* Boston, Marshall Jones, 1925. v. 4, p. 1–295.

Kalevala, the Land of Heroes. Tr. by W. F. Kirby. New York, Dutton, 1923–1925. 2 vols.
Probably the best translation of Finland's national epic.

Löwis of Menar, August von.
Finnische und Estnische Volksmärchen. Jéna, E. Dietrichs, 1922.

Sillanpää, F. E.
The Maid Silja; the history of the last offshoot of an old family tree. Tr. by Alexander Matson. New York, Macmillan, 1933.

Wilhelmson, Carl.
Midsummernight. New York, Farrar and Rinehart, 1930.
A novel that gives excellent background material on native customs, such as midsummer night, funerals, weddings, bathing contests, etc.

FRENCH

Bentzon, Th.
"Christmas in France." *Century,* v. 63 [new series, v. 41], December, 1901, p. 170–177.
Charming illustrations by Boutet de Monvel.

Dobrée, L. E.
"The Brittany Pardons." *Ecclesiastical Review,* v. 43, October, 1910, p. 399–412.

Law, Margaret L.
"Welcoming Spring in Brittany." *Travel,* v. 52, April, 1929, p. 34–37, 64.

Le Braz, Anatole.
Au Pays des Pardons. Paris, Calmann-Lévy, 1900.

Le Goffic, Charles.
Fêtes et Coutumes populaires. Paris, A. Colin, 1923.
Excellent material on all types of French folk festivals.

Selected Bibliography

Mistral, Frédéric.
Memoirs. Tr. by C. E. Maud. London, Arnold, 1907.
Ch. 3, "The Magi Kings," p. 32–37; ch. 14, "Journey to les Saintes-Maries," p. 235–249.

Peck, Anne M., and Méras, Edmond A.
France, Crossroads of Europe. New York, Harper, 1936.
Ch. 8, "Round the Year with Holidays and Customs," p. 123–146.

GERMANS

Grimm, Jacob.
Teutonic Mythology. Tr. from 4th ed. with notes and appendix, by James Steven Stallybrass. 4 v. London, Sonnerschein and Allen, 1880–1888, v. 1–2; v. 2–4 published by Bell.

Gronow, A. S.
"Old Spring Customs in Germany." *Elementary School Teacher,* v. 8, April, 1908, p. 413–422.

Kück, Eduard, and Sohnrey, Heinrich.
Feste und Spiele des deutschen Landvolks. Berlin, Deutsche Landbuchhandlung, 1909.

Peck, Anne Merriman.
Young Germany. New York, McBride, 1936.
Ch. 9, "Heydays and Holidays," p. 162–182.

Reichhardt, Rudolf.
Die deutschen Feste in Sitte und Brauch. Jena, Hermann Costenoble, 1908.
Good descriptions of the folk customs connected with the principal holidays.

Rydberg, Viktor.
Teutonic Mythology. Gods and Goddesses of the Northland. Tr. from the Swedish by R. B. Anderson. London, Norroena Society, 1906. 3 vols.

Reinsberg-Dueringsfeld, Otto von.
Das festliche Jahr. In Sitten, Gebräuchen, Aberglauben und Festen der germanischen Völker. 2 ed. Leipzig, H. Barsdorf, 1898.
An excellent month by month calendar of German holidays with comparative material on holiday customs of other countries.

The Book of Festivals

Stelmachowska, Bożena.
Rok Obrzędowy na Pomorzu. Toruń [etc.], 1933. Instytut Bał-
tycki, Thorn, Pamietnik. Ser.: Balticum, Zeszyt, 7.
Holidays, customs and social life in Pomerania.

GREEKS

Abbott, G. F.
Macedonian Folklore. Cambridge, University Press, 1903.
Excellent material on customs, festivals and folk beliefs of Greek-speaking
parts of Macedonia.

Fox, William Sherwood.
"Greek and Roman." In *Mythology of All Races.* Boston, Marshall Jones, 1916. v. 1.

Gilder, R. W.
"The Miracle of the Greek Fire." *Century Magazine,* v. 53, n.s.
31, April, 1897, p. 950–954.

Harrison, Jane E.
Ancient Art and Ritual. London, Butterworth, 1927.

Lawson, John C.
*Modern Greek Folklore and Ancient Greek Religion; a Study in
Survivals.* Cambridge, University Press, 1910.

MacCallum, Frank Lyman.
"The Great Blessing." *Asia,* v. 27, July, 1927, p. 583–585.
Description of blessing the waters on Epiphany morning in Constantinople.
Good plates.

Rodd, Rennell.
Customs and Lore of Modern Greece. London, David Stott, 1892.

HINDUS

Crooke, W.
"The Dasahra: An Autumn Festival of the Hindus." *Folk-Lore,*
v. 26, March, 1915, p. 28–59.

Selected Bibliography

—— "The Dīvālī: the Lamp Festival of the Hindus." *Folk-Lore*, v. 34, December, 1923, p. 267–292.

—— "The Holi: a Vernal Festival of the Hindus." *Folk-Lore*, v. 25, March, 1914, p. 55–83.

Forster, E. M.
A Passage to India. New York, Harcourt, Brace, 1924.
Ch. 33–36, p. 183–316. A description of the festival in honor of Krishna's birth.

Keith, A. Berriedale.
"Indian." In *Mythology of All Races.* Boston, Marshall Jones, 1917. v. 6, p. 1–250.

Lee, Frank Harold, ed.
Folk Tales of All Nations. New York, Coward-McCann, 1930.
"India," p. 598–663. These old folk tales explain many native customs and festival practices.

Noble, Margaret E. (The Sister Nivedita).
Cradle Tales of Hinduism. London, Longmans, Green, 1907.

—— *Myths of the Hindus and Buddhists.* New York, Holt, 1914.

—— *The Web of Indian Life.* London, Longmans, Green, 1918.
These three books by Margaret Noble afford rich background material essential to the understanding of Hindu festivals.

Roy, Satyananda.
When I Was a Boy in India. Boston, Lothrop, Lee and Shepard, 1924.
Ch. 13, "Hindu Festivals," p. 183–197. Other chapters deal with social life and native customs.

Ryder, Arthur W.
Kālidāsa; translations of Shakuntala and other works. New York, Dutton, 1933.
"The Seasons," p. 211–216.

—— *The Bhagavat-Gita.* Chicago, University of Chicago Press, 1929.
An excellent translation of one of the most influential of Hindu sacred writings. Helpful in understanding the background of Hindu religious festivals.

The Book of Festivals

Sarkar, Benoy Kumar.
The Folk-Element in Hindu Culture; a Contribution to Socio-Religious Studies in Hindu Folk-Institutions. London, Longmans, Green, 1917.

Yazdani, Ghulam.
Ajanta; the Colour and Monochrome Reproductions of the Ajanta Frescoes Based on Photography. London, Oxford University Press, 1930–1933. Part 1–2.
Each part is in 2 vols., one of text and one of plates. The plates, which are exceptionally fine, illustrate native mythology and customs, festivals, religious dances and processions.

HUNGARIANS

Holme, Charles, ed.
Peasant Art in Austria and Hungary. London, 'The Studio,' Ltd., 1911.
The artistic background of festival customs is well described and illustrated.

Pulsky, Ferencz, and T. Pulszky.
Tales and Traditions of Hungary. London, H. Colburn, 1851. 3 vols.

Róheim, G.
"Hungarian Calendar Customs." *Royal Anthropological Institute of Great Britain and Ireland. Journal,* v. 56, 1926, p. 361–384.
Well-organized material accompanied by unusual bibliographical references.

Szendrey, Ákos.
"Symbolic Dances in Hungarian Folklore." *Hungarian Quarterly,* v. 1, Spring, 1936, p. 124–135.
Excellent material on festivals and dances.

Viski, Károly.
Hungarian Peasant Customs. Budapest, G. Vajna and Co., 1932.

—— *Transylvanian Hungarians, Peasant Art.* Budapest, Popular Literary Society [191–?].

Wlislocki, Heinrich von.
Aus dem Volksleben der Magyaren. Ethnologische Mitteilungen. München, K. Fischer, 1893.

Selected Bibliography

ITALIANS

Ashby, Thomas.
Some Italian Scenes and Festivals. London, Methuen, 1929.

Fox, William Sherwood.
"The Mythology of Ancient Italy." In *Mythology of All Races.*
Boston, Marshall Jones, 1916. v. 1, p. 285–307.

Heywood, William.
Our Lady of August and the Palio of Siena. Siena, E. Torrini,
1899.

Holme, Charles, ed.
Peasant Art in Italy. London, 'The Studio,' Ltd., 1913.
This book, which describes peasant arts and has beautiful illustrations, fur-
nishes excellent background material for the study of native festivals.

Marinoni, A.
"Popular Feasts and Legends in Italy." *Sewanee Review,* v. 24,
January, 1916, p. 69–80.
A good résumé of some typical feasts.

Marzio, Cornelio di.
"Italienische Volksfeste." *Der Querschnitt,* v. 10, November,
1930, p. 725–729.

Opera Nazionale Depolavoro.
Popular Italian Costumes, Music, Dances and Festivals. Rome,
National Leisure Hours Institution, 1931.
See particularly "Specimen Calendar of Italian Popular Festivals." Brief
but authentic account of some of the most characteristic native festivals.

JAPANESE

Anesaki, Masaharu.
"Japanese Mythology." In *Mythology of All Races.* Boston, Marshall Jones, 1928. v. 7, p. 207–387.

Erskine, W. H.
Japanese Customs, Their Origin and Value. 3d ed. Tokyo, Kyo
Bun Kwan, 1929.

—— *Japanese Festival and Calendar Lore.* Tokyo, Kyo Bun Kwan, 1933.

Greenbie, S.
The Romantic East. New York, McBride, 1930.

Holtom, D. C.
The Japanese Enthronement Ceremonies. Tokyo, Kyo Bun Kwan, 1928.

Kincaid, Zoë.
Tokyo Vignettes. Tokyo, The Sanseido Co., 1933.

Kiyooka, Chiyono Sugimoto.
Chiyo's Return. Garden City, New York, Doubleday, Doran, 1935.
Charming descriptions of such festivals as the Seventh Day of the Seventh Moon, O Bon, New Year, etc.

Lee, Frank H.
A Tokyo Calendar with Impressions of an Impressionable. Tokyo, Hokuseido Press, 1934.

—— *Days and Years in Japan.* Tokyo, Hokuseido Press, 1935.

Okakura-Kakuzo.
The Book of Tea. New York, Duffield, 1912.

Sugimoto, Etsu.
A Daughter of the Narakin. London, Hurst and Blackett, 1933.

—— *A Daughter of the Nohfu.* Garden City, New York, Doubleday, Doran, 1935.

—— *A Daughter of the Samurai.* Garden City, New York, Doubleday, Doran, 1925.

JEWS

Adlerblum, Nima H.
A Perspective of Jewish Life through its Festivals. New York, Jewish Forum Publishing Co., Inc., 1930.
An excellent résumé of Jewish festivals and how they are celebrated. Contains many suggestions for program planning.

Selected Bibliography

Burnaby, Sherrard B.
Elements of the Jewish and Muhammadan Calendars. London,
Bell, 1901.
Part I, "The Jewish Calendar," p. 1–364.

Cohen, Simon, ed.
*Essence of Judaism; Based on Morris Joseph's Judaism as Creed
and Life.* New York, Behrman's Jewish Book House, 1932.
A good condensation of an important work on the Jewish religion and the
ideals and practices it represents.

Greenstone, Julius H.
The Jewish Religion. Philadelphia, Jewish Chautauqua Soc., 1920.

Hooper, Franklin H., and Bloch, Joshua.
*Story of the Jewish People, as Told in the Encyclopaedia Britan-
nica.* New York, Encyclopaedia Britannica, Inc., 1936.
An authoritative guide to material in the *Encyclopaedia Britannica.*

Idelsohn, Abraham Z.
The Ceremonies of Judaism. Cincinnati, National Federation of
Temple Brotherhoods, 1930.
Popular illustrated work on the customs of Judaism. Music included.

Kohler, Kaufmann.
Jewish Theology, Systematically and Historically Considered. New
York, Macmillan, 1918.

Lehrman, S. M.
The Jewish Festivals. London, Shapiro, 1936.
A simply written, attractively illustrated treatise on Jewish festivals and
symbols. A valuable handbook for those wishing to learn the inner significance of outward forms.

Melamed, Deborah M.
The Three Pillars. New York, Women's League of the United
Synagogue of America, 1931.
A brief exposition of the aspects of Jewish life which hold special signifi-
cance for women. Dietary laws, prayers, symbols, festivals, etc.

The Book of Festivals

LATVIANS

Endzelīnam, J.
Filoloģijas Materiāli. Rīgā, Izdevusi Latvijas Ūniversitātes Filoloģijas un Filozofijas Studentu Ramave, 1933.

Gray, Louis Herbert.
"Baltic Mythology." In *Mythology of All Races.* Boston, Marshall Jones, 1918. v. 3, p. 317–330.

Loorits, Oskar.
Livische Märchen- und Sagenvarianten. Helsinki, Suomalainen Tiedeakatemia Academia Scientiarium Fennica, 1926. (Folklore Fellows: FF communications no. 66.)

Urch, R. O. G.
Latvia, Country and People. Riga, Walter and Rapa, Ltd., 1935. Ch. 2, "Lāčplēsis," p. 18–27; ch. 3, "Imanta," p. 28–46. Folklore and customs.

LITHUANIANS

Benedictsen, Åge Meyer.
Lithuania, "the Awakening of a Nation." Copenhagen, Egmont H. Petersens Kgl. Hof-Bogtrykkeri, 1924. Part III, "The Customs and the Festivals of the People," p. 62–83; Part IV, "Lithuanian Folk Lore," p. 84–121; Part V, "The Fight Against Christianity," p. 122–135.

Bezzenberger, Adalbert.
Litauische Forschungen. Beiträge zur Kenntniss der Sprache und des Volkstumes der Litauer. Göttingen, R. Peppmüller, 1882. Contains music.

Gray, Louis Herbert.
"Baltic Mythology." In *Mythology of All Races.* Boston, Marshall Jones, 1918. v. 3, p. 317–330.

Mierzyński, A.
Zródla Mytologii Litewskiej. Warsaw, 1892–1896.

408

Selected Bibliography

Sruoga, Balys.
"Lithuanian Folk Songs (Dainos)." Tr. by E. J. Harrison. *Folk-Lore*, v. 43, September, 1932, p. 301–337.

MEXICANS

"El Dia de San Juan en la Alberca Pane," *Mexican Folkways*, v. 3, no. 3, 1927, p. 173–174.

Fergusson, Erna.
Fiesta in Mexico. New York, Knopf, 1934.
Colorful and charming descriptions of many of Mexico's feast days and holidays.

—— "The Merry Festival of the Dead," *Travel*, v. 63, June, 1934, p. 9–14, 53–54.

Montenegro, Robert.
"El Carnaval en Zaachila, Oaxaca." *Mexican Folkways*, v. 5, January, 1929, p. 28–29.

Montes de Oca, José G.
"La Fiesta a la Virgen de Los Remedios." *Mexican Folkways*, v. 3, August, 1927, p. 203–210.

—— "The Festival of St. John." *Mexican Folkways*, v. 2, June, 1926, p. 34–35.

Núñez y Domínguez, José de.
"El 'Corpus' en mi Terra; Corpus Christi in My Native Region." *Mexican Folkways*, v. 3, August, 1927, p. 191–202.

—— "Los Judas en Mexico; the Judases in Mexico." *Mexican Folkways*, v. 5, April, 1929, p. 90–104.

—— "The Christmas Eve of the Tolonacos." *Mexican Folkways*, v. 1, December, 1925, p. 22–23.

Peck, Anne Merriman.
Young Mexico. New York, McBride, 1934.
Ch. 6, "Markets and Fiestas," p. 142–169.

The Book of Festivals

Ramírez Tovar, Delfín.
"El Carnaval en Huixquilucan." *Mexican Folkways*, v. 5, January, 1929, p. 35–49.

Redfield, Robert.
"El Carnaval en Tepoztlan, Mor." *Mexican Folkways*, v. 5, January, 1929, p. 30–34.

Salas, Angel.
"La Batalla del 5 d Mayo en el Peñón; the Battle of the Fifth of May in Peñon." *Mexican Folkways*, v. 8, April, 1933, p. 56–76.

Toor, Frances.
"Carnavales en los Pueblos." *Mexican Folkways*, v. 5, January, 1929, p. 10.

—— "Christmas in Mexico." *Mexican Folkways*, v. 2, December, 1926, p. 31–43.

—— "Fiesta de la Sta. Vera Cruz en Taxco; Festival of the True Holy Cross of Taxco." *Mexican Folkways*, v. 6, no. 2, 1930, p. 84–94.

—— "Fiestas Patrias." *Mexican Folkways*, v. 2, August, 1926, p. 42–43.

—— "Judas Lives." *Mexican Folkways*, v. 2, April, 1926, p. 18.

—— "Neighborhood Christmas in Mexico City." *Mexican Folkways*, v. 1, December, 1925, p. 16–17.

—— "Semana Santa; Holy Week." *Mexican Folkways*, v. 3, February, 1927, p. 53–61.

—— "The Festivals of the Dead." *Mexican Folkways*, v. 1, October, 1925, p. 17–19.

MOHAMMEDANS

Burnaby, Sherrard B.
Elements of the Jewish and Muhammadan Calendars. London, Bell, 1901.
Part II, "The Muhammadan Calendar," p. 367–508.

Selected Bibliography

Dwight, H. G.
"Mohammedan Holidays." *Scribner's Magazine,* v. 54, July, 1913, p. 102–118.
Well-written, entertaining account of Mohammedan holidays witnessed by the author.

—— "Turkish Coffee Houses." *Scribner's Magazine,* v. 53, May, 1913, p. 620–632.
Contains much charming information on Turkish coffee houses and their relation to native holidays and customs.

Encyclopaedia Britannica (11th edition). Cambridge, England, University Press, 1910.
V. IV. "Mahommedan Calendar," p. 1001–1003.

Haig, Thomas Wolseley.
Comparative Tables of Muhammadan and Christian Dates. London, Luzac, 1932.
Useful for computing Mohammedan holidays. Tables to 2000 A.D.

Lane, Edward William.
An Account of the Manners and Customs of the Modern Egyptians. London, Murray, 1860.
Ch. 24–28 contain much interesting material on Mohammedan festivals and religious rites.

NETHERLANDERS

Boulger, Demetrius C.
Holland of the Dutch. London, Pitman, 1913.
Ch. 17, "Amusements and Fêtes," p. 157–167; ch. 18, "Costumes and Weddings," p. 168–178.

Hough, P. M.
Dutch Life in Town and Country. New York, Putnam's, 1901.
Ch. 9, "Rural Customs," p. 99–113; ch. 10, "Kermis and St. Nicholas," p. 114–131; ch. 11, "National Amusements," p. 132–144.

NORWEGIANS

Bosworth, Abbie L.
"Life in a Norway Valley." *National Geographic Magazine,* v. 67, May, 1935, p. 627–648.
Christmas foods and customs.

Hall, John Oscar.
When I Was a Boy in Norway.   Boston, Lothrop, Lee and Shepard, 1921.
Descriptions of popular superstitions, holy days and festivals.

Jungman, Nico.
Norway.   Text by Beatrix Jungman.   London, Black, 1905.
Detailed description of wedding customs in the Hardanger district, p. 135–145.

MacCulloch, John Arnott.
"Eddic."   In *Mythology of All Races.*   Boston, Marshall Jones, 1930.   v. 2.

Undset, Sigrid.
Kristen Lavransdatter: The Bridal Wreath, The Mistress of Husaby, The Cross.   New York, Knopf, 1930.

POLES

Gardner, Monica M.
Peeps at Many Lands: Poland.   London, Black, 1917.
Ch. 2, p. 14–25.

Jarecka, Louise L.
"Bright Pageantry in Poland."   *Travel,* v. 63, June, 1934, p. 32–36, 57.

Kennedy, H. E.
"Polish Peasant Courtship and Wedding Customs and Folk-Song."
Folk-Lore, v. 36, March, 1925, p. 48–68.

Kreuter, Victoria de.
"The Legacy of Custom and Traditions."   *Poland America,* v. 12, December, 1931, p. 555.

Mason, Violet.
The Land of the Rainbow; Poland and Her People.   London, Hodder, 1933.
"Lingering Faiths," p. 75–86.   A charmingly written book "just about Poland," with much information on festivals and folk survivals.

Selected Bibliography

Morawska, Jadwiga.
"Christmas in Poland." *Poland*, v. 7, December, 1926, p. 728–729, 761–762.

New, Barbara.
"Harvest Time in Poland." *Poland America*, v. 13, September, 1932, p. 408–409.

Otto, Gerhart F.
"Gniezno, Holy City of Pagan and Christian." *Poland America*, v. 12, July, 1931, p. 333–340.
Historical background of some of the old festivals.

Reymont, Ladislas St.
The Peasants; a Tale of Our Own Times. New York, Knopf, 1924–1925. 4 vols. "Autumn," "Winter," "Spring," "Summer." ". . . a panorama of the whole round of peasant life, a brilliant picture of Polish nature through the circles of the year."

PORTUGUESE

Braga, Theophilo.
O Povo Portuguez; nos seus Costumes, Crenças e Tradições. Lisboa, Livraria Ferreira, 1885, 2 vols.
v. 1—Costumes e Vida Domestica.
v. 2—Crenças e Festas Publicas, Tradições e Saber Popular.

Gallop, Rodney.
Portugal; a Book of Folk Ways. Cambridge, University Press, 1936.
A popularly written account of Portuguese folk practices, festivals and music.

Gordon, Jan and Cora.
Portuguese Somersault. London, Harrap, Ltd., 1934.
A popular travel book containing interesting glimpses of native festivals.

Martins, Padre Firmino A.
Folklore do Concelho de Vinhais. Coimbra, Imprensa da Universidade, 1928.

The Book of Festivals

Urtel, Hermann.

Beiträge zur portugiesischen Volkskunde. Hamburg, Friederichsen & Co., 1928. (Hamburg Universitaet. Abhandlungen aus dem Gebiet der Auslandskunde, Band 27.)

RUMANIANS

Beza, Marcu.

Papers on the Rumanian People and Literature. London, McBride, 1920.

—— *Paganism in Roumanian Folklore.* New York, Dutton, 1928.

An accurate picture of Rumanian folk life and ceremonies as described from the personal experience of an authority.

Bibesco, Marthe Lucie, Princess.

Isvor, the Country of Willows. Tr. by Hamish Miles. New York, Stokes, 1924.

Hall, Donald John.

Romanian Furrow. London, Methuen, 1933.

Contains colorful descriptions of a wedding, harvest customs, feasting the dead, etc.

Jewett, Sophie.

Folk Ballads of Southern Europe. New York, Putnam, 1913.

"The Sun and the Moon," p. 22–29; "Bujor," p. 154–159; "Shalga," p. 170–177; "The Little Lamb," p. 260–267.

These old folk ballads illustrate the classic background and romantic spirit which pervade Rumania's peasant superstitions and festal practices.

Murgoci, Mrs. A.

"Customs connected with Death and Burial among the Rumanians." *Folk-Lore,* v. 30, June, 1919, p. 89–102.

Pamfile, Tudor.

Sărbătorile de Vară la Români; Studiu Etnografic. București: Socec & Co., C. Sfetea şi Librăria Naţională. Acad. Romảna. Din Vieaţa Poporului Român Culegeri şi Studii, v. 11, 1911.

Stratilesco, Tereza.

From Carpathian to Pindus. Boston, Luce, 1907.

Ch. 4; "The Peasant and His Religion," p. 156–204. A good résumé of Rumanian feast days and their celebration.

414

Selected Bibliography

Van Teslaar, James S.
When I Was a Boy in Rumania. Boston, Lothrop, Lee and Shepard, 1917. p. 82–96.

RUSSIANS

Hindus, Maurice.
Red Bread. New York, Jonathan Cape and Harrison Smith, 1931. Ch. 3, p. 52–56; ch. 5, p. 186–209.

Holme, Charles, ed.
Peasant Life in Russia. London, 'The Studio,' Ltd., 1912.
Good text and handsome plates. Excellent background material for old festivals and customs.

Kohl, J. G.
Russia and the Russians in 1842. London, Henry Colburn, 1843. 2 vols.
V. 2, ch. 25, "The Butter Week," p. 121–150; ch. 26, "The Great Fasts," p. 151–169; ch. 27, "Easter," p. 170–198. An old book, but interesting because of the picture given of festival life under the Tzars.

Rappoport, A. S.
Home Life in Russia. New York, Macmillan, 1913.
Excellent material on festivals, superstitions, marriage ceremonies and peasant life.

Selivanova, Nina N.
"They Ate Once in Russia." *Asia,* v. 32, December, 1932, p. 608–614, 656–658.
Recipes for some of the holiday foods famous in Tzarist Russia.

Sheddon-Ralston, William.
Songs of the Russian People. London, Ellis and Green, 1872.

Walter, L. Edna.
Peeps at Many Lands: Russia. London, Black, 1910.

SPANIARDS

Bensusan, S. L.
Home Life in Spain. New York, Macmillan, 1910.
Ch. 6, p. 61–75; ch. 11, p. 137–146.

415

The Book of Festivals

Cabal Rubiera, Constantino.
La Mitología Asturiana: los Dioses de la Muerte. Madrid, J. Pueyo, 1925.
Folklore, legends and popular beliefs about death.

—— *Del Folk-lore de Asturias; Cuentos Leyendas y Tradiciones.* Madrid, Voluntad [1923?].

Carreras y Candi, Francisco, ed.
Folklore y Costumbres de España. Barcelona, A. Martín, 1931–1933, 3 vols.
V. 2 contains music. Excellent illustrations.

Knott, Harrison K.
"Valencia Welcomes the Spring." *Travel,* v. 63, May, 1934, p. 32–33, 58.

Moreira, Joan.
Del Folklore Tortosí; Costums, Ballets, Pregaries, Paremies, Jocs i Cançons del Camp i de la Ciutat de Tortosa. Tortosa, Imprenta Querol, 1934.
Music included.

Nixon-Roulet, Mary F.
The Spaniard at Home. Chicago, McClurg, 1910.
Colorful material on marriage customs, fiestas, amusements and folk life.

Pan, Ismael del.
Folklore Toledano. Toledo, Imprenta A. Medina, 1932.
Tome 1, "Supersticiones y creencias. Papeletas folklóricas comentadas."

Spence, Lewis.
Legends and Romances of Spain. New York, Stokes, 1920.

Vazquez, José Andrés.
"The Festival of Spring in Seville." *Theatre Arts Monthly,* v. 13, March, 1929, p. 202–206.

Williams, Leonard.
The Land of the Dons. London, Cassell & Co., Ltd., 1902.
Ch. 7, "The National Fiestas," p. 154–170.

Selected Bibliography

SWEDES

Cyriac, A. Kellgren.
"Swedish Christmas Customs." *Folk-Lore*, v. 44, December, 1923, p. 314–321.

Hagberg, Louise.
"Old-Time Christmas in Sweden." *American-Scandinavian Review*, v. 14, December, 1926, p. 744–750.

Holm, Thora.
Svenska Helger: Högtider och Bemräkelsedagar i Svenska Hem. Stockholm, T. Holms Förlag, 1931.
An excellent volume containing much valuable information on home customs and festivals, and the holiday foods typical of each season.

Holme, Charles, ed.
Peasant Art in Sweden, Lapland and Iceland. London, 'The Studio,' Ltd., 1910.
Native folk arts and costumes are described in connection with old folk practices such as weddings, feasts, etc.

Lagerlöf, Selma.
Mårbacka. Tr. by Selma Swanston Howard. Garden City, New York, Doubleday, Doran, 1925.
Recollections of the author's youth.

——— *Memories of My Childhood; Further Years at Mårbacka.* Garden City, New York, Doubleday, Doran, 1934.
Ch. 16, "The Easter Witch," p. 163–173.

——— *Gösta Berling's Saga.* Tr. by Lillie Tudeer. New York, American-Scandinavian Foundation, 1918.

Lloyd, L.
Peasant Life in Sweden, London, Tinsley, 1870.
An old but useful collection of peasant customs observed in many different parts of Sweden.

MacCulloch, John Arnott.
"Eddic." In *Mythology of All Races.* Boston, Marshall Jones, 1930. v. 2.

Olson, Alma Luise.

"Sweden, Land of White Birch and White Coal." *National Geographic Magazine*, v. 54, October, 1928, p. 441–484.

Posse-Brázdová, Amelie.

"Country-House Life in Sweden; in Castle and Cottage the Landed Gentry Gallantly Keep the Old Traditions." *National Geographic Magazine*, v. 66, July, 1934, p. 1–64.

Description of Christmas and other holiday customs.

Simpson, H. F. Morland.

Southesk and Other Rune Prime-Staves, or *Scandinavian Wooden Calendars.* Edinburgh, Neill and Co., 1892. (Reprinted from *Proceedings of the Society of Antiquaries of Scotland.*)

An interesting and scholarly description of how time was reckoned on the ancient Scandinavian wooden calendars.

SWISS

Grosvenor, Melville Bell.

"An August First in Gruyères." *National Geographic Magazine*, v. 70, August, 1936, p. 137–160. Plates 1–16.

A well-illustrated account of the Swiss Independence Day as celebrated in Gruyères.

Guerber, H. A.

Legends of Switzerland. New York, Dodd, Mead, 1899.

Valuable legendary background for the festivals of different cantons.

Patteson, Louise S.

When I Was a Girl in Switzerland. Boston, Lothrop, Lee and Shepard, 1921.

Ch. 14, p. 141–152.

Vincent, John Martin.

Costume and Conduct in the Laws of Basel, Bern and Zurich, 1370–1800. Baltimore, Johns Hopkins Press. 1935.

Interesting historical background material for modern festivals and customs.

Widmer, Marie.

"Christmas Customs in Switzerland." *All About Switzerland*, v. 6, December, 1929, p. 3–6.

Selected Bibliography

SYRIANS

Curtiss, Samuel Ives.
Primitive Semitic Religions Today; a Record of Research, Discoveries and Studies in Syria, Palestine and the Sinaitic Peninsula. Chicago, Revell, 1902.
An excellent book, helpful in the understanding of ancient folk practices. The author has taken as his sources of information the old people and the keepers of shrines in the interior of Syria. He has made his own deductions from the facts thus gathered.

El-Khoury, Ibn.
"Celebrating Carnival in Lebanon." *Syrian World,* v. 1, March, 1927, p. 7–12.

—— "Christmas in a Lebanon Village." *Syrian World,* v. 1, December, 1926, p. 16–20.

Rihbany, Abraham Mitrie.
A Far Journey. Boston, Houghton Mifflin, 1914.

—— *The Syrian Christ.* Boston, Houghton Mifflin, 1916.

Spicer, Dorothy Gladys.
"Christmas-tide Customs of the Syrian Immigrant." *Adult Bible Class Magazine,* v. 27, December, 1932, p. 67–70.
An account of some of the holiday customs and survivals still observed among Syrian communities in the United States.

Wilson, H. B.
"Notes on Syrian Folklore Collected in Boston." *Journal of American Folklore,* v. 16, July, 1903, p. 133–147.

YUGOSLAVS

Adamic, Louis.
The Native's Return; an American Immigrant Visits Yugoslavia and Discovers His Old Country. New York, Harper, 1934.

—— "Death in Carniola." *Harper's Magazine,* v. 167, November, 1933, p. 693–704.

The Book of Festivals

—— "Wedding in Carniola." *Harper's Magazine,* v. 166, January, 1933, p. 170–180.

Lazarovich-Hrebelianovich, Prince.
The Servian People. New York, Scribner's, 1910. 2 vols.
V. 1, ch. 1, "The Servian Race," p. 1–90. Good material on customs, traditions and ceremonies.

Mijatovich, Chedo.
Servia and the Servians. London, Pitman, 1908.
Ch. 2, "Religion and the Religiousness of the Servians," p. 38–53; ch. 3, "Servian Peasants' Notions About God," etc., p. 54–69; ch. 4, "National Customs," p. 70–114.

Murko, Matthias.
Bericht über eine Reise zum Studium der Volksepik in Bosnien und Herzegowina im Jahre 1913. Sitzungsberichte der Kais. Akademie der Wissenschaften in Wien, Band 176, Abhandlung 2, 1915.

Petrovitch, Woislav M.
Hero Tales and Legends of the Serbians. London, Harrap, 1917.
Superstitions, beliefs and national customs.

Roller, Nettie Huxley.
"Notes on Some South Slav Beliefs and Festivals." *Folk-Lore,* March, 1926, v. 37, p. 35–75.
Excellent description of Feast of St. John at Jajce, p. 54–75.

Schneeweis, Edmund.
Grundriss des Volksglaubens und Volksbrauchs der Serbokroaten. V. Celju, Družba sv. Mohorja, 1935.

INDEX OF FESTIVALS

INDEX OF FESTIVALS